A WORLD OF OPPORTUNITIES

SUNY Series in New Social Studies on Alcohol and Drugs
Harry G. Levine and Craig Reinarman, Editors

A WORLD OF OPPORTUNITIES

*Life-Style and Economic Behavior
of Heroin Addicts in Amsterdam*

Martin Grapendaal
Ed Leuw
Hans Nelen

STATE UNIVERSITY
OF NEW YORK
PRESS

Published by
State University of New York Press, Albany

© 1995 State University of New York

All rights reserved

Production by Susan Geraghty
Marketing by Nancy Farrell

Printed in the United States of America

No part of this book may be used or reproduced in any manner whatsoever without written permission. No part of this book may be stored in a retrieval system or transmitted in any form or by any means including electronic, electrostatic, magnetic tape, mechanical, photocopying, recording, or otherwise without the prior permission in writing of the publisher.

For information, address State University of New York Press,
State University Plaza, Albany, N.Y., 12246

Library Of Congress Cataloging-in-publication Data

Grapendaal, M.
    A world of opportunities : life-style and economic behavior of heroin addicts in Amsterdam / Martin Grapendaal, Ed Leuw, Hans Nelen.
       p. cm.—(SUNY series in new social studies on alcohol and drugs)
    Includes bibliographical references (p.) and index.
    ISBN 0-7914-2241-0 (hc : acid-free).—ISBN 0-7914-2242-9 (pbk. : acid-free)
    1. Narcotic addicts—Netherlands—Amsterdam. 2. Heroin habit-
-Netherlands—Amsterdam. 3. Narcotics, Control of—Netherlands-
-Amsterdam. 4. Drug abuse surveys—Netherlands—Amsterdam.
5. Amsterdam (Netherlands)—Social conditions. I. Leuw, Ed.
II. Nelen, J. M. III. Title. IV. Series.
HV5840.N42A64 1995
362.29'309492352—dc20   94-815
                                                                                          CIP

10 9 8 7 6 5 4 3 2 1

And so I found out just what heroin addiction is about. No dangerously dancing life, but a common day to day existence focused on the most one-sided of breadwinning. The most primitive, most elementary, existence imaginable. Or rather: a metaphor of that existence. After the rhythm of prison had taken the grandeur and shine off living on heroin, while my fascination with it disappeared at the same time, the worst of the addiction was over. Coming off was no great problem. I kept telling myself: "heroin, big deal! If I fancy it again I'll have some, like other people have a cigarette. But Egberts, stop thinking it's something special. It's no more glamourous than a plate of sausage."

Advocaat van de hanen (The Cockrels' Advocate)
—A.F.Th. van der Heyden

CONTENTS

Acknowledgments	xi
Chapter 1 Introduction	1
Goals and Research Questions	1
The Drug-Political Context	5
Normalization of Illegal Drug Use	5
Rejecting a "War on Drugs"	5
Dutch Drug Laws and Law Enforcement Policy	7
Epidemiology of Deviant Drug Addiction	10
Principles of Dutch Social Drugs Policy: Towards a Cultural Integration of Drug Problems.	11
Chapter 2 The Connection Between Drug Use and Crime: Facts and Explanations	15
Empirical Connection Between Drug Use and Crime	17
A Historical and Ecological Perspective	17
Comparisons Between Groups	21
Individual Connection Between Drug Use and Crime	24
Explanations	27
The Perspective of Causality	28
The Perspective of Functionality	34
Chapter 3 Careers in Deviancy and Drugs	41
Starting to Use Hard Drugs	43
Social-Economic Background	43
Place of Birth	44
Primary Phase of Socialization: Family and Childhood	45
Secondary Phase of Socialization: Education, Friends, Starting on Drugs	49

Course of a Drug Career	58
A Theoretical Model of Development	58
The Building of a Drug Career: From Recreational User to Full-Time Junkie	60
Dismantling a Drug Career: The Addict Calms Down and Looks for a Way Out	68
Continuity of criminal patterns in life histories	74
Very Criminal Prior to First Drug Use	75
"Moderately Criminal" Prior to First Drug Use	76
Noncriminal Prior to First Drug Use	77
Conclusion	78
Chapter 4 The Amsterdam Drug Scene	**81**
The Drug Scene in Amsterdam's Inner City	82
Actors in the Scene and Their Mutual Relationships	87
Interactions Between Addicts	87
Interactions Between Addicts and Public	96
Concluding remarks	97
Chapter 5 Income Acquisition	**99**
Ways of Acquiring Income	99
Social Security	99
Acquisitive Crime	100
The Market of White and Brown	103
The Business of Prostitution and Sex	108
Miscellaneous	112
Income in Kind	114
A Quantitative Picture of Income	115
Different Sources of Income and Their Relationship.	115
The Figures for Amsterdam Compared with Other Studies	117
A Closer Look at the Different Offenses	119
Periods of Abstinence and Income from Crime	120
An Economic Typology	123
Construction of the Typology	123
Illustrations of the Typology	125
The Typology in Time	128
Summary and Conclusions	131

Chapter 6 Spending and Drug Use	135
Spending	135
Categories of Expenditure	135
Expenditure in Figures	136
Drug Use	138
Heroin and Cocaine	139
Psychopharmaca, Alcohol, and Cannabis	140
Little-Used Drugs	141
Methods of Drug Taking	143
The Functions of the Different Drugs in the Scene	145
The Function of Heroin	145
The Function of Cocaine	147
The Functions of Psychopharmaca	149
Patterns of Use	150
Polydrug Use	150
Variability in Consumption	153
Summary and Conclusions	157
Chapter 7 Methadone Maintenance, Illegal Drug Use, and Acquisitive Crime.	159
Methadone Maintenance Programs and Crime: The Theory	161
Methadone and Crime According to the Orthodox Theory of Methadone Maintenance	161
Methadone Maintenance and a Reduction in Crime	164
Methadone Maintenance and Nonreduction in Crime	167
Methadone Maintenance Programs in Amsterdam	169
Methadone Use and the Use of Illegal Drugs	171
Methadone Use	171
Methadone and the (Illegal) Use of Heroin and Cocaine	173
The Distribution of Methadone and Crime	178
The Distribution of Methadone and the Economic Typology	182
Summary and Conclusions	186

Chapter 8 Conclusions, Theoretical Implications, and Possible Policy Consequences	189
The Most Important Results	190
The Relationship Between Drug Use and Crime	195
Possible Policy Consequences	199
Two Radical Policy Models	199
Reformation of Drug Policy	205
Epilogue	*213*
Some Considerations for the International Prohibitionistic Policy Perspective	213
Appendix	*217*
Methodology	217
Nature of the Data	217
Weekly Questionnaire	217
Reliability and Validity of Research Data	220
A Closer Look at the Sample	222
References	*225*
Index	*237*

ACKNOWLEDGMENTS

The work on which this book is based was done within the research program of the Research and Documentation Centre of the Dutch Ministry of Justice. Part of the project was funded by the Amsterdam Municipality. The translation from Dutch to English was possible thanks to a subsidy from the Dutch Ministry of Welfare, Health, and Cultural Affairs. We found the necessary criminological expertise and bilingual skills combined in the person of Chrisje Brants, who quickly, accurately, and enthusiastically translated the Dutch manuscript.

Thanking the people and institutions who made this project possible is not just a matter of form, considering how often we made far-reaching demands on their cooperation and trust. That applies primarily of course to the most important people who figure in this book: the group of drug users in Amsterdam with whom we had such frequent (and often good) contact. Although we were after sensitive information, it is surprising how few reservations and little distrust we encountered. Some respondents admitted us further into their world, giving us an opportunity to become better acquainted with the world of drugs than would have been possible on the basis of verbal contact only. We often spoke to our respondents in the privacy of their homes, and we were able to observe at close quarters the daily routine and rituals of living with, dealing in, and using drugs.

We would also like to thank the Public Health Service (GG&GD) and the Alcohol and Drugs Consultation Bureau (CAD) of Amsterdam for their most loyal cooperation in every stage of the project, especially those who work at the community stations and on the methadone-buses. Their efforts were crucial to the recruitment of respondents and to retracing them later when necessary.

The active and ardent contribution of our field-workers not only prevented us from ever giving up, but also provided a wealth of information. Roberto Aidala, Eva Schoone, and Gerben Kroese were all indispensable.

CHAPTER 1

Introduction

This is a study about the life-style and economic behavior of deviant heroin users in Amsterdam, the biggest city of the Netherlands. The local and national context of the research is particularly relevant. Just as in any other country hard drugs such as heroin and cocaine are prohibited by law. Yet, the Dutch have adopted their own "pragmatic" approach to illegal drug use, which involves decriminalization on the demand side and some (limited) tolerance for the hard drugs scene to become open and visible within "normal" society. Before embarking upon our main theme, some major assumptions and methodology of our project are introduced. Subsequently we will give a brief historical account of Dutch drug problems and the Dutch drug-political climate.

GOALS AND RESEARCH QUESTIONS

There has been a great deal of interest in illegal drugs for a long time, with attention focusing on both the trade in and the use of drugs. One important reason is that both seem to bring countless problems in their wake, especially crime committed by drug users and the nuisance they cause. Although there is a broad consensus on the connection between crime and the illegal use of hard drugs (mainly heroin and cocaine), there has been very little research in the Netherlands into the actual nature of that connection. Again, systematic knowledge about the amount of crime committed by drug users is surprisingly sparse. This research project is partly meant to fill that gap, although its general aims are broader, namely the acquisition of knowledge on and insight into the economic behavior of regular opiate users. When examining that behavior, we have especially highlighted crime. For the user, crime forms the most explicit expression of his marginality. For society, crime forms the most explicit expression of the injurious effect and nuisance value of illegal drug use. As we shall see in more detail in chapter 2, the literature offers several explanations for the evident relationship between drug use and crime. According to a prevailing notion, crime results from the fact that drugs are an illegal and scarce commodity. This reduces illegal activities to purely instrumental behavior, the inevitable result of addiction to expensive drugs. In other words: drug use causes crime. A second explanation turns the causal relationship around: crime causes drug use, because this behavior belongs to a criminal subculture. A third approach to the relationship between crime and drug use has it that crime is deeply motivated, (socially) expressive behavior connected with the identity of the drug user. It is, therefore, of paramount importance for structuring and making sense of his life. This approach sees drug use as but one of the expressions of a deviant existence.

These different frameworks of interpretation have important implications for social policy on drugs and related problems. For some time now, policy has centered around methadone maintenance treatment. Reducing the crime rate has typically been a more or less implicit aim of the different methadone programs. If a direct causal relationship between crime and drug use is assumed, one may also assume that illegal activities will decrease if the drug ceases to be a scarce commodity: replacing an expensive drug like heroin with a drug that has more or less the same effect, in this case methadone, should therefore lead to a reduction of crime. Looked at from a different theoretical perspective, however, such a reduction in the crime rate is less self-evident. If one's interpretation is based primarily not on addiction, but on deviant life-style, it is quite plausible that a heroin user whose craving has been legally satisfied by methadone, will then organize his/her deviant life-style around the use of another drug (such as cocaine). In that case there is no logical reason why the drug user's crime rate should decrease.

Obviously then, it is important, for both theoretical and practical-social reasons, to gain more insight into the economic behavior of regular opiate users. This general aim can be translated into five specific questions:

- In what way(s) do regular opiate users obtain their income and how do these relate to each other?

- In what way(s) do regular opiate users spend their income and how do these relate to each other?
- What is the effect of methadone maintenance treatment on the economic behavior of regular opiate users?
- What is the function of crime and/or heroin and other drugs in the user's day-to-day existence?
- Is this related in any way to the user's life history?

A "regular opiate user" is defined as "a person using heroin, methadone and/or another opiate at least on four days a week." This definition therefore limits this project to the group of users generally considered to be the most problematic.

For the purpose of this research, "economic behavior" was taken to mean all behavior with regard to the acquisition of money, goods, or services on the one hand, and the spending of that income on the other. In this context, the concept of crime is restricted to those criminal offenses that provide the offender with some sort of economic gain. In other words, our attention was focused exclusively on income-generating crime, ignoring "expressive" violence such as assault and battery and rape.

In the practice of drug use, the term "income-generating crime" refers to the illegal production of income by means of drug dealing or one of several types of theft. For reasons that we shall explain later, we have chosen to deal with both sorts of crime separately. The property crimes of the criminal code are being referred to as "acquisitive crime."

In this book, we frequently and unconcernedly use the word "addiction." It will become clear that we use the concept of addiction in the sense of subjective experience, not as a psychiatric disorder or a pharmacologically induced pathology. This corresponds to Peele's psychological concept of addiction (1985 and 1989), whereby the object of the addiction (drugs, alcohol, sex, gambling) is scarcely relevant for its essential nature. "It is the cycle of desperate search, temporary as inadequate satisfaction, and renewed desperation that most characterises addiction" (Peele 1989, p.152).

Our approach combined qualitative and quantitative methods, namely a questionnaire, a cohort study (following a fixed group of respondents for a certain length of time), and ethnographic fieldwork in the city.

Any "hard" research material derives mainly from interviews according to a standardized questionnaire, completed in principle seven times by each respondent. Every interview provided information on their economic behavior during the seven days prior to the interview. During the following two weeks, the questionnaire was repeated twice. Thereafter less frequently, namely four times during a whole year (once every quarter).

Each respondent was also interviewed about his/her life history. Together with our field observations, this interview played an important part in putting our hard data into perspective.

With a view to obtaining comparative data, this research was designed to correspond closely with a research project in New York, "Taking Care of Business" (Johnson et al. 1985).

Our population was made up of all opiate users who meet the qualifications for participation in methadone maintenance programs. That means, among other things, that foreign drug users were excluded. The sample consisted of 150 regular opiate users. Because one of our central questions concerns the effects of methadone maintenance treatment on economic behavior, we distinguished between users registered with a regular methadone program and users who did not participate in such programs. Publications by the Public Health Service of Amsterdam (GG&GD) show that about 65 percent of all users receive methadone at some point during the year (see Buning 1986). We attempted to match that percentage in our research group. The sample eventually contained 105 participants in a methadone program and 45 nonparticipants.

See the Appendix for more detailed information on the methodology and the nature of the sample.

The book is organized as follows. The next chapter explores the relationship between drugs and crime in general terms, not only looking into the empirical evidence on the basis of the literature, but also examining existing theory in this field. In chapter 3 we start to present our empirical data, focusing on the routes by which the respondents came to use hard drugs and the careers they have developed. Chapter 4 concerns the situation in Amsterdam and contains descriptions of the day-to-day worries of the drug scene. Chapters 5 and 6 deal with the use of (illegal) drugs and ways of income acquisition, chapter 7 with (the distribution of) methadone. The first part of chapter 7 goes into the theoretical reasons for providing methadone, while the second part attempts to answer the important question of whether and to what extent methadone maintenance treatment affects the crime rate of drug users. Chapter 8 contains the conclusions and examines their theoretical policy implications and consequences.

In any study on life-style and economic behavior of deviant drug addicts both the national and the local sociohistorical context has to be taken into account. The culture of illegal drug taking can only be understood against the background of drug policy and the general sociocultural climate, both nationally and locally. In order to put the reader of this book on the right track, this chapter is concluded by an outline of the way(s) the Dutch are dealing with the drug phenomenon.

THE DRUG-POLITICAL CONTEXT

Normalization of Illegal Drug Use

The Dutch Parliament enacted the revised Opium Act in 1976. This penal law is part of the Dutch drug policy framework that includes tolerance for nonconforming life-styles, risk reduction with regard to the harmful health and social consequences of drug taking, and penal measures directed against illicit trafficking in hard drugs. This multifaceted approach established the basic principles and operating practices of contemporary social and criminal drug policy in the Netherlands.

Dutch drug policy is pragmatic and nonmoralistic. It has been conceptualized within a "normalizing" model of social control, aiming at depolarization and integration of deviance as opposed to a "deterrence" model of social control, aiming at isolation and removal of deviance (van de Wijngaart 1991). Within this ideology of normalization, illegal drugs are considered a problem which is an inevitable, but limited and manageable social problem of modern Western society. Thus within the ideological context of normalization, drug addiction is not conceived as an alien threat forced upon an otherwise innocent society.

Rejecting a "War on Drugs"

During the parliamentary debate preceding the adoption of the revised Opium Act, the major elements of national drug policy were summarized as follows:

- the central aim is the prevention and amelioration of social and individual risks caused by the use of drugs;
- a rational relation between those risks and policy measures;
- a differentiation of policy measures which will also take into account the risks of legal recreational and medical drugs;
- a priority of repressive measures against (other than cannabis) drug trafficking;
- the inadequacy of criminal law with regard to any other aspect of the drug problem (Handelingen 1976, p. 3088).

These essentials of Dutch drug policy have been upheld till the present day, although at times practical policy measures have been reconsidered and adapted.

Apart for a short period preceding the adoption of the revised Opium Act in 1976, illegal drug use has not been a moral or political issue in the Netherlands. Consequently, the drug problem has never been instrumental for promoting political or moral power, or the specific institutional interests of law enforcement agencies. Political speeches elaborating on the abhorrence of illegal drugs are virtually absent; they would appear as quite misplaced in the Dutch political culture. In a comparative analysis of the development of drug policies in the Netherlands and western Germany it was concluded that "a low degree of politicization of the issue was the most important prerequisite for successful decriminalization" (Scheerer 1978, p. 603).

Within the context of the Dutch pragmatic and normalizing drug policy, the basic contradictions of any attempt to reach practical solutions are readily appreciated. A study on "the Dutch Approach" observed that within the Ministry of Public Health, which carries the primary responsibility for national drug policy formulation, there is no pledge of "solving the problem." Instead, policy efforts are understood as pragmatic attempts to cope, meaning the management and, if possible, the minimization of the risks and the damaging effects of the drugs phenomenon and the preparation of society to optimally live with it (Baanders 1989). On the one hand this pragmatism requires the recognition of moral and life-style pluralism of modern Western society, on the other it requires a clear dissociation from the stringent moral reductionism of the radical prohibition ideology.

Within this normalizing model of social control the ultimate paradox of all drug policy can be acknowledged. The basic predicament is that attempts to limit the availability of illegal drugs tend to increase their damaging (social) effects as well as their psychological and economic attractions. The more drugs are tabooed and forcefully repressed, the more its users will tend to be marginalized, criminal, bearers and sources of diseases and the more the world of drug use will offer attractive perspectives for earning money and living a meaningful life in deviant subcultures. Thus the real challenge of pragmatic drug policy may be perceived as striking a balance between limiting the availability of "dangerous substances" and augmenting their secondary risks.

In the course of this endeavor, the Dutch approach has not gone beyond certain clear limits. There is a continuing debate on the feasibility of radical abolition of all criminal law interference with drugs. This option has some prominent proponents among penal law professors, law enforcement authorities, and local politicians (Rüter 1986; Baanders 1989). Nationally and officially, however, the flexibility of Dutch drug policy has stopped short of formal legalization or even further practical decriminalization of illegal drugs. Engelsman described the "Dutch model" as a "compromise between a war on drugs and legalization to which he adds that the Netherlands want to operate between the boundaries of the international drug conventions (Engelsman 1988).

Dutch Drug Laws and Law Enforcement Policy

The Revised Opium Act of 1976 is a compromise between outright prohibition and social integration of illegal drugs. The largely decriminalized status of cannabis (marihuana and hashish) is the most explicit expression of the normalizing approach, as is reflected in the differentiation of the act in two schedules. In Schedule I a number of substances (among which opiates, cocaine, amphetamines, LSD, etc.) is listed under the heading "drugs presenting unacceptable risks." Schedule II mentions cannabis only, without the qualification of unacceptability. Penalties for forbidden actions pertaining to Schedule II are considerably lower than those for Schedule I.

Laws in practice are more relevant than laws in books. The social reality of penal law involvement with illegal drugs may be described as de facto abolition with regard to (possession for own) use of all illegal substances. Normally there is no investigation, arrest, or criminal prosecution for the use of hard drugs, no more than for the use of soft drugs (Rüter 1988). In the last case there has also been a de facto legalization of the retail market. Hashish and marihuana are officially permitted (though not officially "licensed") to be traded in limited quantities. During the last decade this has mainly taken the form of small commercial outlets, "coffee shops." In these cannabis parlors exotic brands of hashish and homegrown brands of "Netherweed" are offered for sale, to take home or for consumption on the spot, in an openly and undisguised manner. Basically, the establishments operate just like "normal" bars or coffee shops (Jansen 1989).

For commercial trafficking in hard drugs, Dutch policies and practices resemble those of most Western countries. The Dutch drug policy conforms to the international agreements to combat drug trafficking: importation, exportation, and transportation (Albrecht and van Kalmthout 1989; Rüter 1988). In 1989 the U.S. Embassy in the Netherlands observed: "Dutch attitudes towards trafficking closely mirror those of the United States government and of the neighbouring states in the European Community" (U.S. Embassy 1989, p. 2).

Law enforcement policy in the Netherlands operates within the framework of the more comprehensive social drug policy except for wholesale drug trafficking where law enforcement agencies act autonomously. In other realms of the drugs problem, such as the control of street markets for hard drugs, meeting places for drug users, and the supervision over commercial establishments for the sale of soft drugs, crime control interests are coordinated with other interests of public order, public health, and welfare. Typically, police authorities will take part in local drug policy formulation under the responsibility of the city administration, thus attempting to integrate law enforcement activities into the central priorities of (local) drugs policy. In such real-life situations the interest of law enforcement will yield to public order or public health interests. This has for instance resulted in an agreement of the Amsterdam police to refrain from investigating or arresting criminally suspected methadone clients in the vicinities of the methadone posts.

The necessary flexibility of law enforcement to be integrated in the general social drugs policy is warranted by the "expediency principle," which authorizes the prosecution office to decide whether or not to prosecute or initiate criminal investigation. Those decisions can be made "in the public interest." They are ultimately based on the political responsibility of the minister of justice.

In 1976 guidelines for the investigation and prosecution of drug offenses were issued by the Ministry of Justice. They thus form a translation of the intentions of drug policy to the practical execution of law enforcement. These guidelines direct the law enforcement actions of the public prosecutor and of the police. The prosecutor is instructed with a summoning and penalty demanding policy. On his part the head prosecutor has the authority to direct the police investigation activities within his district by stipulating the priorities of police actions with regard to specific violations of the law. For instance, the police operates on the base of the "stumble principle" when small (30 grams or less) but commercial amounts of cannabis are involved. The police will not initiate investigations on having knowledge of such violations. But it may act if it happens to stumble on such an amount (Rüter 1988). In 1987 the commissioner of the police in Amsterdam wrote a letter to all "coffee shop" keepers in the city, warning them of possible police actions if they traded in quantities larger than 30 grams (de Beaufort 1989, p. 74). Obviously this implicitly signals the fact that those shopkeepers do not have to fear police actions if they only keep a limited stack of soft drugs.

The guidelines give prosecutors some latitude in reacting against small-scale dealers of hard drugs who provide for their own use. Those cases are intended to be met by demands of imprisonment, although no standard for length of imprisonment is specified. The actual absence of specified instructions for prosecution in this category of hard drug trade offenses provides a leeway for a differentiation of practical law enforcement policy between addicted street dealers and more businesslike dealers of hard drugs. Thus, the relatively low priority of acting against occasional, petty street dealing of hard drugs allows opportunity for some tolerance of the street market of hard drugs in the drugs quarter of Amsterdam. Such a pragmatic level of tolerance may be called for in order to realize the "higher" drug policy aims of medical and social risk minimization. For all other traffic offenses involving hard drugs, the guidelines stipulate actions of the police and prosecutor, including minimum terms of imprisonment to be demanded by the latter. Under the guidelines simple use or no trade related possession of hard drugs do not require specific police investigation, nor pretrial detention or prosecution (Rüter 1988). In fact, this principle has more or less immunized this kind of drug offenses against interference with law enforcement.

Epidemiology of Deviant Drug Addiction

The number of deviant drug addicts in the Netherlands has increased sharply from 1974 until the present level was reached in 1980. According to most estimates there are between 15,000 and 20,000 "addicts" who use opiates, cocaine, or both. A survey that infers the number of drug addicts from estimates of methadone providing institutions arrives at a somewhat higher level of approximately 23,000 addicts in 1988 (Driessen 1990). All sources agree that for the last ten years the average age of this population has substantially increased (Driessen 1990; Buning 1990; van de Wijngaart 1991). This indicates that fewer young people are becoming drug addicts and that earlier cohorts are ageing.

The prevalence of deviant drug addiction in the Netherlands is within the same range as the figures for some neighboring countries. Inferences from German drug treatment and assistance institutions led to an estimate of approximately 100,000 drug addicts in the former Federal Republic (Leune 1992). In England the estimate ranges between 75,000 and 150,000 (Pearson 1991). Converted to rates, these numbers suggest 100 to 153 addicts per 100,000 population in the Netherlands. The German rate of 164 and the English rate of 132 to 264 are somewhat higher than the Dutch. Moreover it has to be noted that the Dutch figure is probably substantially inflated by the inclusion of foreign drug addicts. Due to the relatively "friendlier" Dutch situation for drug addicts the "foreign element" is certainly more significant than in the other countries. In Amsterdam about 44 percent of the drug addict population is estimated to be of foreign citizenship (van Brussel and van Lieshout 1992).

The few sources available suggest that epidemiological development in several European countries has been as comparable as the levels of prevalence (Hartnoll 1986). The stabilization of the number of drug addicts may have occurred somewhat earlier in the Netherlands than elsewhere. For instance drug addiction in Italy, Western Germany, and England sharply increased until the middle of the 1980s (Ibid.).

The Dutch prevalence figures for deviant drug use are probably reasonably reliable because of the easy accessibility of socio/medical agencies for drug addicts. This makes it unlikely that the Dutch figures are an underrepresentation relative to other countries.

Principles of Dutch Social Drugs Policy: Towards a Cultural Integration of Drug Problems.

In a letter to Parliament in 1983 social drug policy was reformulated in the light of the more serious drug problems which had developed in the previous years. This policy plan reflects the rather more sceptical and less idealistic attitudes which came to predominate the social and criminal justice policy of the eighties. Harm reduction was established as the basic principle of drug policy: "The basic aim has not been to combat drug use itself or to prosecute persons because they are drug users, but to reduce these risks" (State Secretary for Welfare, Health and Cultural Affairs 1983, p.2). For the implementation of this aim there has been a heavy reliance on existing or especially created social work and medical institutions. Due to the traditions of the welfare state and to the booming economy of the sixties and early seventies, an extensive, easily accessible network of medical and social assistance facilities existed in the Netherlands. Inexpensive and comprehensive (public) insurance covers the expenses for virtually all people.

The letter to parliament argued that aiming at abstinence and complete rehabilitation was generally unrealistic and ineffective because: "Addicts who do not, or do not primarily, feel the need to kick the habit or are not capable of doing so will remain beyond the reach of assistance" (Ibid, p.7). The secretary stated that effective social policy aiming at reduction of the risks of drug use will have to acknowledge that deviant drug use has important functions for the addict. Thus, conceiving no alternative for a (provisional) acceptance of drug use (addiction) as matter of fact in many individual cases, the letter stated that ."...there must be increasing scope for forms of assistance which are not primarily aimed at curing the addiction as such, but at improving the social and physical functioning of addicts" (Ibid, p. 7).

Based on this perspective, in recent years a stronger accent has been put on operating so-called low-threshold facilities which offer limited but easily accessible services for a broad population of drug addicts. Basically those programs offer unconditional support, based on the acceptance of drug addiction as an explicit individual choice. They include shelter projects, free methadone maintenance, free needle exchange programs, material support (free meals, housing projects), social guidance programs, and psychomedical care. Methadone programs form the core of most help-providing institutions for drug addicts. Registration figures of the ministry in charge indicate that the strategy of establishing regular, frequent contacts between the hard drugs using population and socio/medical institutions has been rather successful. "Methadone has proved itself an instrument for establishing contact. Concomitant social assistance is tailored to the needs of the clients, both with regard to content as well as intensity. Assistance varies from incidental contacts concerning one-time problems, to referral to intensive treatment services" (van de Wijngaart 1988).

On a national scale a survey was conducted among all extramural drug treatment and assistance institutions. Based on their knowledge of drug addiction in their own region, the institutions estimated an average of 70 percent of the local drug addict population to have some contact with the institution. A combination of methadone provision, social casework, and limited psychomedical care was the prevailing "treatment" model for 73 percent of all the addicted drug clients (Driessen 1990). Within the Dutch approach in social drug policy there is only limited scope for clinical treatment of drug addicts aiming at abstinence. Compared to an estimated number of 17,000 persons with contacts with extramural drug assistance and treatment agencies in 1988 there were no more than some 1,300 admissions in that year to treatment clinics for drug addiction (Driessen 1990; WVC 1992). Treatment to abstinence is considered to be a sensible option only on the explicit and unrequested demand of the addicted person. Consequently there are no compulsory (clinical) treatment programs for (criminally apprehended) drug addicts in the Netherlands (WVC 1987).

Summarizing we conclude that official Dutch drug policy has attempted to neutralize the drug problem as a moral and a political issue. It has embarked upon a strict harm reduction course, which to a large extent is achieved by easing law enforcement pressure on users and petty traders of illegal hard drugs. The consequences of this approach will hopefully become visible from the theoretical considerations and the empirical data that will follow.

CHAPTER 2

The Connection Between Drug Use and Crime: Facts and Explanations

"Opiate use itself is the principle cause of high crime rate among addicts" (Jarvis and Parker 1989). This statement was made about young heroin users in rundown inner-city areas. In Great Britain, this present generation of problem drug users is known as the "new users" (Pearson 1991). At the beginning of the eighties, a review of research results on drug use and crime from the previous twenty years led to a quite different conclusion: "addicts are no more likely to be convicted than are non users. Opium addiction has never been regarded as a major source of criminal behavior in the United Kingdom" (Mott 1980).

Such a drastic difference in the consequences of heroin use in one and the same society can only mean that the significance of the relationship between drug use and crime is formed within a specific historical/cultural context. In other words: the statement "drug use *causes* crime" may only be valid in certain circumstances. A comparison of the cultures of "old" and "new" heroin use in Great Britain provides some important indications of the circumstances which may be relevant.

About 1970, heroin users began taking heroin at a much later age than in 1990. More importantly, there were no epidemic concentrations of drug use in lower class areas. The junkies of the sixties and seventies were seen as "dropouts," loners and nonconformists of varying sorts. To a certain extent, the values of the anticulture provided some legitimation for their life-style. Junkies were not merely down and out desperados, personifications of losers in society. To an extent they could be seen as "cultural rebels," who symbolized the final consequence of individual autonomy pitted against respectable society and its tying conventions.

In England, just as in the Netherlands, a split in the heroin culture was completed around 1980. It occurred against the background of large-scale social-political developments. To put it simply: the development of heroin use as a problem in underprivileged lower class areas runs parallel to the economic depression at the end of the seventies and the subsequent rise of Thatcherism (Pearson 1987 and 1991).

Although there was no comparable drastic change in socialpolitical climate, the same process of coinciding social deprivation and deviant drug use has also taken place in the Netherlands (Gerritsen 1991). Like elsewhere in the (Western) world, current Dutch drug problems are strongly related to (relative) social and cultural deprivation. Indeed, deviant drug addiction has become established in groups that are also problematic for various other reasons. A bird's-eye view of the distribution of problem users shows a concentration within certain age categories (adolescents and young adults) in the lower social economic classes, in (ethnic) minority cultures, and often even in certain geographical areas (inner cities and certain housing estates). This merging of cultural and structural adversities with problematic drug use, in the Netherlands (as well as in other Western European countries), has conduced to more similarity with the traditional patterns of deviant drug addiction in the United States, which have been known for a much longer period (Duster 1970; Musto 1973).

Also for this reason it is difficult to avoid emphasizing American work, in discussing the theory of illegal drug use and criminality. Deviant drug use is very much an American problem, with regard to both its origins and its size. The same applies to modern social scientific research of empirical orientation. However, the nature of addiction to illegal drugs may be similar in all modern Western societies, and we have therefore assumed that English language research on drugs and crime also has significance for the Netherlands.

In this chapter we shall be taking a closer theoretical look at the relationship between hard drug use and crime. The first half of the chapter deals with the empirical connection between drug use and crime that appears in research results, while the second half delves more deeply into the interpretation of that relationship. After that, we shall concentrate on three theoretical models. Two could be said to be causal explanations; the third focuses on the functionality of living on drugs and the significance of crime for such a life from a perspective of deviance. The concept of career, which occupies an important place in this perspective, is examined at the end of the chapter.

EMPIRICAL CONNECTION BETWEEN DRUG USE AND CRIME

A Historical and Ecological Perspective

The development of problematic drug use and crime runs parallel in time. Drug use began to be a problem in the Netherlands about 1973. As has been described in the previous chapter the prevalence of deviant drug use increased steeply in about ten years. Registered (acquisitive) crime shows a similar development. Between 1975–1985 it increased by about 150 percent (from approx. 346,000 offenses to approx. 850,000; CBS 1986).

However, comparisons as to (acquisitive) crime between cities and towns with different drug problems are more relevant than such broad trends. If there is a strong connection between hard drugs and crime, this should be visible in comparisons of cities where the degree of problematic drug use differs. We have compared Amsterdam with two other major cities (Rotterdam and Utrecht), with much less concentration of hard drug use. Until 1970, the development of crime in Amsterdam is quite comparable to that in other cities. These developments begin to diverge after 1973—a crucial year in the distribution of problematic drug use. After that year, registered crime in Amsterdam *increased* two or three times as fast as in the other cities (Berghuis 1987).

Analysis of more detailed data for the years 1980–1984 is even more revealing. Moreover, these crime figures are reliable, because they are based partly on dark number research.[1] The differences between Amsterdam and other cities can largely be explained by several kinds of income-generating crimes. These types of petty opportunistic offenses such as bicycle theft and stealing from cars are generally known to be drug related. Whether this picture of junkie crime is confirmed by this research will be described later. We first take a closer look at the offense known as mugging. Although, in absolute figures, it occurs less

---

1. Research based not on officially registered offenses but on information gained from, for example, perpetrators and victims of crime.

frequently than many other offenses, this violent and intimidating offense greatly influences feelings of (in)security and therefore the livableness of the city. Mugging is not a "typical" form of junkie crime in the sense that many delinquent drug users resort to it. But on the other hand, it is quite likely that a relatively large number of addicts are involved in this sort of desperate crime. The literature offers some indications of this (Goldstein and Brownstein 1987; Goldstein et al. 1989). In any event, the figures show that four times as many muggings are reported in "drug city" Amsterdam than in the other big cities (Berghuis 1987). This fits the broad pattern of a connection between drug use and acquisitive crime. On the other hand the level of registered "expressive" violence, which is not known to be drug related, is rather similar in the Dutch cities mentioned. Violent crimes such as (indecent) assault, rape, and vandalism in Amsterdam occur to more or less to the same extent as in the other cities. On the whole the existence of a connection between illegal drug use and (some types of criminality) on a macrostatistical level seems to be evident. What does this connection mean in a more qualitative sense?

Since the beginning of the century, problematic drug use in the United States has been concentrated within precisely definable geographical and social-economic boundaries (Chein et al. 1964; Duster 1970). As we have seen, the same social phenomenon has been visible in Great Britain for about a decade. It is hardly surprising that drug problems develop within groups that are socially deprived in several ways. Deviant drug addiction is typically reported for groups and for areas characterized by unemployment, lowest incomes, worst education, worst housing, worst state of health, highly instable family situations, etc. Much more typical in the United States than in most Western European countries, such economic and cultural deprivation is localized in ethnic minority communities. In the United States these are traditionally the black or Spanish speaking ghettos. It is this manifestation of the drug problem that has given rise to an ecological approach in the United States.

The object of ecologically oriented descriptions and explanations is not the individual drug user or the specific subculture of drug users, but rather the social system in a certain housing area. A complex of socially problematic phenomena is explained against the background of dominant social-economic and cultural conditions within a given area. Almost as a matter of course, such analyses of housing areas lead to the conclusion that while there is no causal link between drug use and crime to be traced at the collective level, there is a significant relation between both phenomena. Both " . . . are the products of a constellation of variables in the ecological environment and (. . .) both behaviors are an attempt to adapt to such an environment" (Dobinson and Ward 1985).

The results of a social-geographical study on the connections between indications of social pathology in Baltimore are typical for the ecology of problematic drug use (Nurco et al. 1984). Epidemiological data on the distribution of hard drug use over the different census-tracts[2] fitted into a collective pattern with a variety of other phenomena, which were all indications of social disintegration and (economic) deprivation. In the different areas, there was a high correlation between drug problems and the presence of ethnic minorities, inadequate housing, incomplete families, dependence on social security, venereal disease, arrests by the police, and serious violent offenses.

Recently, this tradition of drug research has been carried on in England. Drug research and drug therapy in impoverished working class areas in London and Liverpool are placed explicitly in the ecological perspective. As we have seen, the term "the *new* heroin users" ("of the 1980s") refers to the new generation of young drug users from poor urban areas (Burr 1987; Pearson 1987; Parker et al. 1988). A sociological case study in a social problem area near Liverpool combines historical and ecological perspectives (Parker et al. 1988). It compares crime trends in five of Liverpool's surrounding districts. In one, Wirral, an epidemic of problematic drug use developed between 1979 and 1986. Just as was described for the Netherlands in the one district with the heavy concentration of drug addiction, crime increased much more sharply than in the other four districts (114 percent as against 50 percent). Closer analysis based on the nature of crime

---

2. A housing area of which the sociographic characteristics have been registered.

in Wirral confirms the assumed connection with the drug problem. Like Dutch crime figures, those for Wirral also show a much sharper increase in acquisitive crime, such as burglary and theft from cars, than in more expressive crime such as assault.

Similar results had already been obtained in a former era of illegal drug use in the United States. In the beginning of the sixties, Chein et al. conducted their classic study of the drug and crime problem in the same context of area-related social deprivation. Their book, *The Road to H.*, is about the heroin epidemic that developed in the fifties in a number of poor (black) housing areas in New York. The study showed that the distribution of drug use was strongly related to the severity of social economic and ethnic problems. The rise of a heroin problem between 1949 and 1952 went hand in hand with escalating crime. Areas where hard drug use was well established *always* had a lot of crime. However, according to this study the reverse is not always true: areas with a lot of crime did not necessarily have a big drug problem. According to Chein et al., this reflects cultural resistance to the social pathology of heroin use in some deprived and criminal areas. They state that social and cultural negativism is being expressed in criminal behavior, whereas problematic drug use represents a further escalation of the social pathology. High levels of drug addiction within problematic communities may accordingly be an indication of a social climate devoid of hope and future prospects. "The high delinquency areas most vulnerable to the spread of drug use are the ones that are most heavily populated by the two most deprived and discriminated against minority groups in the city, and they are the areas with the highest poverty rates" (Chein et al. 1964, p. 64). This New York study also revealed a shift in the type of crime after heroin had appeared in certain areas. Like in Wirral, there was a relative decrease in expressive crime and an increase in acquisitive crime.

Turning to the Dutch situation, it is important to ask to what extent the ecological approach is relevant for explaining drug use and crime. The Netherlands do not have the ghettos and traditional, large-scale poverty in certain housing areas that are the subject of American and British ecological research. On the other hand it would be wrong to exclude social conditions in certain areas as a determinant of the development of both drug use and crime in the Netherlands. We shall return to this point in chapter 3.

Comparisons Between Groups

If we compare both certain periods of time and certain housing areas, it would seem that there is a clear and consistent connection between problematic drug use and crime. For a more direct exploration of the empirical connections between deviant drug use and crime we leave the ecological or historical perspective and turn to differentials of groups that vary on both phenomena. Here a general distinction between two types of research strategies should be noted. In the one case, groups whose drug use varies are compared as to criminality. As we are looking for a connection between the two variables and not for an explanation, it is also possible to look for the same connection by comparing the drug use of groups who vary in crime.

The main purpose of the other type of research is to specify the connection between drug use and crime. This centers around the question of which patterns of (illegal) income acquisition are typical for which patterns of drug use. Rather than comparing groups with different general patterns of drug use in this type of research the (co-)variations in time of income acquisition and drug use are examined, within one and the same group of users. We shall be returning to this type of research that is closest to our own in the next paragraph.

The biggest problem of research into different groups using drug use as a variable is the requirement of comparability. Leaving aside for the moment the question of the reliability of the distinction between users and nonusers, there is a real risk that drug users may differ from nonusers in other ways that are significant for crime. This is true for the simple fact that illegal drug use is an indication of deviant attitudes in itself. In one of the few known studies of this type, the risk was decreased by recruiting a research population with relatively homogenous social backgrounds. The respondents were all Mexican-American detainees in a county jail. This study found a big difference in the level of crime between users and nonusers of heroin. In the year prior to their detention, the users committed more types of (income-generating) crime. Moreover, the offenses within these types were more frequent and more likely to involve firearms (Chambers et al. 1981). The results of an Australian study among detainees are comparable (Dobinson 1989). Here, the relationship between the levels of drug use and crime during the six months prior to detention were determined for eighty-eight respondents. Those who had been users during that time had committed ten times as many burglaries as the nonusers.

Apart from use and nonuse, also the type and level of drug use (kinds of substances used and the intensity of drug use) is important for the connection with crime. Strangely enough, little research deals directly with this obvious question: To what extent do groups with differing patterns of problematic drug use show different crime profiles? A British study distinguished five patterns of drug use with increasing levels of intensity and "hardness," in a group of 150 criminals (Hammersley et al. 1989). At the bottom we find alcohol use only, in the middle poly-drug use, excluding opiates, and at the top what was designated as the most severe pattern of drug use, namely intensive use of opiates. A positive linear relationship between life-time crime experience and the severity of drug use was observed. Moreover, the group of intensive opiate users also committed by far the most current income generating crime. On the other hand, moderate opiate use was not significantly linked with current crime. So in general terms this study demonstrates a relation between severity patterns of crime and drug use.

Even more interesting may be the fact that almost every crime index distinguished sharply between the exclusive alcohol group and all illegal drug groups. The average weekly income from theft, for example, was £ 12 for the alcohol group, £ 102 for the cannabis group, and £ 303 for the intensive opiate group. These results allow for various interpretations. The fact that cannabis users are rather less criminal than intensive opiate users is compatible with a possible causal effect of psychopharmacological dependence on an expensive drug. On the other hand, a much bigger ratio of crime levels for cannabis users compared to alcohol, than for cannabis compared to intensive opiate users was observed. The alcohol group was relatively far less criminal compared to the cannabis group, than the cannabis group compared to the intensive opiate group. This result leaves open the possibility that the drugs' connotations with illegality and deviance may be even more important than the addictiveness or other pharmacological properties of the substances used. Cannabis is relatively cheap and nonaddictive in a pharmacological sense. The relatively high level of coinciding criminality may be explained by the rather strong social taboo on cannabis in the United Kingdom.

A different type of study in a different geographical and historical context produced comparable results. In the middle of the seventies, Preble (1977) conducted an urban ethnographic study in New York on patterns of drug use and income acquisition among the clients of methadone maintenance programs, then being introduced on a large scale in the United States. Unfortunately, contrary to the optimistic expectations and previous evaluations of those providing the methadone, no evidence was found of heroin users being given methadone and subsequently going on to lead a "normal," integrated, and productive life. Preble found three life-style patterns among this group of clients, in which the nature of drug use and the nature and level of (illegal) income acquisition were linked. Levels of drug use were categorized according to the drugs used regularly alongside methadone. The study distinguished three patterns of use: methadone + wine, methadone + wine + pills, methadone + cocaine. As far as life-style (income acquisition) is concerned, the first group was labeled as apathetic tramps, the second as opportunistic hustlers and petty thieves, while the third group distinguished itself through much more frequent and serious crime, including muggings.

As to the reverse question, are there more drug users among offenders than among nonoffenders, we can be brief. It is immediately clear from simple registration data that drug users are heavily overrepresented, especially at the lower levels of the criminal justice system. Probation service data show that active hard drug users even form the majority of detainees in Amsterdam police cells. According to the Prison Service Directorate of the Ministry of Justice, 25 percent of all prisoners are known to the prison medical staff as drug users (before detention). Research samples reveal even higher percentages: about 40 percent in remand centers and 30 percent in prisons (Erkelens 1987; Grapendaal 1987). This high concentration of drug users in the criminal justice system is by no means a typically Dutch phenomenon. According to a report of the United States National Institute of Justice (1989), more than half of those arrested in sixteen big American cities systematically produce positive results when (urine) tested for hard drugs. Again, British research by Parker et al. (1988) notes a high level of drug use among registered criminals. This study found percentages of drug use for different offenses varying from 55 percent for burglary to 10 percent for vandalism. In the same district, the percentage of hard drug users between sixteen and thirty-four years old was 1.5. This extreme overrepresentation of drug users among registered criminals is certainly significant, for it was found within a relatively homogenous population living in the same area. However, we must be careful here. Problematic drug users may not only commit more or more serious offenses, but they also run a greater risk than nonusers of becoming apprehended by the police. This is partly due to the user's stigmatized identity, which is often easily and outwardly recognizable. Possibly a greater vulnerability of drug addicts for the police may result from a more careless and opportunistic style of offending.

Individual Connection Between Drug Use and Crime

The fact that, "on average," drug users commit more crime, and that offenders take more drugs, says nothing about the (relative) significance of criminality for a drug user's pattern of income and spending. More especially, it does not answer questions concerning the part played by crime in a drug user's total income or the degree to which (illegal) income is connected with drug use. Are an increase or decrease in the intensity of drug use and crime linked? To find out requires a longitudinal element, in which the individual development of relevant behavioral characteristics is followed over a certain period of time.

The usual social circumstances of present deviant drug use imply an exceedingly low level of legal income. Badly educated, often unemployed young people find themselves almost automatically at the bottom of the regular income pyramid—whether they take drugs or not. And any study within the subculture of hard drug users is bound to reveal that regular use of hard drugs is at least partly financed from unconventional/illegal sources of income. This is certainly born out by the English studies of drug addiction in problematic big-city working-class areas. According to the self-report study we already mentioned among forty-six "new" drug users in London, crime formed the primary source of income for 80 percent (of which 65 percent was income-generating crime and 11 percent drug deals). It is perhaps even more striking that, during one research week, ten times more was spent on drugs than was received in legal income (Jarvis and Parker 1989). The Wirral study produced almost identical results. Of the group of active drug users, 65 percent named acquisitive crime as their most important source of income, 11 percent named drug dealing, while 13 percent had primarily legal income (Parker et al. 1988).

The results of Korf's study on the provincial heroine scene in "Noesveen" sharply contrast Parker's findings on young urban drug users in a highly deprived social economic setting. Korf found moderate heroin use, as far as both frequency and intensity are concerned, in (lower) "middle class homes with grey wall to wall carpet, black Scandinavian corduroy furniture and plants everywhere (. . .)" in the provincial residential area of "Heestergaard." According to self-report data, crime in this context forms the most important source of income for no more than 15 percent of the users (Korf et al. 1989, pp.56 and 130).

The fact that problem users in the city derive an important percentage of their income from crime does not in itself imply that this income is spent primarily on drugs. It is, for example, quite possible that much of the easy money of crime may disappear in various patterns of fast spending. Indeed, our society provides almost inexhaustible opportunities for consumer indulgence in the ultra-short term: gambling, "night on the town," sex, taxis, etc. And it should not be forgotten that such expensive pastimes fit a (deviant) life-style in which drug use often plays a part.

Despite all possible alternatives for spending income, an intense relationship between (illegal) income and drug use is very plausible. This is confirmed by research in New York, in which problem users reported on the offenses they committed on any one day and on how they spent the money. Within twenty-four hours, 85 percent of that money had been spent on drugs (Johnson et al. 1988). Some of these researchers also made an extensive study of the economic behavior (generating and spending income) of drug users in Harlem, New York (Johnson et al. 1985). In chapter 5 we shall be comparing the results of this study with those of our own project in Amsterdam.

It is at the individual level that we find the most critical test for the existence of an intrinsic connection between drug use and crime. However carefully groups of users are matched, in comparing them one can never exclude the fact that problem users may be, per definition, more deviant and more marginal. Theoretically, there are even strong arguments to support this assumption. In that case they are incomparable on a point that is directly related to the criterion variable (crime). This is why research that follows individual users during a certain period of time is so important. It allows one to study whether they commit more offenses during active periods of use than during periods of nonuse. The development of patterns of use is usually characterized by shorter or longer periods of abstinence or very low levels of use (Bennett and Wright 1986). This is often due to the influence of some form of treatment or therapy for the addiction. However, such periods also occur as a result of compelling circumstances, such as temporary unavailability of the drug on the illegal market, or they may occur "spontaneously," for example because the user has decided to decrease the use of drugs (temporarily). Because treatment and therapy are assumed to have some effect on the social behavior of addicts in general and not only on drug use as such, the latter types of abstinence are most relevant.

Research (especially American research) has shown that, leaving the possible effects of treatment aside, there is a strongly negative relationship between abstinence and income-generating crime. A group of American researchers undertook several research projects over a number of years, using "crime-days per year at risk" as standard of the drug user's level of criminality. This expresses the number of days calculated per year that the drug user was at liberty and for which he reported at least one specified criminal offense. No account was taken of more than one offense per day. This means, therefore, that the standard constitutes an underestimation of the actual number of offenses committed (Ball et al. 1982; Nurco et al. 1984; Nurco et al. 1988). All these American self-report studies reach the same conclusion, namely that addicts commit three to six times as much (income-generating) crime during active periods of use as during periods of non (or greatly decreased) use. Studies on Australian users show that about 85 percent of those who commit offenses during periods of drug use, stop during periods of abstinence (Dobinson 1989). When interpreting these results, it should not be forgotten that (periods of) abstinence usually form episodes within a lengthy career of drug use. This means that the element of drug use disappears temporarily, while the more lasting social and psychological characteristics of living with drugs (identity, life-style, circle of friends, social position, etc.) probably remain the same. There is, therefore, all the more reason to conclude that the problem user's level of crime is strongly linked to the level of drug use.

In summary, according to, mostly English language, research, it may be said that drug users as a group are more criminal than nonusers, that criminal gains form an important and structural part of the user's budget, that individual patterns of intensity of drug use and crime are synchronic, and, finally, that the user's illegal income is primarily spent on drugs.

All in all, it should come as no surprise that some researchers think it high time to leave out the remarks on "all things being relative" that the social sciences seem to require and to announce decidedly: "it is opiate use itself which is the principle cause of high crime rates among addicts." Perhaps we are even seeing the elevation of "common-sense prejudice" to scientifically established fact: "Common-sense notions about drug takers have long supposed that the so called addicts commit crime to finance their habits. Recent empirical research has born out the truth of this assertion—a somewhat unusual occurrence in the social sciences" (Jarvis and Parker 1989).

We shall be examining the question of whether any niceties of distinction can be discerned in the seemingly inevitable notion that crime is the *necessary result* of drug use.

EXPLANATIONS

Accepting the inevitability of an empirical link between problematic drug use and crime, the next step should be the construction and examination of theoretic models to explore the significance of the coincidence of these two modes of behavior.

Goldstein's "tripartite conceptual framework" forms an example. It has served to explain the drugs-violence nexus in the wake of the developing epidemic of crack use in big American cities. This pragmatic model, based on the examination of instances of homicide, proposes three different kinds of links between illegal drug use and criminal violence: "psychopharmacological, economically compulsive and systemic" (Goldstein 1985). Using crack may be related to violent behavior because this substance generates aggressive behavior as a consequence of its psychopharmacological effects. This comes close to the classical notion of irrational "drug-crazed" behavior. According to the concept of economical compulsiveness violent behavior is instrumentally, but yet inevitably propelled by the urges of addiction. And finally "systemic" drug-related violence is not explained by drug or addiction effects, but by the norms and coping mechanisms within a marginal and illegal social/economic distribution system. According to this notion crack would not be connected to violence if it was legally sold in pharmacies or liquor stores. Successive research projects into the drugs-violence relationship suggested that the psychopharmacological explanation was most plausible for alcohol related homicides, while crack-related homicides were best explained by the "systemic" link (Spunt et. al. 1990; Goldstein et. al. 1989 and 1991).

Departing not from empirical data but from a simple logical model, three types of links between (illegal) drug use and criminal behavior may be assumed:

1. drug use leads to crime;
2. crime leads to drug use;
3. drug use and crime are both symptoms of something else with a common cause.

The first model emphasizes the drug and the addiction. Crime is simply a function of the psychopharmacological (addictive) and economical (the price) properties of the drug. According to the second model, the primary factor is a deviant life-style in which drug use is an inevitable phenomenon. Drug use is seen as a secondary consequence of socialization within a deviant (criminal) subculture. The third model assumes that both drug use and crime are mutually reinforcing expressions of a deviant existence. The basic assumption of this model is that common conditions and processes underlie both drug use and crime.

The Perspective of Causality

The idea that drug use causes crime can be interpreted in several ways. The scope of one's concept of causality is important here. Swierstra uses an illuminating distinction between etiological causality and "causal reinforcement" (Swierstra 1990, p.55). The latter means that, given collective or individual developments of deviant patterns of social behavior, the phenomenon of drug use has a *stimulating effect* on crime. In other words, addiction to drugs is a ""multiplier' of already existing criminal behavior" (Ibid. p.58). " Free cash from crime might determine the amount of heroin used one day, but the need for heroin might determine the amount of crime committed the other day" (Hammersley and Morrison 1987). On the basis of the research results outlined in the section entitled "A Historical and Ecological Perspective," we may assume the existence of an empirical law of "causal reinforcement." As ever, alas, the actual significance of the obvious is small (McBride and McCoy 1982).

The etiological concept of causality is more far-reaching. It centers around the assumption that drug use plays a decisive part in both the long-term development of individual patterns of criminal behavior, and an individual's current criminal behavior. Excluding addiction to drugs would mean that decisive reasons for income-generating crime would disappear. Logically, this implies a drastic decrease in the level of crime in case drug addicts could receive drugs for free.

On the other hand, the term etiological also refers to an aspect of development that cannot be separated from the person committing the crime. The illegal acquisition of income assumes not only a more or less compelling motive, but also, among other things, competence in crime, the availability of noncriminal alternatives, and the relative absence of good reasons for behaving "respectably." The latter category of reasons is also referred to as inhibiting factors. These are constituted by whatever an individual has to lose by his criminal behavior. On a personal level this may be generalized as shame and fear of losing social, affective, and material interests in the conventional order. Etiological causality implies that drug use is decisive in the individual development of such criminal propensities.

Commonsense (and policy) notions about the drug problem do not usually question the truth of the statement that illegal drug use inevitably leads to crime. In this connection Goldman (1981) has referred to the "inevitability hypothesis." This inevitability derives from a theory of addiction in which addiction is seen as a disease. The theory has a strong internal logic and consistency in explaining the social behavior of drug users. The addict's (social) behavior is perceived as predominantly determined by the addiction. Normally, multiple purposes, meanings, and functions are perceived as explanations of or significant for social behavior. These explanations concern social positions and individual aspirations. Acquisitive or violent crime committed by nonaddicts, for example, is attributed to a number of motives and functions: economic gain, confirmation of peer group status, the expression of social frustration and protest, the expression of a need for power or domination, or simply pleasure in performing competently and fulfilling a certain life-style.

Apparently all of this is no longer really significant when addicts are concerned. In that case we see an extreme reduction in the social construction of the meaning of the addict's (deviant) behavior. His motives appear transparent, simple, and compelling. In this socially accepted construction, the drug user or heavy drinker is perceived as a response-machine, subjected to the autonomous and dominating force of the disease called addiction: " . . . the logic of the disease concept leads all concerned . . . to deny, to ignore, to discount what meaning that way of life may have. Seen as an involuntary symptom of a disease, the drinking is isolated from the rest of life, and viewed as the meaningless but destructive effect of a noxious condition, a 'disease'" (Peele 1989, p.86). Within this disease model, the question of *why* illegal drug users should commit crime is scarcely relevant. Indeed, as far as the symptoms of the disease are concerned, questions about purposeful behavior seem misdirected. Would it not be almost rude to ask a sick person *why* he sleeps so much? And so questions about the why of a deviant drug user's criminal behavior disappear from view because it is so obvious what *causes* it. In this frame of reference, the (impoverished) addict's criminal behavior is an inevitable consequence of his addiction. This perspective implies that dealing, stealing, fencing, rip-deals, and forged checks are manifestations of purely utilitarian instrumental behavior, for which the motives are considered to be simple and compelling. "Inevitability" stands for instrumental causality, in which criminal behavior essentially has no other meaning than a necessary condition for satisfying the addiction. The conceptual consequences of this construction are twofold. It means that while on the one hand crime is causally determined, it is of little personal significance for the addict. According to the addiction-causes-crime theory, the drug user is more or less forced to commit crime, but it has no real meaning for him. In commonsense terms this means that the addict goes out stealing simply because he has no choice, but that he would like to stop being a criminal if only he could kick the drugs, or if he could get them free, or if he could be satisfied with legally provided methadone.

This construction seems to be very popular among junkies themselves, but not only there. Its optimistic (?) but rather simplistic view of people and addiction often works as a silent arrangement between the parties in the everyday reality of the drug problem, such as junkies, therapists, and the criminal justice authorities. This construction has its advantages for everyone. Its assumption that criminal behavior is essentially alien to the junkie allows him to avoid moral responsibility for his behavior: he is expected to steal, and therefore excused in advance. It allows therapists to avoid confrontations with addicts about their social behavior and it excuses the police and criminal justice authorities for their inability to exercise any degree of control over crime committed by addicts. In practice, this means that addicts may be set free from a police cell after their twentieth arrest in one year, "because it makes no difference to them anyway."

In the perspective of inevitable causality, the answer to questions about the effect of illegal drug use on crime is simple. Drugs appear here as an independent evil in society that generates another evil, crime. This makes the nature of the problem more tangible and in this construction possible solutions become more credible: if something can be done about addiction to drugs, then crime will decrease 'of its own accord.' Doing something about crime can then take the form of any one of the whole ideological-instrumental range of social reactions. In all of these cases, there may be patent solutions to the problem, however contradictory in themselves. Legalization or consistent repression by means of criminal law, medical, or psychosocial intervention and the distribution of methadone are all rational means of dealing with drug-related crime, if the axiom is accepted that addiction to expensive drugs inevitably leads to crime. However, there is a danger that this obvious and pervasive reduction of the problem will lead to all too optimistic and ritual social (policy) reactions. It is by no means certain that there is any sense in approaching the problem of drug-related crime by solely taking its utilitarian function into account.

The more the development of drug use and crime are connected within groups whose deviance and marginality are historically given characteristics, the more difficult it becomes to find empirical confirmation of the inevitability hypothesis. The basic drawback being that within this social context, the time order between both phenomena that is essential for etiological causality often seems to be reversed. In "traditional criminal" subcultures, patterns of criminal behavior usually develop on average at a younger age than problematic drug use (Burr 1987; Clayton and Tuchfield 1982; Chaiken and Chaiken 1990). According to the extensive summary of relevant literature in Swierstra's study (1990, pp. 50–68), it is so usual for both phenomena to develop together—without being able to say which was first—that etiological causality becomes a meaningless and unprovable construct: "In a causal sense, the question of whether hard drug addiction on the one hand and criminal behavior on the other are mutually explanatory, is a spurious question, a matter of chicken and egg . . . addiction does not cause criminal behavior, but neither is the reverse true. The causal explanation for the connections that have been found lies in a common background."

In this connection, Clayton and Tuchfield (1982) advocate letting go of a simplistic concept of causality in explaining the relationship between drug use and crime. Instead, they assume the existence of "causal chains" (see Figure 2–1) in which there is room for both "antecedent" and "intervening variables."

According to these authors, one cannot assume direct causality between drug use and crime. Rather, the relationship develops as a result of the effect of intervening factors that can explain the connection between both phenomena, a connection that is limited

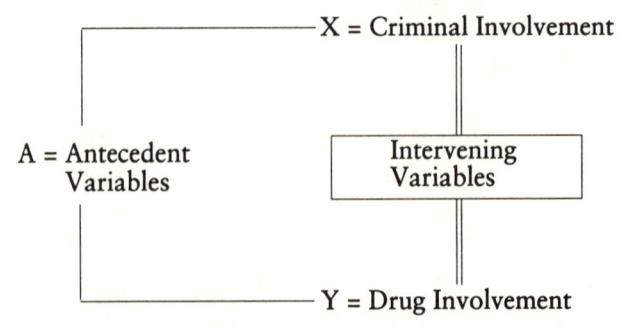

```
                          ┌──────── X = Criminal Involvement
                          │                ‖
                          │                ‖
                          │          ┌───────────────┐
  A = Antecedent          │          │  Intervening  │
      Variables           │          │   Variables   │
                          │          └───────────────┘
                          │                ‖
                          │                ‖
                          └──────── Y = Drug Involvement
```

Figure 2–1: Causal Chains (Clayton and Tuchfield 1982)

and conditional in this model. Unfortunately, this article does not go deeper into the question of which factors actually have such effects. Speckart and Anglin (1986a and 1986b) have subjected the matter of causality to rigorous empirical research, collecting retrospective data on a group of 671 addicts. The data concerned drug use and criminal behavior in the period one year prior to the onset of illegal drug use. They conclude that:

1. there is a certain individual stability in both drug use and patterns of illegal income acquisition (drug dealing and acquisitive crime);
2. crime has strong instrumental connections with drug use, without this necessarily implying a causal connection, because their research does not reveal any exclusive long term effects between drug use and crime.

Finally, they maintain that the results of their study partly confirm all of the causal relationships that are theoretically possible: "The fact that each of these three positions holds some validity is a consequence of the heterogeneity of types or styles within addict samples and reflects the need to segregate addict types in search of lawful relationships and to specify the conditions under which such relationships hold" (Speckart and Anglin 1986a).

It is difficult to reduce the phenomena under discussion here, drug use and crime, to static and isolated elements in a causal order. The perspective shifts away, both prior to the supposed cause and following the supposed effect. If drug use leads to crime, then what is the "cause" of drug use, and what are the effects of the crime so caused? These questions are of particular importance if there are reasons to assume that complex categories of social behavior in real-life social situations are not only "causes" and "effects" in a simple one way causal relationship, but that they also affect and reaffect each other.

Factors upon which the development of the causal factor is partly based (here drug use), may play an independent part in the development of the supposed effect (here crime). This means, for example, that the structural strain inherent in positions of social-economic deprivation may contribute directly both to a criminal existence (whether or not in combination with drug use) and to the development of problematic drug use. This latter effect of social deprivation is, therefore, also a cause of crime. Criminal behavior, however, also provides the conditions that promote drug use. It produces the necessary (financial) means with which to buy illegal drugs and, at the same time, it promotes the necessary social contacts for acquiring access to the illegal drug market. At an individual, psychological level, drug use provides strong motivation and legitimation for criminal behavior. Addicts feel driven to acquire the necessary means (illegally) by their physical and/or psychological craving. As a result, the same craving provides a credible reason for being criminal, both for the addict himself and for society in general. Finally, it is likely that concentration of deviant phenomena in a minority culture will reinforce and perpetuate that culture's marginality. This brings us back to square one: structural marginality underlies such deviant symptoms as crime and drug use, while in their turn these symptoms may reinforce the marginality of the environment concerned.

The Perspective of Functionality

This model proceeds upon the assumption that living with drugs represents a life-style of which both drug use and criminal behavior are important elements. Both forms of behavior are connected, but, contrary to the assumptions of the causal model, crime cannot be traced to the addiction. This approach, that is strongly oriented towards the person of the drug user in his social context, sees social behavior as purposeful and functional, rather than determined. This means that crime committed by deviant drug users has more meaning and serves more purposes than that of mere instrument for acquiring the drug and satisfying the urges of addiction. In an existence with drugs, crime is less inevitable on the one hand, and of greater social and psychological significance on the other, than is usually assumed. It is generally thought to be self-evident that the deviant drug user is strongly involved in his use of drugs. However, it may even be more important to understand that he is also involved in his criminality, as a central element of a deviant-life style. In this view, crime is much more than a "necessary evil" that only serves to obtain drugs. Rather, it makes an essential contribution to the realization of a life with drugs. In other words: crime is one of the attractions of a deviant existence with drugs. The criminal behavior of deviant drug addicts may be understood not so much as *caused* by the addiction, but as *functional* for a life on the rim of society. As (predominantly) independently motivated behavior, crime is linked to the life history of the user and to the situational circumstances of his drug use. Both, in their turn, are strongly related to their social-cultural context.

The concept "deviant career" plays an important part in this deviance perspective. In everyday language and in relation to conventional life-styles, the concept of career implies a certain duration and a number of phases. Its substantive meaning concerns the development of social patterns of behavior. A career has a more or less distinguishable beginning and end and proceeds in stages. In a professional or sports career, for example, this could be described in the following sequence:

- a (preliminary) phase of development, a run up to
- a middle phase in which the pattern of behavior is maintained at a high level and
- a phase of completion, winding down.

This description does not necessarily exclude shorter cycles within a more general and longer time perspective.

In general, biological, psychological, and social factors determine the course of a career. Because these are long-term developments, the biological cycle of life is of some importance. To a certain extent, normal vital processes of growing and aging determine increases and decreases in knowledge, skills, experiences, and physical or mental competence of behavioral patterns that are relevant to a career. This is, of course, most obvious in a sports career, but this cycle of vitality also plays a part in professional careers. Finally, it is important to take the subjective, psychological side of the career concept into account. This is determined by the individual's interest in the social pattern of behavior and by the extent to which he is (emotionally) involved in it.

In brief, this may be regarded as the degree to which a person derives identity from his career. Some authors distinguish here between normative, economic and social involvement (Adler and Adler 1985, p.144). We assume that these psychological elements of involvement have more or less the same cyclicity as the objective characteristics of a career.

In criminology, the concept of a deviant career has long been accepted (Sutherland 1937). Like a professional cyclist or a journalist, a burglar too has a certain minimum and maximum age at which he can ply his trade; he must learn skills and acquire knowledge; there is a period in his life in which his profession is a central and determining factor of his existence; and there comes a time when he gets tired of it all. The term drug career, as well-established as deviant career, can be regarded as a variant of the latter.

As well as similarities, there are also differences between deviant and conventional careers. In sociological labeling theory, the deviant career is, to a great extent, seen as the product of (disapproving) social reactions (Becker 1963; Lemert 1967). This theory is especially relevant for highly socialized deviant careers, whereby moral judgments play an important part. Labeling theory describes the normal development of a deviant drug career as a process of escalation, typically beginning in puberty and adolescence. During this phase of life, the normal psychosocial process of development involves experiments with a variety of forms of behavior, including the sort of behavior that the adult world calls troublesome, risky, morally dubious, or even delinquent.

The first development of a life with drugs is strongly connected to adolescence. Drug careers usually begin between the fifteenth and eighteenth year of a person's life. The further course of a drug career is usually seen as occupying some twenty years. Only some of those who started using illegal drugs in adolescence will actually complete this span. Longitudinal research on drug users over such a long period of time usually concerns users whose deviant drug career was already established when they became involved in the research. Swierstra's summary of twenty-eight non-Dutch longitudinal studies shows that almost all involve hard drug users registered by the criminal justice authorities and/or therapeutic institutions. A curve is extrapolated from these studies, showing that about 20 percent no longer use drugs two years after the start of the research, and that 40 percent abstain after twenty years, while 15–20 percent die during this period (Swierstra 1990, pp. 78–92 and 122–124). This means that about 40 percent of addicted drug users still use drugs after twenty years.

Sociological labeling theory has often described the development of an addiction to illegal drugs as a process in which primary deviance develops into secondary deviance. Primary deviance is formed of normative transgressions, in which the individual has little personal stake. In secondary deviance, however, deviating from normality becomes an essential characteristic of the person and his position in society. "They (the deviant acts) become the central facts of existence for those experiencing them, altering psychic structure, promoting specialised organization of social roles and self regarding attitudes. The secondary deviant, as opposed to his actions, is a person whose life and identity are organized around the facts of deviance" (Lemert 1967, p. 41).

Drug use is one of the types of (risky) behavior that usually arise from tensions, problems, and needs connected with adolescence. Young people must come to terms with the sharp contrast between hedonistic and consumptive needs and the trials and tribulations that must be borne if these needs are to be fulfilled in a respectable way. Illegal drug use offers an escape from this fundamental conflict. In experimenting with drugs, adolescents may satisfy and demonstrate a need for independence. Perhaps most essential of all are the social rewards to be found in the peer group of coexperimenters, (Glassner and Loughlin 1987; Carpenter et al. 1988). Such age-related deviance is usually of a freewheeling and frivolous nature. To a certain extent, adolescents may behave in this way without being identified too closely with their behavior. There is something "innocent" about primary deviance. The (moral) rejection of it concerns the act rather than the person committing it. Fundamental to the explanation of the escalation of deviance is the social-psychological assumption that, to an important degree, an individual's image of self reflects the image of that individual that has been cast and disseminated by the outside world (Mead 1939). Under certain circumstances, this mechanism allows the actor to identify with his deviant acts. The more (morally) objectionable the behavior appears to be (the stronger its taboo properties), the longer it goes on, the more public it is, and the less there are socially accepted circumstances to serve as an excuse and to mitigate the individual's "blame" for that behavior, the more inevitable such deviant identification will become.

In some life histories, such conditions trigger a development from primary to secondary deviance. In this case the distinction between the person and his deviant actions disappears—first for the outside social world and later for the individual himself. That individual then develops (accepts) an identity in which deviance is more durable, more central, and less freewheeling.

Labeling theory has it that behavior that is labeled "immoral" is highly stigmatizing and therefore extremely likely to determine an individual's image of self and style of life (Goffman 1963). Any illegality attaching to the behavior is a coincidental but reinforcing factor rather than an essential one. In the Netherlands for instance, prostitution is a legal form of income acquisition, but as a consequence of its immoral character, it nevertheless often leads to a highly determined deviant development. The addiction to illegal drugs is especially consequential, because it is surrounded with both moral and legal prohibitions. This gives drug addiction properties of an infringement of a social taboo. Such infringements give rise to a double process of isolation and collectivization. Those who perpetrate moral infringements are excluded from "respectable" society and, at the same time, attracted by, and allotted a new place, in a collective of like-minded comrades. This allows a process of marginalization to develop in which conventional society's (re)action of exclusion and the individual's (re)action of retreat to his own "safehouse," are mutually reinforcing.

The formation of deviant subcultures is the more collective dimension in this process. Deviant subcultures may be regarded as structural entities in which deviant forms and behavior exist and survive more or less independent of the individuals who exhibit them. Thus, within a subculture ready repertoires of (deviant) actions are offered to anyone entering such a social circle. These deviant modes of behavior in their turn offer (temporary) solutions for the (daily) social, psychological, and economic needs.

The degree of marginalization that accompanies a deviant career can be regarded as a function of the above-mentioned collectivization and isolation. That is to say, the more an individual is absorbed into the deviant subculture and, on the other hand, the greater the gap between the deviant subculture and conventional society, the stronger marginalization will be. Because of this aspect deviant drug addicts are more completely segregated from conventional society and more intensely enveloped by a marginal subculture than, say, alcoholics. Contrary to junkies, in the course of their career of addiction, alcoholics are able to keep their worlds of bars and cafes on the one hand and work and family on the other separate for quite a long time. This allows them to avoid having their existence completely determined by their addiction.

The following chapter will put some flesh on the abstract bones of deviant career development described here, by looking at the life histories of many of the drug users who took part in this research project.

CHAPTER 3

Careers in Deviancy and Drugs

Life histories, whether they be deviant or not, are products of societies and individuals. Historical-social circumstances play a part in their development, as do the characteristics of the person concerned, such as personality structure and individual experience. An analysis of careers of addiction may emphasize the (deprived) social position of drug users, the lack of attractive, motivating, and realizable expectations of a meaningful existence within the conventional order, or the existence of an individual psychological pathology. The problem, therefore, is the (relative) importance of three types of determinants: structural, cultural, and psychological. This distinction corresponds to three, frequently used, models of explanation which center around a specific form of the functionality of being an addict: an alternative existence "from force of necessity," a rebellion, and a medicine. According to the first model, drug addiction is predominantly the result of poverty and social deprivation. For those who have no chance in the regular social economic order, the world of drugs offers an alternative existence, with its own economy, social contacts, and daily activities. According to the second explanation, an addiction to drugs is an attempt to attribute some meaning to life: drug addiction as a "cultural disease," which appears among groups of the population susceptible to such problems (such as adolescents). In this connection, drug problems among bored young people from respectable backgrounds, but alienated from school and family, are proverbial. But other (nondeviant) forms of (possibly) problematic drug use fall into this category too, such as the use of medicines by housewives, or cocaine by yuppies. The third explanation turns to psychopathologies and regards drug addiction as an expression of individual psychological disturbance. More than in the previous sociological perspectives, the emphasis here is on the psychopharmacological effects of drug use on the user's emotional well-being. Given a certain personality structure, personal problems and traumatic experiences are said to create a strong need for the intoxicating and numbing effects of psychotropic drugs.

Studying individual life histories is especially useful for gaining some insight into the relative importance of, and the connection between, the different types of determinant in the development of deviant drug addiction. The addiction is approached as a long and ongoing process in which, in answer to and in interaction with his or her environment, the individual pursues certain goals, makes choices, and tries to find a solution to the problems of life. Within existing social conditions, deviant drug addicts derive rewards from their behavior, and at the same time they pay a certain price. A drug career may, therefore, be regarded as a dynamic process of development in which a more or less conscious balancing of costs and gains determines both the deviant drug user's daily activities and the long-term course of the career itself.

A deviant life with drugs is functional and sometimes even attractive against the background of alternative options (subjectively) available to the individual for realizing a satisfying existence and planning a meaningful future. The artificial distinction between the different types of determinant disappears in the light of the availability of alternatives. At the level of individual life histories, it is often difficult to separate social deprivation, cultural alienation, and the psychological need for intoxication and numbness. This is especially true of the first two types of determinant. In practice, poverty on the one hand and poorly functioning social institutions (such as school and family) and lack of involvement in the goals of conventional culture on the other, often go hand in hand. But again, in this context there will probably be no lack of traumatic psychological experiences, the alleviation of which may be sought in the effect of drugs.

Using the life histories of our respondents, this chapter provides an outline of the way in which their deviant and drug careers developed. The first section deals with social backgrounds and primary and secondary socialization. This provides us with a picture of the start of the drug careers of the hard drug addicts in Amsterdam who figure in our sample. The second section looks at the further development of those careers. Finally, the last section deals with the patterns of delinquency gradually developed by the respondents in the course of their careers.

STARTING TO USE HARD DRUGS

Social-Economic Background

We have already seen in chapter 2 that deviant drug addiction in the United States and the United Kingdom seems to be predominantly determined by the user's social position. Not all American adolescents from deprived ethnic minority backgrounds become problematic drug users. But, on the other hand, addiction to illegal drugs in the United States is very much concentrated in the culture of poverty of black and Latin American minority groups. We have also seen that the relatively recent development of "new heroin use" in Great Britain is, without exception, to be found in impoverished working-class areas. Both Western examples suggest massive determination of deviant careers of addiction as a result of the structural/cultural problem posed by the "lowest levels" of society. Given such a strong connection with social position, it may well be that no special individual reasons are needed for the development of a deviant drug career. In that case the drug career may resemble other "normal," self-evident ways of life with a tempting beginning and a bad end.

Because the focus of this explanation of drug careers is on the social-economic structure, we shall first examine whether there is such an obvious connection between culture of deprivation and the development of problematic drug use in Dutch welfare society, with its relatively less sharp contrasts.

TABLE 3–1
Social-Economic Background

Social-Economic Class	Percentage
Class 1	42
Class 2	44
Class 3	14

The social-economic background of the respondents was operationalized according to the profession of either or both parents. If both parents were working—which did not occur very often—the highest position was taken as indicative. We distinguished the following three social-economic environments: class 1, with respondents whose parents were either (durably) unemployed or employed as unskilled laborers. Class 2 contains the respondents whose parents could be regarded as respectable working class and lower middle class. Finally, class 3 contains respondents from higher (middle-class) backgrounds. Table 3-1 shows how the classes were distributed in the sample.

Our sample also reveals relative overrepresentation of the lower social-economic classes. Five other Dutch studies, summarized by Korf, show the same tendency: "Persons from working class and lower middle class backgrounds are strongly over-represented among the hard drug users in our country"(Korf 1990). However, it should be noted that more than half of our sample does not belong to the "real" lower class. The relationship between hard drug use and low social position is less pronounced here than in Great Britain and the United States. Our sample shows no significant differences in social-economic status between Dutch and immigrant users, or between men and women.

Place of Birth

A minority of our respondents (38 percent) were born in Amsterdam. At the age of fifteen, exactly half of the respondents were in the capital. Of the immigrants, 32 percent celebrated their fifteenth birthday in Amsterdam; 34 percent of the respondents from Surinam/Netherlands Antilles[1] came to the Netherlands after their twenty-first birthday. The life histories show that many of the respondents born and bred in Amsterdam were from the old nineteenth-century working class areas on the outskirts of the old city. Although these areas can by no means be compared with American ghettos, nevertheless in Amsterdam as well the social environment of one's youth seems to have some effect on the development of a criminal career. Many of the respondents from these areas revealed that their first steps on the path of deviance took place in an area-related setting. As young children they hung about the streets, met like-minded friends of the same age at the community center and formed a sort of gang with them.

---

1. Surinam, situated in South America, is a former colony of the Netherlands. This country became independent in 1975. The five islands of the Netherlands Antilles (and Aruba) are still part of the Dutch kingdom.

Primary Phase of Socialization: Family and Childhood

The parents of 37 percent of our respondents are still together. One-parent families often occurred when the respondents were very young; 41 percent were confronted with divorce, of the other 22 percent (at least one) parent died.

Almost half (48 percent) of the respondents describe their relationship with their parents as poor to very poor. No less than 37 percent of the sample had been in contact with a child protection agency before they reached the age of sixteen: 24 percent were involved with civil courts or the Child Protection Council; 13 percent were sent to a penitentiary for young people as a result of contacts with the criminal justice authorities. By comparison, in the past decades the percentage of young people coming into contact yearly with the civil or criminal branch of child protection authorities has never exceeded 2 percent (Junger-Tas and Kruissink 1990; van der Laan 1990; CBS 1961–1993). So these biographical data alone show that a large number of our respondents grew up in typically problematic family circumstances.

The following is a description of our respondents' childhood years. According to family stability, we distinguish two categories: the more problematic family circumstances and the "normal" unproblematic families according to the respondents. The groups are about equal in size, with about sixty respondents in each.[2]

The Problematic Family Background These respondents were inclined to describe their childhood families in terms of tension, broken marriages, and problems. As a rule, these meant that one of the parents left. The children then usually grew up in one-parent families, or were taken into care.

Problems at home were blamed on many factors, especially addiction of either or both parents, domestic violence, and the regular absence of parent(s) for differing reasons, including illness or psychological problems.

In one in five families, at least one of the parents (usually the father) had an alcohol problem. In these families, the burden of bringing the children up usually fell entirely on the mother. If she too avoided parental responsibilities, the children had to fend for

---

2. Life history interviews were conducted with 136 respondents. In fourteen cases we could not obtain a clear picture of the family situation.

themselves. Annie's life history reveals the extent of neglect that may result from this development:

> Annie[3] never knew her father to do anything but hang around in bars. According to Annie, her mother soon followed her husband. To keep the children quiet, they were regularly fed "space-cake" (cake with cannabis)—for the first time when Annie was four. They also went along to the bars and cafes and often stayed there until two in the morning. After a while, the father turned out to be involved with other women. Mother found out and sent Annie and her little brother out to catch father red-handed in his adultery. Two things could happen if father noticed: he would ignore the children, or fly into a rage. Annie wasn't sure which was worse. Things went badly at school. Annie managed to finish primary school with difficulty. Just after she finished, a radical change took place at home. Mother came into contact with a Jehovah's witness, and spent a great deal of time studying the bible. As a reaction, father spent even less time at home. After a while, mother also went out knocking on doors, taking Annie with her. Annie rebelled and ran away from home. She ended up at an agency providing shelter for the homeless. She was then 14 years old.

Respondents remembered not only excessive alcohol consumption at home, but also the immoderate consumption of psychopharmaca. There was an overrepresentation of mothers here. Parents also regularly used soft drugs. The use of hard drugs, however, was exceptional. Indeed, if respondents remembered hard drugs being used, the users were generally brothers or sisters experimenting with pep pills or opiates.

Of our respondents, 15 percent explicitly mentioned tensions at home developing into violence towards the partner and/or children. The father was usually the aggressor. The picture that these respondents paint of their father reveals extremely authoritarian men using domestic violence in order to give their authority in the family an extra boost.

A number of respondents were not only physically but also sexually abused. Eight women and three men said they had been sexually abused by a member of the family. Confirming Draijer's findings (1988), the respondents reported mechanisms of denial

---

3. Having promised our respondents confidentiality, it goes without saying that the Christian names used in this report are fictitious.

on the part of the mother and intimidation on the part of the father.

All of the respondents who described the situation at home as one of conflict reported feeling emotionally neglected as a child. In a number of cases, lack of interest was directly traceable to the fact that the parents were so busy. One respondent went to live with his grandmother when his parents found it impossible to combine their activities in the red-light district of Amsterdam—mother was a prostitute and father a pimp—with bringing up their son. Neglect, however, was not typical for the lower social-economic classes. It was the respondents from the "better" social backgrounds who complained regularly about being neglected. In these families the father was too busy with his own career and the mother lacked the strength or the heart for worrying about the children.

As we have seen, some failures in upbringing were due to the fact that the parents were ill or psychologically distressed. This was named as an important cause of seriously impairing family life by 20 percent of our respondents. The mothers usually had the psychological problems. Respondents were inclined to connect problems relating to the father figure with long periods of unemployment. In many cases, physical and mental problems led to hospitalization or early death.

Three respondents said that the mother or father had been (temporarily) absent while serving a prison sentence. As far as we know, the fathers and/or brothers of six respondents spent their time committing criminal offenses.[4] Four respondents reported that another member of the family (uncle or cousin) was involved in criminal activities. Only a few, therefore, were brought up to be familiar with crime.

We have seen that almost a quarter of the sample came into contact with civil or criminal child protection agencies at an early age. The great majority of these respondents ended up being taken into care, spending an important part of their childhood in childrens' homes or foster homes. Some respondents regarded such periods as a welcome change from the misery at home, others felt abandoned and felt they had landed from the frying pan in the

---

4. Domestic violence that took place within the home is not, of course, included.

fire. This setting provided an early experience of a highly marginal social perspective.

A substantial number of respondents, although "allowed" to remain at home despite the precarious family situation, developed norms and values that were based more on what they experienced outside than on internalized patterns within the family. These children avoided the oppressive atmosphere at home as much as possible, and their daily life was conducted in the street, the community center, the youth center or the squatters' cafe. Participation in a regular school system was less and less compatible with the deviant life-style they were gradually developing. However, this did not always involve crime at an early age. In a number of cases, their behavior was no more deviant than hanging about in gambling halls, youth clubs, or community centers, while consuming an immoderate amount of alcohol, cannabis, and/or pep pills. For these respondents, crime did not become a serious option until much later—sometimes never.

The Nonproblematic Family Background The use of hard drugs is certainly not always based on a problematic family background. Slightly more than half of the respondents reported a "normal" or even "very nice" childhood. 15 percent of our respondents characterized their family background as "good," seeing no relationship at all between their childhood experiences and the later development of a drug career. Monica:

> If you're asking whether my drug habit has anything to do with the situation at home, the answer is a straight no. I had a fantastic childhood, really. I could have anything I wanted, I was spoiled really, by both my parents. I can't remember them ever being not nice to me.

Only a few were so explicitly positive about their family background. Most said they had had a "carefree childhood," "no problems at home" or a "harmonious family." Further questioning revealed that there had been friction at home in some cases, although not so serious as to fundamentally disrupt the structure of the family. The respondents often criticized their parents for being too strict (sometimes for religious reasons). It was only in adolescence that real conflicts developed. Not doing well at school, the "wrong" friend, going out too much, and the use of soft drugs all led to clashes with parents during this phase.

Secondary Phase of Socialization: Education, Friends, Starting on Drugs

We shall first give the figures for level of education and average age at which the respondents started on different drugs and crime prior to drug use. These data will then be filled in, using our qualitative material.

Level of Education We collected data on both the last type of school attended and the last type of education that was actually finished.

That level is not very high; 49 percent did not finish any school after primary education, while 5 percent did not even finish primary school. Almost a quarter of the respondents did finish some type of secondary, higher, or even college education, with 6 percent finishing secondary professional training. Six respondents started university or college; three finished. We did not find differences in educational level between the sexes and ethnic groups.

First Use of Different Drugs The lowest average starting age is for cannabis (sixteen), followed by LSD/speed at seventeen. Most respondents started on opiates around their twentieth year. The older respondents started on opium (at the end of the sixties or beginning of the seventies). Without exception, these respondents went on to take heroin. Two respondents reported starting on methadone and then moving on to heroin. In general, they did not try cocaine until about a year and half after they had started using heroin. Nevertheless, fifteen used cocaine first and then moved on to heroin. These cases represent an interesting development from recreational, nondeviant use of cocaine in discotheques, etc., to deviant drug use. Medicinal drugs come last in this development. Hard drug users start on psychopharmacological drugs at about twenty-two.

Predrugs Crime A study on imprisoned drug addicts by Erkelens et al. (1979) shows that about half of them had committed (registered) offenses before they started using drugs. Despite the fact that our sample was not taken from a prison population, we found the same result: for 51 percent (64 percent of the men and 13 percent of the women) of the respondents, crime came prior to their first use of opiates. There is hardly any difference between Dutch users and immigrants. More than half of the 51 percent committed fairly serious first offenses, such as robbery with violence, burglary, assault, or some other violent crime. Six respondents were dealers before they became users. There are substantial differences in the frequency with which these offenses were committed. 28 percent of the men (20 percent of the whole sample) started committing serious offenses early. For about the same percentage of the sample, predrugs crime was restricted to "petty" offenses such as shoplifting, vandalism, joyriding, etc. With the exception of one female respondent, the "criminal" women were all involved in petty crime only.

The Different Routes to Hard Drugs The life histories reveal that there are different routes to the use of hard drugs. Some of our respondents developed a deviant life-style at an early age, into which drug use was integrated as a matter of course, others bumped into psychotropic drugs in the recreational sphere. Between these two extremes lie many different routes to hard drug use. The following description has deviant (criminal) behavior as a starting point. We shall first describe the beginning of a drug career in the context of a more general deviant development. We shall then repeat the procedure for those respondents who started from a more conventional way of life.

As we have shown, a considerable number of respondents became alienated from such conventional frameworks as school and family at an early age. These respondents soon carved a niche for themselves in a world of young people with identical problems. From the very beginning they were to be found in marginal youth cultures, in which the (immoderate) use of alcohol and (soft) drugs was a normal phenomenon. The same often applied to committing criminal offenses. Often the development was a collective one, with group behavior shifting from "petty" crime to more serious offenses such as burglary and violence.

The influence of the peer group on such young people—all male in our sample— was of crucial importance for the further course of their criminal career. These ganglike groups usually had strong ties with the neighborhood, a more or less permanent core, and a clear status structure. The position of the members of such groups depended very much on the amount of showing off they did and on the amount of money they had to spend. It is no coincidence that "living dangerously" and immoderate consumption are also central elements in the life of drugs that they later came to lead. Some respondents were the types who became leaders of these youth gangs. John is one of them:

> At the age of 16, John was a recognised leader of a notorious neighbourhood gang that often figured in the newspapers. They committed burglaries, prised cigarette machines from walls and, more especially, fought ferociously with other gangs and with the Hell's Angels. Later the local authorities gave them their own club-house. Once, the Hell's Angels came to take revenge: they were angry because the authorities had given them less subsidy than John's gang. They also stole cars on a regular basis. On average they drank between 20 and 30 glasses of beer a night, but in the weekends, when things really got going, it could have been twice that much. John says that he once stole a few thousand guilders from the safe in his own club-house.

Hard drugs soon entered these criminal subcultures. The pressure to conform to group norms played a significant part here. Losing face had to be avoided at all costs. This does not, however, mean that these young people nurtured ambivalent feelings about drugs and had to be helped over the threshold. On the contrary, most described the process of initiation as "exciting" and indicated that curiosity as to the effects of the different drugs was one of their strongest motives to experiment as much as possible. Sometimes these respondents did not even know what they were using. "We thought it was a sort of pot, it wasn't until later that we found out it was heroin."

The youth gang plays a less prominent part in the development of drug use by women in a deviant context. As far as the female respondents are concerned, starting on hard drugs is connected with relationships and (the exploitation of) sexuality. It sometimes seems to be a process that the women sought actively. Hard drug use may be rooted in a pattern of sexual victimization. Here are two examples:

> When she was ten, Nicole and her five brothers were taken into care. A few years later she ran away from the children's home together with some other girls. They made straight for Amsterdam, and smoked their first joint with the hippies on Dam Square. Nicole is lyrical about this time: "I lived like the queen in paradise." Nicole lived on the street and in the Vondel Park for a while. The JAC[5] found her somewhere to stay on a boat. The man who ran the boat also dealt in hash and he let the girls

who lived there get stoned for nothing. Nicole wanted to earn her own money and became a prostitute through a friend. She was 14 years old. The police soon got on to her and she was sent to a home for difficult girls. Indeed, she says herself: "Society couldn't deal with me."

For some time, Karen had been sexually abused by her stepfather. When she was 15, she ran away from home and went to live with a Chinese boy she had met in a disco. Shortly before that, she had used heroin for the first time in that disco. At that point Karen was as green as grass as far as drugs were concerned. "I didn't even know what hash was, never mind heroin. The only thing I can remember about the first time was that it knocked me out." Karen's Chinese friend dealt in drugs on the Zeedijk and soon she was there herself. She had no idea what the eventual consequences of using heroin might be. The only thing she knew immediately was that heroin gave her a great feeling.

Karen started taking heroin of her own free will and was not encouraged by her boyfriend. Undoubtedly many of our female respondents encountered force. Boyfriends tried to make these girls dependent on them by giving them heroin, so that it would be easier to force them into prostitution or pornographic modeling. This sometimes involved violence, or locking the girl up. After a while, these women usually managed to get away from their "boyfriend" (now turned pimp), be it that by then they were hooked on heroin. Having to take care of themselves, things soon went from bad to worse and they continued their career in prostitution in a second-rate streetwalkers area.

It should be noted that considerably more women than men cited individual (psychological) motives for starting on heroin. Many women sought to legitimate their use of opiates by saying that they wanted to push their problems away for a while. Some girls also related how they had tried desperately to help their boyfriends kick the habit. When these attempts failed the girls themselves started. For most men, the process of initiation involved excitement, curiosity, and fear of losing face. It was not until much later in their drug career that they saw heroin not primarily as a means of enjoyment, but as a means of escape.

---

5. An organization that provides assistance for young people in trouble.

The Development of a Drug Career in a More Conventional Context Up till now we have been looking at the secondary socialization of those respondents who went off the rails almost immediately and with a vengeance. For many respondents, however, the development towards a career of drugs was much more gradual. Although some deviant characteristics became visible during adolescence, at the same time ties with conventional society remained reasonably close. These respondents, balancing on the edge, participated in regular education for longer than the fringe groups described above. However, only a few actually managed to successfully finish any education. Here too, the picture is one of lack of interest in the curriculum, conflicts with teachers, and truancy. After the untimely demise of their school career, many did attempt to find a regular job, but in most cases this acquaintanceship with the job market did not last very long. These young people found it very difficult, if not impossible, to find a workable combination that allowed for deviant interests and a regular working life. Soon they failed to come up to standard, staying away from work, arriving late, smoking cannabis on the shop floor despite the boss's disapproval, or coming in drunk. As a result they were fired.

It is characteristic of these respondents that, for a while, they were living in two worlds as it were. Gradually the elements of their deviant existence blotted out those of convention. This was not always a straightforward process. Sometimes they were active in crime for a short period, and then temporarily absorbed in a conventional existence, such as finishing school, or taking a job.

> After primary school, Chris went to a lower technical training school. He had little contact with his classmates and felt more comfortable with his friends in the neighbourhood. "We were a bit like hippies; we had a youth centre in an old shed and we hung about being groovy with loud music." In this atmosphere a joint was a necessity, of course, and at 13 Chris had his first experience with hash. Soon he was smoking joints every day. He was dependent on his friends' generosity, for his parents kept him short of money. By this time he had little contact with his parents. In the same year as he started smoking hash, Chris experimented for the first time with LSD and speed: "I wanted to belong, but looking back I must say that everything went so fast." These outside activities soon meant that Chris played truant from school regularly. Nevertheless, at 16 he left school with

a baker's diploma. At this point, the moped-age began, and this was accompanied by even more boasting and fighting with other boys in the neighbourhood. Round about this time he also started shoplifting with a friend. Chris describes this now as "playing games": "We did it for kicks." Thanks to his father's influence, Chris found a job as a cook in a neighbourhood hotel after the summer holidays. He kept this job for just under two years. He gave satisfaction during the first year, but during the second his use of drugs was an increasing handicap—by this time heroin had been introduced into his circle of friends—and he started coming in late, or not at all. Eventually he was fired.

A number of the (older) respondents remember when heroin first came onto the Dutch market at the beginning of the seventies. They belong to the generation that was able to provide some sort of ideological foundation for their use of heroin: a protest against "square society." In Janssen and Swierstra's terminology (1982), these are the "cultural rebels." Although their style of life was indeed defined as deviant then, today hippy behavior is regarded as reasonably innocent and even remembered with fond nostalgia, not in the least by these respondents themselves.

We shall finish this casuistic description of the different approach routes to hard drugs with a fairly large group (20 percent of the sample) who had not developed any kind of deviant life-style before they took to drugs. The older generations can be regarded as "ex-night-on-the-town boys" from conventional working-class backgrounds. The younger respondents are "respectable boys" from middle-class families (Swierstra et al. 1986). The first group is distinctive because of their conventional work ethos and conformistic morals: these young people usually finished their—predominantly low level—school successfully, found a job, thought it was important, and dreamed of starting a family. After being introduced to hard drugs, they had to make substantial changes to this dream of the future. They often had their first experiences with drugs during an ordinary night on the town.

Our representatives of "respectable youth" also bumped into drugs when out in town, although in more trendy scenes. As they were usually quite young, they did not have a settled picture of their future and in the beginning they viewed drug use as a fairly innocent source of fun. As long as the consumption of different psychotropic drugs did not adversely affect schoolwork or contacts with parents and friends, they had no objection to experimenting now and again. Although this group had strong ties with conventional society and was in no way keen to develop a deviant life-style, they were unable to introduce much principle of organization into their existence. They had integrated several elements of regular society into their own lives as a matter of course, but were unable to discover why this should be meaningful. These problems of identity, together with the ready availability of drugs in their own environment, eventually resulted in them overstepping the line and entering the world of drugs.

> After primary school, Ellen went to a comprehensive school. The club of friends that she had collected was often to be found in a neighbourhood sports hall in their spare time. Ellen, who at that time had never smoked a joint or even a cigarette, was offered a sniff of heroin when she was 16. She took it readily, but she was not thrilled by the effects of heroin: "I didn't like it at all. It made me feel sick." Despite this disappointing experience, Ellen nevertheless said "yes" a few weeks later when offered first cocaine and then heroin. By now Ellen was well away and taking heroin (and sometimes cocaine) almost every weekend. "I became weekend user, only the weekend got longer and longer and I was still using the stuff on Tuesday and Wednesday."

Finally, we end this section with a description of the routes that took our respondents of Surinam origin to drug use.[6] The approach routes to a drug career taken by immigrants have their own specific characteristics. One relevant distinction is the fact that some respondents were born and bred in the Netherlands, while some spent their childhood and adolescence in Surinam. Let us start with the latter.

As we have already seen, more than two-thirds of the respondents from Surinam spent the first fifteen years of their life in this former Dutch colony. With only one or two exceptions they grew up in the capital, Paramaribo. Most come from large families, often without a "steady" father figure.

---

6. We have left the respondents from the Netherlands Antilles out of this section, because we cannot justify making general statements on the basis of the life histories of just three drug users.

A quarter of our Surinam respondents—exclusively male—had already developed a delinquent life-style in their country of birth. Without fail their family background was fairly precarious, sometimes very authoritarian, often neglectful, and lacking clear supervision. Because their school careers all ended at a very early age, they came to live their lives on the street, surrounded by like-minded children of the same age. In this group, the normal repertoire of behavior included a lot of drink, a lot of soft drugs, and crime. All of the respondents in this category had already been in contact with the criminal justice authorities in Surinam.

They usually report two motives for the move to the Netherlands. To start with, reunion with other members of the family who had already emigrated. Secondly, the hope that they would be able to build a better future in affluent Holland. Many of these respondents belonged to the large group of immigrants that had opted for Dutch nationality in 1975—the year that Surinam became independent.

This group of young men from Surinam, with their criminal antecedents, found themselves in a marginal position very soon after arriving in the Netherlands. Lacking adequate education and sufficient job experience, they were unable to integrate easily into Dutch society. Disappointed about losing the future as they had imagined it would be, they turned their backs on the white components of society and turned primarily to the world inhabited by others from Surinam who shared the same fate. Through them, the respondents soon came into contact with hard drugs. None of them had used heroin or cocaine in Surinam, for the simple reason that these drugs were not available there at that time.

Such rapid marginalization not only affected the young people from Surinam with a criminal career behind them. A substantial number of the immigrants who had not touched crime at home succumbed to the temptations of drugs soon after arriving in Holland. These respondents found a legitimation for the speedy start of their drug career in the same arguments as the others: disappointment about the lack of opportunities in Dutch society, a strong orientation towards their "own" Surinam world, and—within that world—experimenting with different drugs as a matter of course.

A minority of the respondents who grew up in Surinam managed to adapt to Dutch society reasonably well after arriving.

They attended schools and/or looked for a job for a while, before setting out on the road to drugs. The use of drugs was often common practice in their direct environment, but ties with conventional society prevented them from doing much more experimenting than smoking a joint. Dissatisfaction with their own situation eventually led to the barrier against hard drugs coming down. The route taken by one respondent is typical in this connection:

> Mike stepped onto the plane to the Netherlands when he was 17 years old. All his brothers and sisters had already made the move and they helped him to overcome his initial problems in Amsterdam. He worked hard at establishing a circle of friends and acquaintances, and found a job as a house painter. After two years he had enough of this work, and decided to exploit his talents as a musician. He became a drummer in a band that was to become quite well-known nationally. He played with this band for five years. Meanwhile he had married and was the father of two children. During a party after a concert, Mike was introduced to heroin. He was 24 years old. A friend warned him to keep his hand off "that rubbish," but Mike took no notice of any advice. He first "chased the dragon" out of curiosity and to relieve boredom. "Of course, when I was with the band I saw a lot of people take heroin, and at that party I thought, why not try. There was also the problem of not having enough to do at that time. We didn't perform much, my wife had gone to Surinam for a few months and I fancied something nice. Anyway, there were so many people at that party using drugs, you were the odd man out if you didn't."

Young people from Surinam who experienced primary and secondary socialization in the Netherlands were not oriented per definition towards their own cultural background, but also towards the psychological and physical world of white youngsters of the same age. During puberty, the emphasis was even on this white world. However, this process of "becoming Dutch" was full of ups and downs. The boys were reminded regularly of their different background and the "deviant" color of their skin. This merely encouraged them to manifest themselves even more emphatically in their group of friends. Peter's behavior is typical:

> When he was 14, Peter became increasingly involved in the youth club. Alcohol and hash played an important part in his circle of friends. Peter reports that those with the most money enjoyed the greatest respect. He longed for some status, because:

"As you get older you start to understand that as a Surinamese you come second or third, not only in society, but also in your own circle of friends. You have to compensate for it by showing off. I was clever at stealing purses at the swimming pool, and once my friends knew about it they no longer looked down on me."

The respondents from Surinam who grew up in the Netherlands were caught between two worlds: they became alienated from their mother culture that was embodied in their parental home, were unable to fit into regular society, and had to do their utmost best to be accepted by white people of their own age. At a later stage, these identity problems were to lead to a reorientation towards their "own" cultural characteristics as these have been incorporated into the street hustling that goes on in downtown Amsterdam.

COURSE OF A DRUG CAREER

A Theoretical Model of Development

In her study on the life histories of female heroin addicts, Rosenbaum (1981) describes the development of a career of addiction as a phased process, governed by the principle of expanding and narrowing options. She maintains that development of this cost-benefit ratio, which is closely linked with the drug career, runs contrary to that of conventional (professional) careers. Conventional careers usually begin with a highly restricted freedom of decision for the individual; freedoms, options, and rewards all increase as the conventional career develops.

Rosenbaum uses the imagery of a snare. During the first stage, increasing individual freedom from social and moral barriers prevails. The novice drug user discovers a new world of opportunities, challenges, and pleasurable excitement. But as the drug career continues, Rosenbaum's research reveals how it turns into far-reaching restrictions of individual options. First the ties with and opportunities in the conventional world are cut. The restricted opportunities of conventional life, which influenced the attractions of a deviant life in the first place, are drastically reduced even further by the choice to continue a stigmatized life in the drug scene. During the later stages of the drug career, the primary and secondary rewards of a deviant life with drugs are also reduced. The pleasures of consuming drugs become increasingly volatile and dubious as addiction continues. The euphoric effects of the drug disappear. All that is left is the unhappy treatment of painful (physical and psychological) withdrawal symptoms. According to Rosenbaum, at an even later stage the secondary rewards of a life with drugs (such as enjoying successful and autonomous hustling) also become increasingly problematic. The women in her study were increasingly unable to defend themselves against the manipulations and exploitation of the hard world of drugs. Adequate income acquisition became impossible or the price of it became exorbitant at an early stage as the addicts gradually lost their ability to control the risks of prostitution or (drug-related) crime.

Without doubt, these actual drug careers were partly determined by the relatively repressive American reaction to drug use, and by the fact these were female addicts whose position, as the author explains, is more vulnerable than that of the males for a number of reasons. However, the abstract model of expanding but then gradually narrowing options may be an accurate description of the effects of a career of drugs.

In her study, Rosenbaum distinguishes five stages in the careers of female heroin addicts: "(1) an initial stage when people explore drug use life-styles; (2) a becoming stage when regular visits into addict life are made as an apprentice; (3) a maintaining phase, when opiates are used regularly and the individual takes on an addict social identity and commitment; (5) an on again, off again stage when addicts slowly find drug use alternatively functional and dysfunctional; and (5) a conversion phase when the addict intends to become clean permanently" (Rosenbaum 1981, pp.15–16).

The transitions between the stages are marked by the options that face a deviant drug user during his/her development. As the drug career progresses, the addict crosses boundaries as a result of which systematic changes occur in life-style, pattern of drug use, and patterns of (illegal) income acquisition. In each stage there are probably conditions that are necessary for or that promote the transition to the next stage, or that act as a brake on the development of a deviant career (Bennett and Wright 1986). The elements of life histories that determine the level of the threshold for committing criminal offenses are of special importance in research into crime committed by drug users.

In the rest of this section we shall divide Rosenbaum's five stages into two blocks. First we shall describe the building of a drug career, that is to say, the development of the recreational user into a full-time junkie. Then we shall take a closer look at the dismantling of that career, that is to say at the stage in which the costs gradually come to prevail over the benefits.

The Building of a Drug Career: From Recreational User to Full-Time Junkie

One of the most crucial and consequential moments in a career of drugs is the discovery that one is addicted. The transition from controlled drug use to addiction is accompanied by denial, self-delusion, and sometimes extreme naivety. In the beginning, many users are convinced of their own ability to keep the use of hard drugs under control. Many a (drug) addict will recognize himself in the following statement by a respondent:

> I always thought: nothing can happen to me; I'm above all that. I believed all those stories that you didn't need to get hooked. It was the weak ones that got hooked, not me.

Contrary to what the novice user realizes (or allows himself to realize), addiction occurs after the transition from occasional to (almost) daily use. Addiction can be avoided by rigorously moderating the frequency of use, for example by only taking drugs in the weekend. In the social context of (initial) hard drug use, this is a difficult thing to do. The deviant development of many an addict during puberty often results in a speedy transition to an existence as a full-time addict. A substantial number of our respondents considered themselves "addicted" within a relatively short space of time—varying from a few weeks to six months. This initial phase usually took longer if the person concerned still had any ties with conventional society, because of a steady job, a steady partner, nondrug using friends, etc. Some even managed to more or less combine drug use with a partly conventional life-style for years. Only when such stabilizing elements disappeared, for example because jobs or partners were lost, did their use of drugs escalate and did they disappear into the deviant existence of a life with drugs.

After the discovery of withdrawal symptoms and the attributing of these to drugs, a decisive change in the drugs user's identity often occurs. He is often the first to accept the mythology of "being hooked" and "having to live as a junk for ever." Once they have accepted "the inevitable," most junkies experience the most attractive stage in their career. Seen from a cost-gain perspective, the costs of being an addict have not yet come to outweigh the gains at this stage. Drug use becomes intenser and more compulsive, social contacts are increasingly restricted to users. Logically, drug-related ways of income acquisition, such as crime, prostitution, or dealing in drugs reach their highest levels. This stage of a drug career is accompanied by very high levels of activity: earning a lot, consuming a lot, living fast. It is, of course, no coincidence that this phase of life (generally between twenty-four and thirty) is also the one in which professional footballers, traders on the stock exchange, and burners of the midnight oil also experience their most productive period. During this middle stage of the drug career, there may be many short term changes. Generally, there is no strongly stabilized pattern of drug use. Most involved users vary their life with drugs episodically, trying to kick the habit, cutting down, having therapy, going on holiday, etc. Usually a decrease in income acquisition also occurs during such, mainly consciously controlled, episodes.

What are the functions of deviant drug use at this stage, and do they reveal any links with crime? Preble and Casey (1969) undertook pioneering work with regard to clarifying the functionality of the traditional heroin problem for the lowest levels in society. They used the notion of the functional rationality of position related crime, that derives from Merton's (1957) anomie theory. They describe the life with heroin that young men in a ghetto lead, as a way of realizing central values and goals of (conventional) society that is adapted to their own social reality. According to these authors, such heroin users are far from being losers, driven on by disease, and ending up despite themselves in a vicious circle of crime and an inevitable process of social and psychological decline. Rather, they regard these addicts as a subcultural variation on the (American) prototype of conventionality, the hardworking, independent little man. In a deviant way, the illegal drug user is conforming to a dominant social model of conventional consumption culture: acquiring consumer goods by diligence and perseverance and in doing so, earning self-respect and a place in society. "When I'm on the way home with the bag safely in my pocket, and I haven't been caught stealing all day, and I didn't get beat and the cops didn't get me—I feel like a working man coming home; he's worked hard but he knows he's done something, even though I know it's not true" (Preble and Casey 1969).

Junkies realize a meaningful existence through the role model of heroin addiction. This reflects an active transformation of social reality, rather than a pathological one "(. . .) euphoric escape from the psychological and social problems of ghetto life." "On the contrary, it provides a motivation and rationale for the pursuit of a meaningful life, albeit a deviant one" (Ibid.). As one of the most deviant roles in Western society, paradoxically an addict's existence is motivated by entirely "normal, good reasons," such as having a social environment in which (self) respect can be gained, an unambiguous position in society, an (economic) perspective of the future and structured day-to-day activities.

Of course, the heroin addict of the sixties as described by Preble and Casey is an ideal type and is not immediately applicable to the hard drugs scene in Amsterdam at the end of the eighties. Nevertheless, the following functions of the complex of addiction and crime are typical elements of the basic conditions of (Western) social-economic and cultural marginality. There is no reason to suppose that the addiction to illegal drugs in a big Dutch city is any exception.

- The user derives excitement and status from his deviant life-style.
- A life with drugs offers both short- and long-term structure and predictability.
- The user finds a place in a social circle and obtains an identity for the outside world.

We shall now take a look at these elements in the light of our empirical material.

Excitement and Status As long as everything is going well for a user, that is to say, as long as his sources of income allow him to acquire drugs with a certain regularity, he experiences his life as adventurous and successful. In this stage of their career, many are proud of being "free men," not having to account for themselves to anyone and having enough money at their disposal. Consuming, dope or anything else, seems to be a fairly fixed measure of success. As we reread our notes on conversations of "successful" drug users among themselves, it became quite obvious that addicts enjoy comparing themselves favorably with members of their own generation who have to turn up to work every day.

> If you see these guys working for a boss, the pittance they earn compared to us, well, I know who's got the best deal. But I must say that the money comes in handfuls here, but goes out again just as fast. If I think about how much money I could have had in my account if I'd put everything I ever earned into the bank, I could go mad.

The transition from a relatively stable life-style to the feverish existence of a junkie, often starts when a good source of income is found so that the availability of drugs increases automatically. In this connection, Faupel and Klockars (1987) refer to the "big sting" or "big hit." According to these authors, the transitions in a drug career are mainly determined by two factors: the user's life structure and the availability of drugs. These may vary from high to low. Table 3–2 shows a typology based on these factors.

TABLE 3–2
A Typology of Four Career Stages (Faupel and Klockars 1987)

Availability of Drugs	Life Structure	
	High	*Low*
High	Stabilized User	Freewheeling Junkie
Low	Occasional User	Street Junkie

The availability of drugs is not defined in terms of "objective" availability. That is to stay, availability does not depend primarily on market mechanisms, but also and especially on personal choices and competence. For example, the street junkie may be found every day at the scene where dope is widely for sale, but his competence in actually acquiring heroin has decreased; he is dependent on what he finds in the gutter; "objective" availability is high, personal availability low. Availability may also be low if an addict elects to stay at home and not to go to "where it's at."

"Life structure" stands for the way a dope user structures his/her life. If a person brings a certain regularity into his life and enters into certain obligations—for example because he has a job, or a child to take care of, but the same applies to a junkie keeping himself alive through his activities on the drug market—then his/her life structure is high. Vice versa, the user who has scored a big hit and has a great deal of money at his disposal during a certain period of time has little or no "life structure." Spurred on by an urge for immediate satisfaction of their needs, these successful users will spend their newly acquired income as soon as possible. This means that temporarily their level of drug consumption will be very high, at the cost of the stabilizing elements in their lives.

Although most of the gains from a big sting will be spent on drugs for their personal consumption, these users regularly allow others to share in the profits. The "big spender" grows in stature and is confirmed in his own successful actions. Now and then there is exorbitant spending in entirely other areas. One respondent bought a sports car after successfully ripping off a dealer and toured about in France for six months.

It is therefore the degree of success with which income is acquired that determines to a large extent the place a junkie occupies in the hierarchy of the scene. At the same time, junkies with certain specialisms in the field of income acquisition, or with plenty of muscle power, are also regarded with respect. The following are examples of these two types, taken from the fieldworkers' diaries.

> Got Harry from the bus. He hasn't got much time, because he has to go to "work." He puts off seeing his friends for an hour. "Everybody wants to work with me" Harry says, "because they know that they can always earn something with me. I'm cheeky, and I'm the fastest." (This is confirmed later by other drug users; Harry commands a lot of respect). Harry is famous for breaking into cars. He gets two or three car radios a day. He shows me some of the tools he uses: screwdrivers, scissors, a centrepoint and special (partly home-made) hooks for getting the radios out of the dashboard. He considers himself a cut above just kicking in a window and destroying the whole dashboard. He calls people who work like that "bunglers."

As I cross Nieuwmarkt Square,[7] I just catch a glimpse of Eddy, Martin and Hans having a row with two other addicts. Martin and Hans seem to be verbally involved. In the beginning Eddy keeps in the background, but suddenly he steps forward and fells one of the opponents with a dreadful blow. The victim is then counted out by his female companion. By this time Eddy has moved on, though without batting an eyelid. His faithful companions dance round him enthusiastically and are as loud-mouthed as ever. We had already heard from several sources that Eddy is feared for his terrible strength: apparently both customers and dealers put money and dope away fast when they see Eddy coming.

Social Circle and Identity In the subculture of drugs, ties of friendship are often utilitarian and precarious. Relationships between users—especially those of Dutch origin among themselves—are instrumental partnerships. Nevertheless, one should not underestimate the importance of group ties. As we have explained, these ties provide a certain social integration—especially at the beginning of a career of addiction. The feeling of definitely belonging gives dope users a place in society, an identity that is confirmed by conventional society. Drug users receive a flattering amount of attention from the police, therapists, the media, and, last but not least, researchers. They may be considered a public enemy by society, but for that very reason they are no longer a "quantité négligable."

The label of drug user offers an addict numerous opportunities to escape from conventional norms of behavior and responsibilities. He parries recriminations about crime effortlessly by pointing to the high price of drugs. The biopharmacological perspective on addiction provides him with the legitimation of his deviant behavior: he himself is the victim of addiction and he cannot really be called to account for the criminality that inevitably accompanies it.

As long as a life of addiction is experienced as adventurous, interactions with the police are all part of the "game." Of course addicts try to keep these contacts to a minimum, but being arrested is seen as just one of the risks of the trade. Moreover, the knowledge that they will usually be set free after a few hours

---

7. One of the centers of the drug scene.

makes the prospect of an arrest much more bearable. The following is typical of the rather nonchalant attitude of many addicts towards the police, although in this case Dick's arrest had more far-reaching consequences than normal.

> It was one of those Friday afternoons that everything was going like clockwork. I had just scored with my friend and we were on the way home. I said to him: if you get a video, I'll go and get something to eat at the supermarket (read: steal). When I came out of the shop two policemen were waiting for me. One asks: aren't you Dick X.? Well, I know the guys from that area and they know me, so there was no point in denying it. I tried saying I was in a hurry, but they didn't care and they got me in the car. I went back to the station with them and I thought: Dick, give it to them, the sooner they'll let you out. So I got out the cans of beer and the cheese and the sausages from under my coat and I said: ok boys, congratulations, this is for you. They looked real surprised, it wasn't what they'd got me for. I had an old sentence still outstanding and now I had to serve it: four months instead of an hour.

In many cases there are no regrets at being locked up. The penalty is turned into one of the facilities that goes with being an addict. If life has become so hectic that the addict can no longer cope, a short stay in a penitentiary makes a welcome change: for life in the penitentiary stands for a certain regularity; food and other comforts are adequate and, if one is lucky, dope is available.

The majority of addicts who are still in the middle of drug life regularly return to the facilities offered by therapeutic agencies. They integrate these facilities—especially those with a low threshold—into their lives, and are very satisfied with them, as long as no serious obligations arise in return. From the perspective of the addict, his relationship with therapists at this stage is take a lot and give a little. But they complain frequently about their dependency on the therapists and on the condescending attitude they have to put up with. Appreciation of therapists seems to depend on the degree in which they are prepared to meet the addicts halfway, or in which they can be manipulated. Take, for example, Otto's behavior as described in the field notes.

> Otto finds himself in the luxurious position of having methadone prescribed by two different agencies, in T. and in Amsterdam. He more or less labels one set of medication for personal

use and the other for street trade. It takes a while before I can interview Otto, because he has to make a call to a social worker in T. "The bastard wants to contact the medical services in Amsterdam. Then he'll hear that I get methadone here and I'll lose the pills in T." It takes a while before he manages to get through to the social worker at the other end, but having established the contact, Otto shows how tenacious he can be. Swearing: "Jim, you know I never lie to you," he spins the social worker a complicated tale in order to prevent him from ringing Amsterdam.

Some users do not want any contact with therapists at all. They refute any interference in their lives and are afraid of being registered. More than anything else they detest methadone, because they regard it as more addictive than heroin and they say that the one addiction is more than enough. We shall return to this aspect in chapter 7.

Addicts who do not participate in regular replacement therapy programs usually regard themselves as superior to their colleagues who have turned to the medical or other services: the feeling that one can go it alone improves status.

I don't need methadone, but it's a good thing they distribute the stuff. There are enough junks around who just wouldn't make it without methadone.

Regularity and Predictability of a Life of Addiction In his book *The Meaning of Addiction*, Peele (1985) draws attention to the value that addicts attach to the simplification of experience. He emphasizes the importance of rituals in the scene, not only in connection with the great diversity of ways in which to take drugs, but also with the addict's life-style in general: the predictability of daily actions such as hustling and scoring are in themselves a reward for the addict.

If external circumstances cause alterations to the familiar pattern of behavior, this severely taxes the addict's mental resilience. During our fieldwork we came across a striking example:

Last night we put the clocks back an hour. As we discover at the bus stop, several addicts still have to get used to the difference. They are all complaining like mad about withdrawal symptoms coming on. One respondent, superior and aloof from his wailing colleagues, puts the problem of withdrawal into perspective: "You know what's the matter, they've all got it into their head that they'll be sick if they don't get their methadone on time. It's the fear that's making them all sick."

The functionality of rituals in the drug scene is expressed especially in the diverse ways of consuming drugs. The actual taking of drugs is preceded by a range of preparations that the addict must carefully perform. The performance of these actions alone gives the use of drugs an extra dimension. Take, for example, the way in which cocaine is taken in the scene. When used recreationally, this drug is sniffed, but in the subculture of drugs people "chase the dragon," "shoot" or "base." The latter seems to have its own special magic.

> The interview with Carol threatens to get out of hand, for she says she wants to base first. I wait my turn and this gives me the chance to watch all the preparations that Carol and her boy friend Ramon have to make. Ramon has brought a glass of water and this is covered by a piece of taut aluminium foil with two perforations. One is for sucking through while prepared coke and cigarette ash is heated up with a lighter on the other. The cocaine is prepared thus: A small amount of ammonia is poured onto a teaspoon, the coke is put in and the whole business is boiled with the aid of a lighter. When it is ready, the coke crystals sink to the bottom and are fished out with a potato knife. The big crystals are ground up with the knife and placed on the foil to be smoked. All these actions are performed by Carol and Ramon smokes. The interview doesn't seem to be coming along very well. When I ask why the cigarette ash is necessary, Carol replies: "Yeah, why, I wonder?"

This passage from a diary illustrates how the addicts' behavior is influenced by collective conviction. They copy each others' actions, even when there is no obvious need for them. But group culture influences not only the addict's pattern of behavior, but also his assessment of the different drugs he consumes: if others say they are affected by a certain drug in a certain way, the addict will soon think he notices the same effect on himself.

Dismantling a Drug Career: The Addict Calms Down and Looks for a Way Out

> Henry compares his present life in the scene with being in jail. "You're really tied onto the same carousel; after a while the rut is the same."

The words of these respondent reveal that one of the most important components of a life with drugs loses a lot of its significance at a later stage in the addict's career. Life in the scene, such a challenge in the beginning because of the adventure and excitement, becomes routine after a while. And gradually the motivation to chase after income and dope all day long disappears. Although they do not want to give up their entire existence as addicts, many seasoned drug users calm down a bit after a while. Patrick's development during the period in which we followed him is highly illustrative of this point.

> *Passage from Diary at the Time of the First Interview* Patrick has just got out again. He has been in jail for six months. During the past seven years, he has been in contact with the police 71 times; they told him that the last time he was arrested and he repeats it, not without pride. He has been homeless for four years. Once in a while he sleeps at an organisation that provides shelter, but usually he lives on the street. He gets his income mainly from acquisitive crime.

> *Passage from Diary at the Time of the Last Interview (A Year Later)* Looking back on the year with Patrick, I come to the conclusion that there have been certain changes in his life. A social worker has helped him to find a home. His social benefit is administered by the same person. He has become much calmer, and it shows in a decrease in criminal activity. He's not entirely "clean" yet, but compared to 13 months ago he is committing far fewer offenses. Patrick admits himself that he's had enough of this hurried junkie existence. As far as that is concerned, it is immensely important to him to have his own home. He must not lose that, whatever happens, because otherwise the road downhill is way open again. Patrick has also stopped shooting. Not out of health considerations, but more because this way of using dope contradicts his attempts to lead a quieter life. In his own words: "You know how fast you go downhill if you start shooting and there comes a time when it's not worth it anymore." Patrick has talked about kicking the habit a few times during the past year, but has never actually done anything about it. The past few months he has been working at the Junkie Union as a result of a community service order. He doesn't really feel at home with this organisation, but at least it gives him something to do again. And that is very important at this stage, because his main problem has been boredom.

In Patrick's case there is some progress, but he is still on a tightrope. If the stabilizing elements described above were to be taken away, there is a good chance he would fall back on the familiar hassled life-style. During our fieldwork, we also saw many a respondent develop in the opposite direction: in the beginning we regarded them as addicts trying to shake off their life of addiction, but later their behavior became so hectic that we had to revise our judgment.

Despite the fact that many dope users fall back on their old habits after a period of relative calm, their perception of the addict's life nevertheless changes. The longer they have been around, the more that life loses its attraction. It appears as more of a rut, and the problems and deprivations of a life with drugs come to outweigh its usual attractions. Undoubtedly this is related to the fact that the competence needed to stay upright in the drug scene slowly but surely diminishes. Quite a lot of "older" addicts (older than thirty) indicated that their heydays of crime were over. They themselves blamed this on many factors. Several respondents spoke of increased difficulties in committing crime as a result of crime prevention measures. Another important factor seems to be the disappearance of a fellow hustler. We have already explained in the previous section how addicts in the scene make use of each other, if there is anything to be gained from it. These functional relationships are common in the field of crime. In the course of their career, different drug users join forces with a suitable colleague to become a pair of expert criminals. However, if either partner in crime drops out, for whatever reason, the other is not usually able to continue the "successes" of the past. Take for example the change that occurred in Freddy's life after the arrest of his—highly expert shoplifter—girlfriend.

> Kitty was the one with the most guts. She usually did the dirty work, I just acted as a look out and carried the stuff. When Kitty was arrested I tried it alone once or twice, but I was always caught. Somehow I've lost my touch.

Diminishing competence in crime usually results in an increasing amount of contact with the police. These interactions are no longer seen as all part of the "game," but give rise to an increasing feeling of loathing. Some users even feel the need to lie low (for a while). In order to avoid the police/criminal justice authorities, some of our respondents even started to buy tickets for public transport, an exceptional step for an addict to take.

Addicts not only come to regard contacts with the police and criminal justice authorities as troublesome, they gradually develop an aversion to the whole dope scene. This negative view cannot be separated from the social isolation that envelopes many older addicts. In the beginning there are group ties, but at a later stage these increasingly fall apart. This applies more to white addicts than to those of Surinam or West Indian origin.

Although, after a while, there are hardly any ties left with fellow addicts, this does not alter the fact that most dope users have a circle of acquaintances almost exclusively made up of fellow users. Lacking strong ties with conventional society, they still need each other.

Although most addicts bump into more and more negative aspects of being an addict as their career progresses, a number of factors prevent them from getting out entirely. One of the most important elements that makes continuation of a life of addiction still an attractive option is connected with the structuring influence that life has. Even if the addict no longer wants to chase money and drugs every day, he still wants something meaningful to do. Most drug users are very aware of the fear of boredom, or— as many respondents put it— "falling into a black hole," and for this reason they attach great importance to a more or less predictable rhythm of life. In their attempts to give some structure to their day, many fall back on the facilities offered by therapeutic organizations. A visit to a methadone maintenance program, for example, not only provides some very necessary methadone, but satisfies other needs too: a visit to the methadone bus or to the community station provides a start to the day for many addicts, a good reason for getting out of bed. It also gives them a chance to talk to somebody, an important factor considering the social isolation that befalls many of them. Contrary to the segment of the population described before, who keep visits to maintenance programs to an absolute minimum, the more staid users hang about in the waiting room at the bus or community station. Some are even able to make themselves useful there, as this passage from a diary reveals.

> Albert and Rudy are regular customers at the community station. They hang about for hours in the waiting room every day

and talk to everybody who comes in. This morning they got permission to get the bucket and mop out of the cupboard to give the floor a good scrub. Both are visibly proud of this assignment. This is the second time this week that Albert has been given a job at the post. Last Monday the guard and "chef de cuisine" asked him to do some shopping. Albert was given money and the cook's bicycle. Some of those present remarked scathingly that the cook "had better say goodbye to his bike and his money" and one—slightly annoyed—even said frankly that this "was asking for trouble." But despite such scepticism and annoyance, Albert returned after three quarters of an hour with bicycle, shopping and change.

The maintenance programs are not the only places that addicts use as a meeting place; they also do so at several "shelter" organizations in the center of town. Besides visiting these places frequently, many of these addicts spend a great deal of time hanging about downtown. They are not particularly active there anymore: they do small jobs, scour the streets for little balls of dope that have been lost by a colleague or thrown away when he was arrested, or they move on to the area where medicinal drugs are being bought and sold.

Judging by the change that takes place in their life-style, at some point in their career most addicts become "retired junkies." They return, as it were, to a more or less conventional and only slightly stigmatized existence in Dutch society. Once an addict has calmed down, he joins the legions of the "normal" segments of the Dutch society, which for various reasons are not employed. In 1989 more than one-third of the Dutch labor force was inactive. This group comprises housewives as well as recipients of unemployment, sickness, or social benefits. Elements from their previous life with drugs are incorporated into the less problematic lifestyle of a socially regulated methadone customer. The importance of contacts with the "respectable" outside world—often occasional and usually with members of the family—grows. In this connection it should be noted that a substantial number of our respondents went back to live with their parents after years of being away, or at least had a meal there frequently.

There is also a much more problematic way in which a drug career can end, albeit that it concerns only a small percentage of all addicts. This is what could be called psychosocial deterioration. These addicts often find themselves in a downward spiral of psychological and physical health problems, neglect, and social isolation (homelessness, etc.). In the scene they are sometimes known as "pill freaks," but for the same money (literally) they may be into excessive alcohol use. Those who belong to this group have a big need for drugs but little ability to acquire any (criminal) income. In the eyes of the public, these are the "worst junkies" because of the way they look; however, they are often unable to obtain heroin or cocaine. Their condition also means that they are usually unable to pull off much successful crime and they restrict themselves to occasional petty offenses if the opportunity presents itself. Everybody is watching them, again because of the way they look, and they lack the energy for successful crime. There is a good chance that this notable, but criminally ineffective, fringe of the dope scene is the most frequent but misdirected target of crime prevention.

> Bennie totters into the community station. He is a tramp in the very last stage. He was a customer at EPD,[8] but even there they now regard him as hopeless and/or intractable. He hardly uses heroin, but fills himself full of pills, especially on Mondays when he gets his money for the week. He gets $75 and for that he immediately buys $30 worth of sleeping pills and he swallows them all at once. "If I get my money on Monday, I want to go right out," he said the other day. By the look of him, Bennie's had quite a lot of psychopharmaca already. Nevertheless, he manages to produce quite a bottleful of urine to be tested for dope on the side. He takes it, balancing precariously, to the window and on handing it in announces that he is "quite clean." However, he doesn't get any methadone, the doctor thinks that would be completely irresponsible at the moment. Bennie doesn't quite understand. He lets us know that he is off to the "pill bridge," for more pills or for methadone, what we don't know.

Although comparisons based on research are practically nonexistent, drug careers appear to finish in a different way in Holland than in a harder society such as the United States, where there is less patience with addicts and there are therefore far fewer facilities for therapy and aid. In the American situation, an addict's career probably ends more as it should according to the principles

---

8. A special program for "extreme problematic drug users."

of soap opera—damnation or salvation (Biernacki 1986). In the former case the addict dies (violently) or is locked away in prison for a long time. In the latter he finds Jesus in his heart and renounces all dope for ever. He marries his childhood sweetheart who has waited for him all this time and accepts a job as manager in his uncle's laundry.

Many a drug career may end like this damnation-salvation scenario in the Netherlands too. But years of continuing drug use at a much lower level is probably more typical. Swierstra's study (1990) confirms this picture. The great majority (twenty-nine) of his forty respondents in this follow-up study were still using dope after a drug career of some twenty years. Most of these—still addicted—users, however, no longer committed criminal offenses. So it seems that a fairly large group of addicts makes the transition to a sort of integrated drug use, after a hectic and involved middle phase in their career. However, this way of being an addict does not imply "real" resocialization, but rather it is the life-style within the regulated drug scene of someone on social security. An involved middle stage, lasting perhaps from four to eight years, is not followed by resocialization to a conventional life of abstinence, but by the life-style of a "retired junk."

CONTINUITY OF CRIMINAL PATTERNS IN LIFE HISTORIES

This section will examine whether different conventional/deviant starting points retain their significance for criminal patterns of behavior during the development of a drug career. In theory two contrasting developments are possible, with an emphasis on socialization prior to drug use, and the effects of the illegal drug career respectively. This is an important question, both theoretically and practically. Does a drug addict's criminal pattern of behavior always depend on the degree of deviant socialization in his youth, or are original differences lost under the hard conditions of being an addict (White Raskin et al. 1985; Shaffer et al. 1987). If we assign a determining influence to addiction and drugs, we must expect a fairly homogenous pattern of crime once heroin addiction has become established. We shall try to learn more about this from the qualitative information provided by the life histories of our respondents.

Our respondents' years of puberty and adolescence, as described before, allow us to distill three types of crime profiles prior to drug use: frequent and relatively serious crime, more or less frequent but usually "petty" crime, and no more than occasional "petty" crime. We shall describe the development of criminal patterns of behavior during the drug career of these three types with their different starting points.

Very Criminal Prior to First Drug Use

The fact that these dope users are such competent criminals leads to rapid escalation to a full-blown life with drugs early in their career. Contrary to the other types, they barely need a warming-up stage in order to adapt to the conditions of the drug scene and the demands of being an addict. The transition from the survival strategies of delinquent marginality to those of hard drug use is a smooth one.

Serious criminals not only differ from the other types because of their stormy entrance into the world of drugs, but also because their criminal career covers a fairly long period of time. They are inclined to value their deviant life-style positively for longer than the other users and within it crime is regarded as self-evident. In this connection the statement, made by a number of addicts, that they "are not only addicted to drugs but also to stealing" is significant. Indeed, abstaining from drugs does not necessarily imply abstaining from crime.

During their drug career, most serious criminals (of Dutch origin) specialize in the type of offense they have been familiar with since adolescence. There is a strong emphasis on (serious) acquisitive crime. One or two side steps into drug dealing, but activities in this field are usually temporary: after an arrest and/or detention they go back on their tracks in the direction of acquisitive crime.

It is in this group of serious criminals that we find criminal specialists: burglars, car thieves, check forgers, and robbers (with violence). And it is in this group that the moral boundaries that determine whether they find their own behavior acceptable are highly elastic. With the exception of selling one's own body, distasteful to most of these respondents, almost anything goes. In many cases violence too is legitimated. As their careers come to an end, so these very criminal addicts draw their moral boundaries more firmly again. Violence (against outsiders) is no longer justified. The standard expression for an offense like mugging usually produced by these respondents was: "I used to, I don't any longer." Burglary is fine, but it shouldn't be violent.

Almost without exception, the serious criminals of Surinam origin take to drug dealing. Besides that, quite a few have sidelines in prostituting girlfriends or illegal gambling. For these dope users, the transition to drugs is a turning point in the sense that they now start to commit other offenses. For, like their white counterparts, in the past they committed mainly acquisitive crime.

"Moderately Criminal" Prior to First Drug Use

In principle, the crime committed by this group during puberty and adolescence is little more than serious wantonness. They shoplift, joyride, commit acts of vandalism, and fight with other youths. It is exceptional for them to commit more serious offenses. Moreover, offenses are committed with changing frequency.

It is among these moderate criminals that we see the most notable shifting of moral boundaries as their career progresses. For example, as their drug careers escalate, women in prostitution start to rob the punters every now and then. Male addicts from this originally moderately criminal group turn to more serious crime, adding burglary or mugging, but also male prostitution to their (criminal) repertoire.

At the height of their drug career, differences in patterns of criminal behavior and their justification between the groups of originally serious and moderate criminals have all but disappeared. However, a difference remains in the time span of the stage of maximum deviancy in their careers. The stage in which involvement in being an addict and therefore also drug use and deviant income acquisition are at their height is over sooner. This group seems to develop (moral) resistance to intensively criminal behavior at an earlier stage. Crime was always less self-evident in their case, and this inhibition returns after the intoxication of drug life has worn off. Without necessarily giving up all crime immediately, nevertheless most offenses are simply no longer opportune: most regard offenses without individual victims, such as shoplifting in big stores, as the only type of morally acceptable crime.

Noncriminal Prior to First Drug Use

Almost half (49 percent) of our sample indicated that they had never committed a criminal offense prior to using opiates. This group is far from homogenous: it encompasses young people with both socially marginal backgrounds and relatively protected childhoods. We shall deal with each group separately, in order to do justice to this diversity.

About one-third of the group of respondents with extremely problematic family backgrounds originally committed no more deviant acts than playing truant frequently, hanging around in youth centers and (immoderately) consuming alcohol, cannabis, and/or pep pills. But they were also younger than average (about seventeen or eighteen) when they first came into contact with opiates. Except for those with a rich source of income such as prostitution, their drug careers usually develop gradually. However, as their careers progress, these respondents too develop a highly varied pattern of opportunistic income acquisition, in which crime has a place. Their offenses, for example shoplifting, do not usually require any special skill. The members of this group, from problem backgrounds but not especially criminal before they started taking drugs, are less specialized in the more serious forms of crime.

Finally there are the respondents with conventional starting points (n=43). Their past socialization is reasonably stable and nonproblematic and they commit few offenses before starting on drugs. This subgroup contains representatives of two generations, namely the "old hippies" and members of a younger generation of hard drug users, already referred to as "respectable youth" (Janssen and Swierstra 1982; Swierstra et al. 1986). It is true of both generations that crime played no part of any importance for a long time. As far as the "old hippies," "cultural rebels," or whatever one wants to call them are concerned, in the beginning criminal behavior was incompatible with the ideology of the hippy subculture. "Respectable youth" has a lot of resistance to crime, because they have always been taught that it simply does not "become them." Eventually, as their careers progress, some give in. Some shift their boundaries so far that they are hardly distinguishable from the other two types as far as the sort and frequency of crime they commit are concerned.

Most of these addicts, with their nonproblematic/noncriminal starting points, find the thresholds of morality and fear too high to engage in intensive and more serious crime. They restrict themselves to a bit of shoplifting, a bit of drug dealing, and a bit of hustling.

Hustling is more often restricted to the "victimless" sorts. Our respondent Philip always managed to pay for his drug habit with a bit of dealing on the drug market, letting other addicts stay at his place in exchange for drugs, and, besides his social benefit, a bit of moonlighting." Going out to nick something, I would have thought that was a real moral defeat.' Respondent John used to earn a lot of money in the sex shop he ran with his father and this allowed him to pay for his addiction. When this source of income disappeared, he established contact with an old invalid neighbor, for whom he keeps house daily. This earns him about $85 a week including meals. Together with his social benefit, enough for the two grams of heroin he uses each week.

CONCLUSION

The development of a career in drugs only partly wipes out the differences in life-style prior to an addict's first use of opiates. For a large majority of dope users, crime is simply part of being an addict at a certain stage in their career. The choice of means of income acquisition is strongly determined by the discovery that one is hooked on the one hand, and by the addict's history of socialization on the other. The addict's identity acts as a legitimation (excuse) for committing crime. In general, this is also true of other social behavior that is disapproved of, such as earning money through prostitution. To a certain extent, admitting to a drug addict's identity means liberation from the moral restrictions of conventional existence. Our research data show that the majority of hard drug addicts in Amsterdam have few objections to committing theft. However, there are addicts who indicate that they would consider stealing a "moral defeat."

As with techniques of drug use, the addict also sets boundaries with regard to the nature of offenses (or prostitution). Although such boundaries are set at a certain stage in his/her career, the addict will cross them, albeit with more or less difficulty, at a different stage. But this certainly does not imply a point of no return.

On the contrary, boundaries that were once crossed are often respected again at a later stage. The boundaries of types of crime determine who might be a justifiable victim and what type of crime will be used to acquire income: "I will never steal from: my mother/my family/friends/small shopkeepers, etc." Not only are there boundaries as far as justifiable victims are concerned, they also exist with regard to the type of crime that an addict thinks suitable for earning his living. Undoubtedly, conventional moral judgments play a part here, and it is often violent crime that is deemed unacceptable. In other words, the dope user's moral justification of crime usually covers theft, but not violence.

The life histories of our respondents reveal the relevance of socialization and environmental factors for the nature and development of criminal behavior. Dope users from backgrounds where delinquency is more "normal" and usual generally opted later as addicts for a more criminal form of income acquisition than those from more conventional backgrounds. Addicts with a "highly" criminal background seem to value their deviant lifestyle or criminality more positively than the other types, and to continue in it for longer. Competence and specialisms in crime are best represented in this group. The category of "respectable youth" contains relatively more addicts for whom crime never becomes a central issue in their lives. They may commit a petty offense now and again, but not with any enthusiasm.

CHAPTER 4

The Amsterdam Drug Scene

Amsterdam is a special case. The city is the largest in the country, the most cosmopolitan and the main cultural center. It has its own atmosphere, history, and traditions that may all be relevant both to the character of its drug problems and social reactions. Amsterdam easily qualifies as the drug capital of the country. It has the largest concentration of drug users, some 40 percent of the total Dutch number, the highest visibility of drug use, the highest level of social debate on the phenomenon, and, to put it neutrally, the strongest reputation.

Since 1981, the estimated number of deviant drug users in Amsterdam has stabilized around 7,500. In 1991, this number dropped considerably to a total of about 6,300. Within the drug addict population in Amsterdam three groups can be distinguished: foreigners (44 percent), Dutch autochthons (33 percent), and Dutch ethnic minorities (23 percent). Among the ethnic groups, black people from Surinam constitute about 80 percent. Among the foreigners, Germans and Italians are especially represented. The average age of the population of heroin addicts has gradually increased from 26.8 years in 1981 to 33.1 years in 1991. During the same period of time the percentage of addicts under 22 years decreased from 14.4 to 2.3 (Buning 1992). This has been interpreted as an indication that levels of entry into heroin addiction among the Dutch population may be declining.

There is a fairly well defined area in the old city center that is regarded as junkie territory. Here countless small drug deals are transacted every day, in full view of all and sundry. The presence of such an open scene affords the life-style of many addicts an extra dimension. For a better understanding of the way they shape their lives, this chapter will highlight the social context of hard drug use in Amsterdam's inner city.

The first section outlines developments during the past years in junkie territory. The second section deals with interactions between the most important "actors" in that territory. First we shall look at the way in which addicts treat each other, then at interactions between addicts and the police, and finally at the relationship between drug users and the members of the public who live and work in the area.

Although also mentioned in the previous chapter, we would like to point out again that a substantial number of addicts never show their face in the city center. They have a decent home of their own, or they have had enough of the hassle of inner-city life. The picture we paint in this chapter is not, therefore, representative of the life of an average Amsterdam junkie.

THE DRUG SCENE IN AMSTERDAM'S INNER CITY

> I was clean for two months and I was fine. I thought, this time I'll pull through, but one visit to Amsterdam and I'd had it. I fancied chasing the dragon before I even got off the train. When I walked out of the Central Station, I turned left straight away towards the scene, while I really should have turned right. When you're in Amsterdam you simply get sucked towards the drugs.

Although there are other districts in other towns with a high concentration of addicts, the area around Nieuwmarkt Square in Amsterdam has always had the doubtful honor of being called the Mecca of Dutch and foreign junkies. Other areas of Amsterdam (Bijlmermeer, Oude Pijp, Staatsliedenbuurt, and a number of others) have also been increasingly confronted with a drug problem during the past years. But Nieuwmarkt and the adjacent Zeedijk still form the drug paradise of the capital.

Leaving aside the question of why the area should have this reputation, it can be said that many addicts do indeed regard the Nieuwmarkt area as their "natural territory." It is easy to substantiate this statement, with a reference to the use of the word "scene" in the world of drugs: in addicts' jargon, this term not only refers to their own subculture, but also, and even more often, to a certain place. In the latter sense, "scene" refers to the area seen in Figure 4–1 and enclosed by Warmoesstraat, Damstraat/Oude Hoogstraat, Kloveniersburgwal, and Zeedijk.

The most prominent street in the scene is the Zeedijk. Not even so much because most drugs deals are said to take place here, but more because the street is different from the others. It is the only street that has rows of the cast iron posts known as Amsterdammers

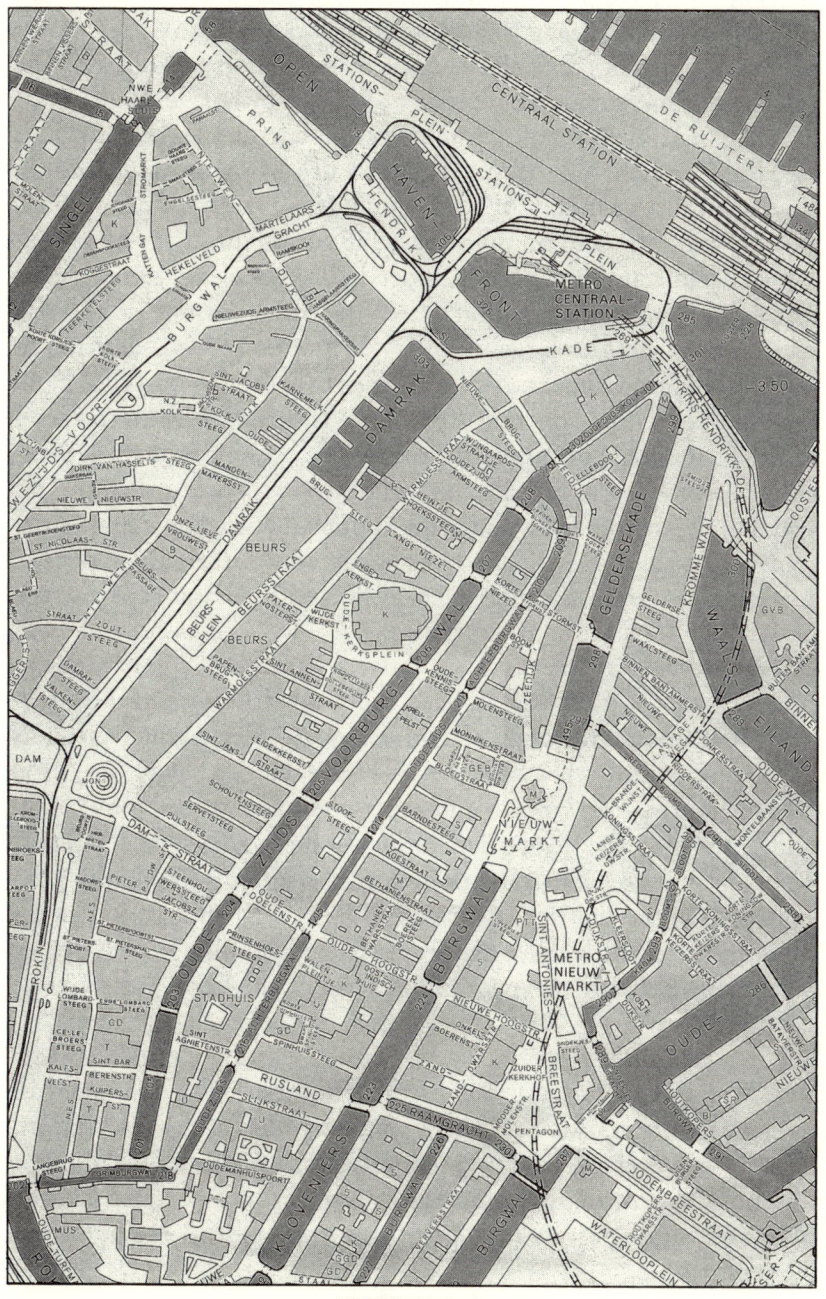

FIGURE 4–1
Map of Amsterdam Inner City (Source: Dienst Stedelijk Beheer, Sector Landmeten en Vastgoed informatie.)

marking the pavement, from beginning to end and on both sides.[1] The direct result is that it is impossible to park there, so that no unacceptable things can take place between and behind parked cars. The Amsterdammers make the Zeedijk look somewhat desolate.

The old inner city of Amsterdam that surrounds the Zeedijk is not only known for the trade in and use of drugs that goes on there, but just as much for a blooming trade in prostitution (both behind windows and on the street) and for the presence of a number of illegal gambling houses. Indeed, the area attracts many sorts and is also a tourist attraction of the first order because of its lively atmosphere. Besides large numbers of foreign tourists desiring to see Sodom and Gomorrah with their own eyes, this part of the old city also receives a constant stream of visitors who want to spend their (abundance) of spare time there. The center of the drug/prostitution scene is the Liesdelsluis, with heroin prostitutes and their (potential) customers wandering about and waiting impatiently and old men, more relaxed, hanging about for hours on the bridge, chatting to the girls every now and then and enjoying the activities taking place all around.

A few bridges further and we arrive at the meeting point for alcoholics. Armed with bottles of beer, they cruise through the area several times, always finishing up with fellow drinkers at the Oudezijds Achterburgwal. Free meals are available at the Salvation Army nearby; coffee, tea, warmth and peace and quiet at the House of St. Vincentius on the Kloveniersburgwal—nicknamed the "Kloof." Many a drug user integrates these facilities into his existence.

Because the red-light district and Nieuwmarkt area is a street scene, addicts and dealers are more visible here than in other parts of the town (with the possible exception of some parts of the Bijlmermeer).

Amsterdam's official drug policy has mainly operated by setting limits on manifestations of the drug market. Thus, over all else, it has aimed at preserving public order and achieving an acceptable level of livability in this part of the city. Different amounts of policing pressure have been put into practice to produce the varying levels of control that were considered as neces-

---

1. The purpose of these is to prevent parking on the pavement. They are about a yard high and derive their name from the fact that they have the emblem of Amsterdam, a vertical row of three X's, cast into them.

sary or as feasible at different times during the last fifteen years. During some periods, large crowds of addicts were left undisturbed while they occupied parts of the area and openly traded and consumed hard drugs. In other periods, often responding to protests and demonstrations of the "normal" inhabitants of this and neighboring city areas, tolerance was reduced. During these periods of low tolerance, the petty participants in the retail trade were deterred out of visibility, their clients were forced to keep moving, and those who had succeeded in obtaining drugs were discouraged from overt consumption. The policy of control for the sake of maintaining public order has, however, stopped short of forcing the hard drug scene from its "natural" habitat. This could have been easily achieved in such a limited area. There is, however, a recognition that if undesirable realities are suppressed in one part of town, they will pop up in another. Some decades ago, there was an unhappy attempt to put pressure on prostitution in this same vice area. In no time, street walkers appeared in the most unexpected parts of town.

In a control policy that aims at striking a balance between reasonable tolerance and necessary suppression, law enforcement objectives, such as arresting and prosecuting persons in possession of hard drugs and persons participating in the retail trade, may receive a lower priority. A municipal report stated that police actions against the hard drug scene should be evaluated in light of whether "a more stringent enforcement of the Opium Act would produce less public nuisance and violent crime than a less stringent enforcement" (Gemeente Amsterdam 1985, p. 25). In an evaluation, the head of the subdivision of the Amsterdam narcotic squad operating in the drugs area rejected the idea of more intensive police actions against the drug-using population. According to his experience, this would only lead to adaptions in the drug market, making it even more elusive. "Instead of removing the rotten parts of a drug organization the police would relapse to 'junkie hunting' as before" (Gemeentepolitie Amsterdam 1986).

Looking back at the last fifteen years, there has been a clear tendency toward decreasing official tolerance for the hard drug market in the drugs quarter of Amsterdam. The city administration has appeared to be responding to two kinds of pressure in adopting a less lenient policy. International media reports on the alleged drugs anarchy in the area have had some impact, mainly because of a concern that they would damage the city's reputation as an international trade and tourist center. The growing indignation of local interest groups concerned with safety and livability in this part of town has probably played a more important role. Shopkeepers and the "normal" dwellers of the affected neighborhoods have put increasing pressure on the police and the city administration to act against the drug market.

In the early eighties, a policy was initiated of rolling back the well-established power of the drug trade on the Zeedijk. For several years, this street had been dominated by collaborating bar owners and drug dealers. The hard drug trade operated openly in numerous bars on the Zeedijk. The Surinamese drug dealers and customers were constantly present. This attracted many more addicts who could be assured of successful transactions any time they wanted. The city administration started a policy of revoking business licenses of all commercial establishments where involvement with the drug trade could be proved. A city bylaw gave the police more powers, specifically aimed at allowing them to tackle the drug trade on the Zeedijk: it was prohibited to carry knives there, to gather together, and, in some cases, individuals could be forbidden to enter the area for a certain period of time (usually two weeks).[2] The city authorities also came up with a plan for "economic restoration" of the Zeedijk. The plan provided for restoration of a number of buildings and aimed at attracting small shopkeepers back to the area, in order to improve the image of Holland's "most notorious" street and to make the area more livable again.

Since these measures, the situation on the Zeedijk has changed visibly. Restoration of the buildings is almost finished and a number of small shopkeepers have already set up a shop. The concerted actions of the city administration and the police have had a clear impact on the drug market. Some effects may be considered favorable, others are definitely not. Hard drug dealing in the Nieuwmarkt area has become a much more fragmented, volatile, and elusive phenomenon. In effect this represents an adjustment by the drug trade to protect itself against interference from law enforcement (van Gemert 1988). For example, after the bars were boarded up, the trade in heroin moved into the street, but dealers and users no longer conduct most of their business on the Zeedijk. Nowa-

---

2. The Council of State later suspended this provision, because it contravenes Article 219 of the Municipalities Act.

days, most gather in the small streets running off from the Zeedijk, such as the Stormsteeg and the Molensteeg, and especially the Gelderse Kade. Only quick deals can be transacted on that part of the Zeedijk itself that has the Stormsteeg at one end and Nieuwmarkt Square at the other (the so-called "tail"). But more often than not the police will have sealed off this part hermetically.

This description of the scene is incomplete, because it only refers to locations where the (street) trade in heroin and cocaine takes place. Addicts interested in (illegal) methadone or psychopharmaca will be disappointed here, and must move on to the "pill bridge." This nickname, although still used in the scene, is a reminder of old times,[3] for there has not been much trade in medicines on a bridge for some years. At present, most deals are transacted—often on the move—in the Oude Hoogstraat or at the corner of this street and the Kloveniersburgwal. There is no longer any fixed location for the sale of pills.

In the Damstraat and moving on in a southeasterly direction, the emphasis is on the trade in pills, but in the summer season heroin and cocaine are also regularly offered for sale. The most important customers then are foreign tourists, for whom the atmosphere of the Zeedijk and its adjoining streets is too threatening. Because these foreigners are often interested in buying large amounts of hard drugs and do not know the ropes in the Amsterdam scene or are afraid of being ripped off, in the summer many Dutch addicts are pleased to offer their services as an intermediary, or, as one of our respondents preferred to think of himself, as an agent.

ACTORS IN THE SCENE AND THEIR MUTUAL RELATIONSHIPS

Interactions Between Addicts

In the previous chapter we remarked that one of the rewards of being a junkie is the esteem that goes with it. Such aspirations are

---

3. The bridge across the Oudezijds *Achter*burgwal in Damstraat was called the "pill bridge" in the middle of the eighties. The guild of users and dealers was evicted from the bridge by a group of "bouncers" hired by the local shopkeepers and driven to the bridge over the Oudezijds *Voor*burgwal. Here too the shopkeepers enlisted the help of the bouncers, and once again trade moved on in the direction of the Kloveniersburgwal (see van Gemert 1988 for a more detailed description).

everywhere in the Amsterdam street scene. Addicts watch each other carefully, and in seeking to elevate their own position, they always go for a lower point of reference. Those exhibiting visible signs of deterioration can count on scathing remarks from their colleagues. In this connection it was typical that many respondents did their best to convince the field-workers that they themselves were careful of hygiene. Surinamese drug users especially attach great value to a well-groomed appearance: in these circles the sleazy life-style of white Dutch addicts is strongly disapproved of.

As well as appearance, use of language is also a way in which to distinguish oneself from the others. Some addicts use an intellectual sounding vocabulary in order to emphasize that they have more brains than just "any old junk." One respondent told triumphantly of a court case where he had won over the court to his point of view with well-founded legal arguments; this impressive act resulted, so he said, in a considerably milder sentence than the prosecutor had envisaged. Another respondent recited constantly from the famous books and the high-quality newspapers that he read.

Sometimes an addict's reputation is expressed in a nickname. One respondent, for example, said that in the scene he was called after an animal that leads a solitary existence and never bothers people, but is nevertheless respected because it doesn't let anybody mess it around.

Television appearances or figuring in the press are good for status in the scene. National and international media pay a lot of attention to the drug problem in Amsterdam's inner city and plenty of addicts are willing to participate in a program or article, certainly if a financial reward is offered. In a time span of two years, three of our respondents figured in national publicity. The first appeared in a documentary about drugs. The second made the front page, albeit inadvertently, of a national weekly that printed a large photo in which our respondent was to be seen selling medicine. Finally, the third has become one of the best-known addicts in the country since he was both interviewed and photographed for several illustrated magazines. Shortly after he had appeared in one of these, one of the field-workers met him in the street.

> Proudly, but with a hint of irony, Frank tells about there being several photo's of him—and one very big one—in this illustrated magazine, while other lads from the Zeedijk had to be content

with much smaller pictures. Later we see that Frank is posing for the photo with a needle in his arm. The photographer had asked him to do it while he was drinking a can of beer in the children's playground on the Zeedijk. Frank didn't mind, as long as there was something in it for him. Eventually it brought in about $120,-.

Being a street dealer brings respect in the scene, on the condition that customers are not sold rubbish or drugs of bad quality too often. Older addicts who have been well-known in the scene for years are often the most suitable characters who are most easily trusted by their clientele. And then there are the users of Surinam origin for whom especially small-scale dealing seems to offer some sort of perspective. The trade networks seem to be partly organized along ethnic lines, while the street market fits a Surinam culture of street corners and hustling.

It is, however, impossible to make a clear distinction between the scenes of white and colored addicts. We noticed very little mutual distrust or animosity between white and black in users' circles. It is not unusual for white female addicts to have relationships with male addicts from Surinam, while Dutch and Surinam users sometimes join forces in hustling.

Nevertheless, there are some differences in the way in which the ethnic groups shape their lives of addiction. Conforming to their street corner culture, dope users of Surinam extraction are much more likely to crowd together than white addicts. In Surinam it is common to discuss one's daily affairs in the street and many an immigrant continues to do so in the Netherlands. A factor that drives the Surinamese together is the failure of processes of acculturation—already discussed in chapter 3—that almost all of these young people have experienced in Holland: they are seriously disappointed in society here and they seek support with fellow sufferers. In order to prevent themselves from deteriorating into "real junks" and in order to be able to feel a cut above their white counterparts, they invoke their "own" rules of behavior: any signs of deterioration are abhorred, and there is a taboo on intravenous use. Infection with the HIV virus may also mean that an addict is no longer accepted by his colleagues from Surinam.

The greater solidarity among addicts of Surinam origin is also reflected in the way they "score": they are far more likely to share any available dope. Relationships between white addicts are usually purely instrumental: if there is any sharing, it is because someone owes a debt, or is counting on getting something in return.

It will be clear from the above that ties between white drug users are as easily forged as broken. If there is any necessity, then each will make use of the services of the other; if the relationship is no longer functional, the other is soon dropped. To illustrate how addicts treat each other, let us take a closer look at Paul who is an expert at the exploitation game in the scene. During the two years that our fieldwork took, he managed to exploit or rip off many another addict. Some of his "victims" were our respondents.

> Paul and Eric seem to be sworn comrades. For months they were inseparable. There were even rumours buzzing around that they had paired off, but these two weren't having any. Eric taught the rumour-mongerer a lesson that he won't easily forget. He's in jail now, but for another offense. There is a tale that Paul has spent $6000 belonging to Eric. There'll be trouble when Eric gets out.
>
> Paul has had a row with his old friend Bert. Both allege that the one owes the other money. According to insiders, Bert is most probably right. All the same, Bert has been transferred to another methadone program, because Paul was threatening him with violence.
>
> Paul is involved in a row again with Rob. The latter was trying to get away from the boys on the methadone bus when—to his annoyance—he found Paul, Albert and Judy in his parents' house one afternoon. The trouble started when Rob found out that Paul had been through the cupboards looking for loot. Rob says he felt like killing Paul. Somehow they all landed up in a meadow. Some of them—Paul certainly—had been taking pills. Paul was unsteady on his legs so that he fell off a dyke into a canal when Judy pushed him. Rob: "He floated past me at my feet. I could have held him under with one foot. I wanted to, and so did Albert, but not Judy. We let him crawl out again."
>
> For some time now, Rosa has had a good home address in the area. When she was there yesterday, Paul was there too. They had put some money together and enjoyed their dope, when Rosa discovered Paul scrabbling in her bag. Before she could do anything, Paul had her purse and he was off. Rosa set off in pursuit, but couldn't manage more than a slap in the face for Paul

who lost his balance and fell down the stairs. Loss: $40 and a bit of brown sugar (heroin).

These field notes reveal that physical violence as a way of repercussion is by no means unusual in the scene. However, compared to the crack scene in American metropoles, the Amsterdam drugs market is probably much more peaceful. Goldstein et al. (1989) describe violence as an almost normative means in the regulation of market relations among dealers and between dealers and customers. Amsterdam street addicts and dealers do not call each other to account by means of violence all the time. To a certain extent the principle of give and take applies as the central norm. Doing someone down is accepted, because everybody does it sometimes. "Rip and be ripped" is the adage by which the scene lives. It is only when certain boundaries have been crossed—for example when someone thinks he's getting a name of being a weak and easy prey—that action is indicated.

> I am talking to Leo on the "streetwalkers bridge" when suddenly an addict comes past of whom neither us have very pleasant memories. Six months ago this bloke managed to sell Leo tap water as fluid methadone and this incident turned into a very nasty row in which Leo was threatened with a knife. I was there when it happened, albeit that I followed the course of events from a safe distance. The addict concerned looks as if he's had a dose of his own medicine, as he's walking on crutches. Leo says that he had sold a few grams of "rubbish" to someone, after which the victim and some friends had some fun with a lump of concrete: they dropped it none too gently on the dealer's toes.

Now and then there is loud trouble between the addicts or between addicts and dealers. They threaten each other with knives or other sharp implements like broken bottles, but they rarely actually hurt each other. Rumor has it that one or two have guns, but we were never able to catch anybody even threatening to use a firearm, let alone actually using it. Respondents regularly looked as if they'd been roughed up a bit. However, often their injuries were not due to any scores being settled in the scene, but to other causes such as marital difficulties or other events in "ordinary" life. Once, for example, three respondents were removed roughly from the tram after they had told the driver—no doubt provocatively—not to close the doors so fast because an old lady wanted to get off. Several female respondents were given a bad time by their partners and were regularly beaten black and blue. One showed a field-worker—very much against his will—a range of burns, the result of a hyped-up row with her husband who had held her for a few seconds against a burning stove. Although women were usually the victims of such ill-treatment, there was one case in which the reverse was true; this time it was a man who had to seek medical attention after being clawed by his impetuous and sharp-nailed girl friend.

INTERACTIONS BETWEEN ADDICTS AND POLICE

The addicts in the inner city of Amsterdam have to be continually on the alert for intervention by the police, because their street trade is so highly visible. Uniformed patrolling has been intensified. Plainclothes policemen also regularly visit the area and the police have a number of strategically placed lookout posts. As Verbraeck (1988) says, a more emphatic presence of police on the streets has meant a greater mobility among users and dealers. It is rare now for a deal to be transacted calmly and peacefully, for at any moment the police may appear on the stage. A constantly moving crowd of addicts, followed at a distance by a couple of policemen, is a fascinating scene for the interested observer.

> From the chemist at the corner of the Gelderse Kade and the Stormsteeg, where I was trying to make arrangements to meet potential respondents, I have a fine view of one of the most interesting meeting points for small dealers and addicts. Outside of the shop there is a shadowy game going on between users and dealers on the one hand, and patrolling policemen on the other. One minute the whole bang lot are gesticulating widely and negotiating a price for the merchandise, ten seconds later everybody has run like a rabbit when four cops arrive from different directions. For about five minutes these officers occupy the street corner, and then split off into pairs again. Not long after they have gone the first addicts are back and the game is off again. After a while the police approach again and the whole company moves off a hundred yards further up, etc.

It is clear from this observation that users and dealers dive into the vacuum left by the departing cops. The addict population and the police follow each other around as it were, through the scene and, as van Gemert (1988) and Verbraeck (1988) have called it, they play a real cat and mouse game. Each party keeps a wary eye on the other, and participants in the drug business must try and profit immediately from the absence of their opponents. Activities on the street reach their highest point especially at times when policemen come and go off duty. Many deals are transacted then at many different locations—but usually at corners or crossroads so that escape in different directions is possible should there be trouble.

As a result of the "keep-moving" system used by the police and because of the way in which drugs are offered for sale in the Zeedijk area—street heroin and cocaine are sold in sealed balls of cellophane—dope users have few ways of testing the quality of what they buy. The risk of buying a pig in a poke is very real and most of the addicts who buy in the street are ripped off sooner or later: thinking they are purchasing heroin or cocaine, they buy coughtablets, ground catlitter, Epsom salt, or lidocaine.[4] If one wishes to avoid such uncertainties, then a good house address is the proper alternative. Here the dope can be tested before it is bought and, if one wishes, taken in peace and quiet.

The uniformed patrols aim at maintaining public order and restricting nuisance value in the neighborhood, but the plainclothes branch is primarily involved in detecting and investigating crime. Their presence on the scene forces those involved in the street trade to be even more alert. A few years ago it was fairly easy—even for an outsider—to spot these "disguised" opponents, because they moved through the scene with a remarkably high level of visibility: their blue jeans were too clean, their sneakers too new, their jackets too short, their clothing as a whole too obvious, and they were regularly sighted riding (police) bicycles that were—by Amsterdam standards—far too well equipped. Nowadays plainclothes policemen dress with more imagination and the result is that they are less easily recognized by the unwary observer. For example, a couple of field-workers watched while two policemen—got up as tourists in Bermudas and floral shirts—arrested and handcuffed a small dealer. However, old hands in the drug world are unlikely to let themselves be surprised by such disguises. William is one of the old hands.

> William belongs to the category of addicts who have learned to watch the gutters, the road, people in front and people behind

---

4. Lidocaine is a bit like cocaine, in that both drugs produce a slight numbness if a small amount is rubbed against tongue or gum. But here the likeness ends.

for any significance for his life as an addict. In evaluating the people he meets in the street, William has a certain sequence. Firstly it is important to determine their status: friend, citizen, or foe. He says he can recognise plain-clothes dicks from a mile off. They look too sporting and, especially, too clean. They move with the sort of self-evident dominance/arrogance that people with power have when they want everyone to know about it. They walk in the middle of the street and don't move aside for anyone, their arms loose beside their body, ready for action. William is not only able to spot plain-clothes policemen, he also has developed a fine sense of who is likely to be a potential customer or who he will probably be able to use somehow. Finally there are the passers-by, to whom he is indifferent: people who live in the neighborhood, sightseers etc. William says that success in the scene depends on how well-developed one's instinct is and how long it takes to put people in the right category.

Finally there are the observation posts. These have been set up at several locations in junkie territory and are in contact with the teams on the street via walkie-talkie. Many an unsuspecting small dealer has been caught this way. During our fieldwork there was at least one addict who, according to the police, was firmly convinced that an observation post had been set up in an empty container used to recycle glass on the Zeedijk. After his arrest he said he was surprised he had been caught, for he hadn't seen any policemen. The arresting officer told him that he had been spotted from this particular container. After he had been let loose, this addict was often seen near the container. He peered into the openings for pushing the bottles through, and shouted down them; once he even put his arm down to feel whether the police were still there.

It goes without saying that, as an institution and considering the job they do, the police are not regarded sympathetically by addicts and dealers. But that says nothing about interactions between individual policemen and addicts. A number of policemen are regarded by the guild of users as friendly and forthcoming, the sort of people it's quite nice to chat to now and then. One of our most extravert respondents, for example, often slapped the policemen she thought were friendly jovially on the shoulder and always called them "hunks." The officers would react with a friendly smile or with another fairly distant but not unfriendly gesture.

As long as they are talking about policemen they like, addicts often show some understanding of the difficult job these people have to do in the inner city.

> It must drive those guys and girls crazy in the end. It's pointless, and it must be so frustrating to be doing something while you know you can't solve the problem. And look what they earn!

But there is no sense of understanding for the officers who have a reputation for being irritating and provocative. The policemen who have made a habit of throwing confiscated drugs into the canal are hated, for example. Most impound the drugs they find. But it is not unusual for officers to return the drugs after a search, or throw them away in a manner that allow the addicts to pick them up again. The plainclothes policemen are also very unpopular, although this has more to do with the fear of being caught. During our fieldwork, one of the plainclothes officers of whom the addicts were afraid was "Blondie." The man with this nickname was not feared for his brutality, but for his unerring instinct: he always knew who was carrying what and nobody to need have any illusions if they were arrested: "Blondie" always found it.

During interactions with police officers, blows sometimes fall. More than once respondents reported being molested during arrest or at the police station.

> Mickey storms into the bus with a face like thunder. He tells everyone who will listen that he has not only been caught red-handed while committing theft, but that the policemen have also knocked his glasses from his nose and broken them. The others start to tease Mickey immediately. The remark that he must surely know that stealing is forbidden by law, is the last straw; he leaves the bus in a rage.

Of course the fieldworkers were unable to check the truth of these stories. As far as we were able to observe, operational policemen behaved correctly, with the exception of one or two incidents. Once or twice their batons were very loose in their hands. Another time we saw the police drive a bunch of addicts apart with a furious police dog—as far as we could tell unnecessarily. But there were only very occasional instances of the police going too far, as during the following incident.

> Two mounted policemen ride down a group of addicts who don't seem to be doing anything more illegal or unruly than sit-

ting and snoozing on the benches of Nieuwmarkt Square. They are enjoying the sunshine, with several pints of beer within easy reach. They are very indignant about such police-intervention. Moreover, two policemen on a foot-patrol apparently thought it necessary to come to the aid of their colleagues and make use of their batons. Muttering angrily, the whole group moves off towards the "pill bridge".

Interactions Between Addicts and Public

Drug users in their "natural territory" not only have the police to deal with, but also the people who live in the area or have economic interests there. These groups have to put up with a lot from the presence of drug addicts. To many, groups of drug users in front of one's door is a source of constant irritation, as is the noise that junkies and dealers make when communicating. This continues through the night and many a resident has had his sleep disturbed. Feelings of displeasure are reinforced when addicts are discovered sleeping or taking drugs in one's street or doorway; dirty needles left behind are a source of extra concern.

Despite a feeling that one's privacy is being seriously infringed, few residents confront the addicts directly. To some extent there exists an "armed peace." As Koster (1987) notes, most residents have a pattern of behavior best described as avoiding the addict population as much as possible and taking steps to ensure the security of one's own interests. Houses—and in some cases whole streets—have high fences meant to keep addicts out and in several places there are signs admonishing addicts to go somewhere else. A small minority of the local population have a warmer relationship with the addicts, in the sense that they sometimes stop for a chat and/or ask them to do a job—like shopping. Almost without exception, the drug users concerned are white: contacts between black addicts and the local population are extremely rare.

It should be noted that those who wish to take active measures against the drug problem in the neighborhood are mostly small shopkeepers or restaurant/bar owners. During our fieldwork, one of them was known as the "Night Mayor of the Nieuwmarkt," because of his habit of going through the neighborhood in the early hours of the morning and getting rid of addicts and homeless sleeping in the streets and parks.

Not all small businessmen are so bothered by the addict population. Some profit from their presence. A number of shopkeepers, for example, have found a new source of income by stocking custard and other liquid food. This provides a service for the addicts, who are very keen on dairy products to which sweeteners and sugars have been added. Another way of profiting from the presence of drug addicts is by selling the paraphernalia that they need: at least two shopkeepers are known to earn a tidy profit from selling individual sized bits of tin foil, ammonia, lemon juice, and other necessities. Another shopkeeper lets some addicts pay for the use of his warehouse as a "shooting gallery." More profitable, but also more risky because it is a criminal offense, is receiving goods stolen by addicts. During our fieldwork we discovered that the managers of several shops were guilty of fencing regularly.

CONCLUDING REMARKS

For some of the addicts in Amsterdam, life consists of repeating short cycles of acquiring income (in kind or cash), buying drugs, and taking drugs. These dope users are to be found in the inner city almost every day and they lead a very hectic existence there, constantly on the lookout for customers, for good dope, or for an opportunity to make money. Moreover, they have to avoid a large police presence as much as possible. For these active participants in the world of drugs, being an addict is more than a full-time job. This was expressed best by our respondent Hugo, who answered a request by a field worker to come and sit in the sun as follows: "But we haven't got time for that sort of thing."

Another part of the addict population leads a calmer existence and these drug users only appear on the scene once in a while to buy dope. Nevertheless, they too must manage to survive economically. There is a great diversity of techniques and means that allow them to do this and these involve not only illegal and semi-illegal, but also more conventional activities, as we will point out in the next chapter.

CHAPTER 5

Income Acquisition

The previous chapters describe the different perceptions that drug users have of their own way of life. Some are drawn to the hassle of being an addict as to a magnet, others are no longer attracted by such a life-style. The different ways in which a life of addiction can be shaped are also reflected in the ways in which addicts acquire and spend income. This and the following chapter deal with economic behavior.

First we shall concentrate on the different ways of generating income, emphasizing the part played by crime. However, in the first section we shall also be looking at (semi)legal income acquisition. The second section weighs the significance of the different sources of income against each other using quantitative data. It also looks more closely at a number of offenses, compares the results with several other studies, and examines the possible effect of periods of abstinence on drug-related crime. In the last section we develop a typology based on prevalent sources of income.

WAYS OF ACQUIRING INCOME

Social Security

The Dutch system of social security ensures that citizens and other (legal) inhabitants of the Netherlands who are unable to earn their own living receive enough social benefit to allow them to exist. Hard drug users are not excepted, and more than 85 percent of our respondents were on social security. During the years covered by this study, an adult individual received about $600 per month. Most receive their money once a month from the social security services. Only a few are able to resist the temptations that go with possessing such a sum of money. As a result, many addicts disappear completely into the scene for a few days. They reappear again as destitute as ever and take up their old routine. Some have had enough of this life, and turn over their social security money to a special foundation for drug addicts that administers it for them, ensuring, for example, that the rent and the gas bill have been paid. Many respondents have the social security services help them with clearing their debts, leaving a smaller sum to spend each month. This sum can then be collected in the form of weekly pocket money from the foundation. In this way, attempts are made to channel the finances of addicts on social security and, therefore, to normalize their existence. Despite these facilities, social security is often not enough to cover monthly expenses and some addicts take refuge in other forms of income acquisition, including acquisitive crime.

Acquisitive Crime

Much of the work on hard drug addiction focuses on acquisitive crime. In chapter 2 we saw that according to the literature, hard drug users as a group commit considerably more crime than non-users. On a group level, acquisitive crime by hard drug addicts is highly diverse, but individually many specialize in one form or the other. We found, for example, two female addicts in the red-light district taking orders from window prostitutes. They go along the windows with pen and paper, writing down their clients' wishes. Considering the nature of the trade these clients ply, it should come as no surprise to learn that most orders are for "stockings like the girl next door" or "a red lace bra with matching suspender belt." Off go the enterprising pair with the orders to steal the required items, usually from a fashionable department store; they do this several times a day. But buyers are not only prostitutes. They are just as likely to be found in more conventional circles such as visitors to local bars and coffee shops, members of addicts' families, friends, and neighbors. Apparently it is easy enough to get rid of stolen goods within "normal" Amsterdam society. Compact discs, electrical appliances, clothing, liquor, and food are all saleable items. One respondent told us that her grocer on the corner regularly bought—at a fixed price—the packets of coffee she stole from the wholesaler's. Another example concerns a garage that bought the daily haul of car radios from two respondents—unseen, and again at a fixed price. The idea that fencing is an isolated phenomenon restricted to a small group of professionals may be reassuring, but is far removed from the reality of everyday life. The informal economy of the conventional and respectable urban citizen forms a ready market for goods stolen by the junkies they detest.

Shoplifting (especially in big department stores) is the crime most frequently committed. Addicts rationalize their choice of victim with the remark that these stores are very rich and, anyway, who's to notice. Often there are other motives too: shoplifting is easier in big shops because one is more anonymous, and there is more choice and a better chance of getting away. In general, addicts specialize in shoplifting if they look reasonably well-groomed and therefore run relatively little risk. Breaking into cars is also a specialization. Although the average citizen is inclined to blame drug addicts if his car radio disappears, this offense is not as popular among the drug-using population as is often assumed. Our data show that only ten respondents (7 percent) regularly steal from cars. Similar results were obtained by a study in Eindhoven (Bureau regionaal coordinator voorkoming misdrijven 1985) of seventy-one perpetrators of thefts from cars, twenty-one of which were drug addicts. In only 10 percent of these cases was the use of drugs reported as a motive for the offense; "going out," "luxury spending" and "gambling" were mentioned far more frequently. Breaking into cars is a risky business that requires a cool head and skill, and not many addicts are willing to run the risk or possess the skills.

Stealing checks and forging the signatures on them is another specialization. The latter can be quite difficult and requires dexterity; those who manage to pass checks with forged signatures have a certain status among fellow addicts. To start with, anyone cashing a stolen check must be sure not to arouse the suspicion of the person at the cash desk. An addict must look clean and decent and not at all like the stereotype of the drug addict. He must have enough self-confidence and make sure that his behavior is as self-confident as that of regular customers at the post office or bank. Checks are obtained in the ordinary ways of stealing wallets and handbags, but there are more devious tactics. In close cooperation, one respondent and his friend acted out the theft of the friend's checks. These were cashed by the respondent, whereupon the friend reported them stolen and was reimbursed by the bank for his loss. Sometimes such operations can count on inside help. In (at least) one case, a post office employee (a nonuser) accepted payment in exchange for checking whether hot checks had already been registered as such.

If the thief is unwilling or unable to cash the checks himself, there are still enough ways of getting rid of them, although the margin of profit is less. Depending on supply and demand, a packet of twenty checks (legally cashed, each check is worth $160) is worth about $125. It is widely known in the scene which shops, bars, and restaurants are in the habit of buying checks. Several times one of our field-workers witnessed such transactions in the cellar of a coffee and sandwich shop: the fence sat behind a table and received the loot. There were no negotiations about the price; apparently the customers knew what to expect beforehand. As well as stealing checks themselves, addicts are also used to cash those stolen by others. They are given a packet of checks to cash, to which end they often visit banks and post offices all over the city, or even in other towns.

Others go for the bold touch. They "simply" walk into offices and other easily accessible locations and make off with what they can carry. They also have a reputation for boldness and brains and command a certain amount of respect, while a whole mythology has grown up around their more spectacular stunts, irrespective of the question of whether these were successful or not.

> There is a story about John—and he is pleased to confirm it—that he once tried to crack a safe. When he discovered that he didn't have the right tools, he decided to carry it home and finish the job in peace. It was too far to walk, so he decided to take the subway, where he was overcome by fatigue. He was woken by the police who had been called by a suspicious driver.

The common characteristic of these offenses is that there is no direct contact with the victim. Offenses where such contact exists are more malignant and sometimes violent. One of these situations may arise from a visit to a heroin prostitute. Usually this fleeting contact proceeds according to expectations. Sometimes, however, the prostitute literally cashes in on the customer's vulnerability: calculatingly she waits until his trousers are down, and then makes off with his wallet. Or she might demand that he takes a shower first. She rifles through his clothes and throws both his address and his keys out of the window, whereupon her partner outside rushes off to see whether the address is in the neighborhood and ready to be burgled. The prostitute makes sure that her services are so attractive as to warrant hiring the room for some time, so that her partner can return the keys and papers before the session has finished.

Street robbery, especially with violence (mugging), was not reported often by our respondents. Nevertheless, it does happen. Sometimes addicts set off to rob someone with premeditation. However, it is more likely to happen on the spur of the moment if the opportunity presents itself: asking a rich-looking drunken bar patron what time it is, to see whether his watch is worth stealing; waiting for passers by inadvertently displaying a breast pocket full of bank notes; relieving a prostitute's customer of his money at the entrance to the hotel.

One very creative respondent made a habit of visiting neighborhood priests in the big cities and telling them a sob story about the situation he had got himself into, of course, without being in any way to blame himself. Eventually he would get round to the loan that would help him overcome all of these problems and that he would, naturally, repay as soon as everything had been settled. He often managed to weedle quite substantial sums this way.

The offenders we have been discussing all have some degree of organization, albeit rudimentary. But addicts do not typically work this way. Most are opportunistic and take advantage of situations that arise: a door left open, a car or bicycle left unlocked, drunken passersby, poor security in shops. The profit is generally small and some addicts commit several offenses a day. Only occasionally do they lay their hands on something big, like one of our respondents who had the good fortune to steal a briefcase in the subway that contained $5500.

The Market of White and Brown

Offers of "white," "brown," or "both" are whispered at many a passerby on the Zeedijk or the Gelderse Kade that runs parallel to it; always followed by "you can taste" if the potential customer hesitates. Addicts not only make this offer to the unconventional looking passerby, but sometimes enjoy surprising respectable older ladies by whispering in their ear and frightening them half to death. The unsuspecting may think they are being offered a loaf of bread, but they would be sorely mistaken; for "white" and "brown" are the easily pronounceable slang names for cocaine and heroin respectively.

Much of the street trade takes place within the fairly well-defined territory of drug users. It has an extensive division of labor and many specialisms. The result is that many users derive some part of their income from the street trade in drugs. On the other hand, this allows the dealer to spread his risks and achieve a bigger turnover.

Two or three times a day, the bigger dealers appear on the market to distribute little balls of white and brown among the middlemen. The latter usually work on commission: for every five packets or balls they sell, they earn one for personal use. Depending on the trustworthiness of the person concerned, direct trade varies from ten to twenty balls, each weighing a little bit more than a tenth or a quarter of a gram. The next time the dealer appears on the Zeedijk, he collects his money and delivers a fresh supply. The middlemen often work for several dealers at once. The advantage to the dealers is as obvious as the disadvantage. The dealers themselves decrease their personal risk and spread the risk of having their merchandise impounded. But their control of the middlemen is limited: it is fairly easy to fabricate a story about being stopped and searched by the police and having the dope confiscated, while in reality they took it themselves.

One of our field-workers was able to observe the methods of one of these intermediaries from very close quarters. A fragment from his diary:

> After I had managed to establish a relationship of trust with Glenn (not, however, without ups and downs: I had to let him search me several times to see whether I was wired), he proposed that I should accompany him one night on his visits to his usual addresses. He appeared at the rendezvous, the corner of the Stormsteeg and the Zeedijk, at about midnight. He was riding a bicycle, and by the sound of the puffing, he must have made quite an effort. "I had to deliver something and it took longer than I thought, but it was worth it; earned quite a bit," was the first thing he said. "How much?" I asked. "He was American, didn't know the price," he answered, "so I charged him double. Profit's about $70."
>
> A quick calculation reveals that he must have sold about a gram (in this case cocaine). Remarking that "it's difficult to cycle carrying all your stuff," he tried to get me to carry quite a few balls of brown and white. Approximately an ounce in all. I had to appeal to his common sense in order to prevent my contraven-

ing the Opium Act. Considering the amount of dope, who ever he gets it from must have a lot of faith in Glenn.

The first address was a crooked little house in an old part of the city. After a signal on the bell, the inhabitant opened the door impatiently. "You're late man," he said, his Surinam accent unmistakable in the dark passage. When he saw that Glenn wasn't alone, he asked a excited question in his own language, Sranan Tongo. Glenn calmed him down, and without further ado the deal was clinched in the passage behind the open door. Two balls of brown and two of white changed hands for $70. Once we were outside, Glenn said that the man had to look after a child on his own and was unable to get out of the house.

The next stop was on a canal a bit further out of town. A quick deal was clinched with four boys of about twenty in front of a tiny, dirty cafe with an exotic sounding name. It all took no more than five minutes. A few swift glances were cast in my direction. They bought seven balls in all for about $90, each paying between $15 and $30. "I am right in thinking you don't charge everybody the same?" I asked as we walked back to our bicycle. "No, that's right. It depends on the customer. Sometimes, if you know them well, or if you like them, or a pretty woman, they pay less than the ones with the big mouth or whatever, they have to pay full price and a bit more if possible." "Do you try to widen your circle of customers by giving reductions?" "No, not really, but sometimes it happens like that, they tell each other, you know, mouth to mouth advertising."

A relatively big deal was clinched in the same part of town. On the first floor of a sparsely furnished house with no more than a table, two chairs and a mattress on the floor, a man speaking broken Dutch bought about $200 worth of heroin, in all about 4 grams. Again we went through the ritual of the customer nervously enquiring about my presence, and Glenn putting him at his ease. There was hardly any negotiating about the price or the amount. The customers seem to trust Glenn too.

"Aren't you afraid of being ripped off carrying all that dope and money?" Laughingly he answers: "I won't get ripped off. They know who I am, they wouldn't live to tell the tale, nobody takes me for a ride. I've got a very good memory. They did it once, but never again." "Why do you do this at night, anyway? It's miles on the bike, it must surely be easier to take the tram?" "It's far too dangerous during the day. The police know me and if they see me they always stop me. If I got caught with all that dope, I'd be put away for a few years. That's why I take the bicycle, they don't expect it, and it gives me more freedom of movement."

A few more addresses, where the turnover was about $300, and we ended up in the Bijlmermeer. By this time it was about four o'clock in the morning. What was left of a very respectable load of dope was sold in a large parking garage. Glenn knew the way like the back of his hand. It was dark, lit only sparingly by one or two neon lights. The spaces in between the cars were in darkness. Every now and then a little flame would flare up underneath a piece of tinfoil, distorting the face bent over it. Having noticed Glenn's arrival, a number of dark shapes came forward from the dark background, retreating as soon as they saw he was not alone. Glenn walked towards them unhesitatingly. Casting nervous glances over their shoulders, they formed a whispering circle around Glenn underneath a neon lamp. I watched from a distance. Judging by his movements, Glenn was counting money and handing over dope. After quarter of an hour he came back, a bundle of notes in his hand. Satisfied, he reported that he had managed to sell it all. All, that is, except for a small amount he was keeping for himself. It had been a good night. On the way back to the bikes, he counted the money. It came to more than $2000. Grinning he remarked that his dealer should be pleased with the 1800 dollars he had earned.

"Isn't it dangerous to cheat your dealer like that?" "Everybody does it, but you mustn't exaggerate and sometimes you mustn't do it. The thing is, you have to get your dealer to trust you and give him what he thinks you owe him." "How does he get his money?" "I'm going back to the _____ now, he'll be waiting for me. Then I'm going home, I'll take some dope, have a drink and get a few hours sleep. I'll get up at about two p.m. and still have enough dope to get through the day. I'll get more stuff tomorrow night about nine, and the whole business will start again. I'm busy."

"Is it like this every day?" "Of late it is, but I also used to be on the Zeedijk. That never did anybody any good. I've worked my self up nicely. Maybe I can start out on my own, maybe my dealer would give me his addresses."'

A variation on this big-time intermediary is the courier. The courier carries the dope, but is not allowed to sell. He works with someone else who collects the money. The division of labor in the retail market of hard drugs is highly differentiated. In this purely commercially organized network, there are not only intermediaries, receivers, and couriers, but also addicts who put dealers in touch with customers, and customers in touch with dealers. Some dope users act as so-called lookouts, shouting "police" at the right moment to let their partner escape with the money, but without delivering the goods. The crowds of summer visitors provide work for the more staid addicts, renting themselves out to foreigners who, not knowing their way on the Amsterdam market, don't want to take any risks. They travel up and down between the market and the hotels where the customers stay. It goes without saying that these intermediaries charge a much higher price than the regular market price.

Up till now, we have been talking mostly about direct transactions between sellers and buyers. However, the provision of more indirect services is also an important activity. The different sorts mentioned below are often combined.

The "garbage men" of the scene play a very useful role. These addicts collect used, "dirty" needles and take them to special locations run by the official health authorities to be exchanged for new, sterile ones for free. Because the number of addicts sharing needles has decreased since the advent of the HI-virus, the total number of used needles has increased (Buning 1990). A considerable percentage of the garbage man's income comes, therefore, from selling sterile needles. Usually, the places where needles can be bought and exchanged are located in the center of the addicts' territory. Still—and this is characteristic of the opportunistic nature of many dope users—they prefer the lesser effort of buying a clean, if more expensive, needle from the garbage men. Although hierarchically this type of income acquisition is way down the ladder, used needles represent a financial value that is attractive enough to some participants in the scene to make them collectable items. The price of needles varies, depending on the time of day at which they are on offer. During the day they cost about one dollar. After the exchange centers have closed, the price can rise to between two and three dollars.

Others allow their homes to be used as shooting galleries, as sales addresses for home dealers, or as overnight shelters for homeless addicts. Some addicts do jobs for the heroin prostitutes, hanging around all day on one of the windowsills near the Liesdelsluis: if a prostitute has earned enough to afford some dope, she will want to take it in the peace and quiet of the room she entertains her customers in. The hotels, however, don't always allow the girls to use the rooms without customers, so the fellow addict acts as a temporary pseudopunter. As a reward he may be paid a small sum, or the girl may share her drugs with him. This brings us to a fourth important source of income: prostitution.

The Business of Prostitution and Sex

Considering the attractions of the red-light district and its direct surroundings, it is hardly surprising that this is where nonregular prostitution has established itself. The Korte and Lange Niezel, with the Liesdelsluis in between, the Central Station and the Ruyterkade that runs behind it, are where the heroin hookers—as they have come to be called—ply their trade. These prostitutes are usually regarded as unhappy victims. Indeed, it is hard to view them in any other way if one considers their physical condition and the way in which they work. The first girls arrive at the bridge at the Liesdelsluis about noon. The last time they took heroin was the evening or the night before, and they start work again driven on by the fear of withdrawal symptoms. If customers are long in arriving, the first symptoms begin to show. Some men observe the girls' condition first, waiting not only to demand a large reduction, but also to make it known that there will be no deals with condoms. Not all of the girls are willing to do "it" without a condom, but they often give in. Prostitutes on the Lange Niezel usually make use of one of the little hotels near by, renting a room for $5 per fifteen minutes.

Most of the women are experienced enough. Without fail they can pick a potential customer from the many passersby. First they fall easily into step beside him, then whisper in passing: "Coming with me?" This is the standard opening, sometimes followed by "darling." The women are not always the ones to make contact, sometimes the man makes the first move. During an interview with one of the prostitutes, sitting on a bench beside a canal, she had to stop for a while to serve a regular customer who lived on the canal. She continued the interview half an hour later.

Earnings vary. The usual price for a "straight up and down number" is about $25 plus $5 for the room. Four to six customers a day allows a girl to pay for a serious addiction. For a prostitute with heavy withdrawal symptoms, the price quickly goes down to $15. That is enough for a small ball of brown. Once she has earned it, she hurries off to buy and take the heroin. After a while she returns and resumes business at the normal rate. Because the women disappear from the bridge regularly to take dope, the population there and at other locations varies. Although heroin hookers earn a lot according to conventional standards, only a few of them really earn big money.

> Lucy is very popular. She mainly takes cocaine. Seven to eight grams a day is no exception. Once or twice a week she takes a bit of brown (one tenth of a gram) to calm down. Despite the hassle of her life and the lack of sleep, she looks good. She takes care of her looks. Well-fed, none of the scratched open spots that so many addicts have, taut brown skin, tastefully dressed. Because she usually free-bases these large amounts of cocaine, she is troubled by her throat. She splutters and coughs, regularly depositing large gobs of frothy sputum in the road. Nevertheless, she has a lot of steady customers. Every time she sees one, she greets him enthusiastically. She persuades a lot of men, snuggling up close in a flattering way. Because she's prepared to do a lot (but not everything: "I don't tongue-kiss anybody") and can take her pick, she charges about $100 a time. On successful days she may serve as many as ten customers, providing an income of $1000. She can even afford a long stay in an hotel. Sometimes she goes to stay with a good customer for the weekend, more as a companion than anything else. During the final period of our contact, she said she had given up actual prostitution. She was taking less dope and was being kept by several men, without there being any obligation on her part, so she said. Of late she had met several rich men who were sorry for her. Indeed, once or twice I saw men giving her money without her going with them.

Although most of the prostitutes hate their work, one or two look at it differently. Apart from the daily hassle of going after good quality heroin and the risks of working on the street, some see good points in being a prostitute. These are girls who are in control from beginning to end, and this gives them self-confidence: "The nice thing about this job is not the sex. I think it's exciting to discover that you have the customer in your power."

Some addicts have developed being kept by a man a few times a year, regardless of any other relationships, into a fine art. The host is usually an older man who belongs to the regular group of visitors to the Lange Niezel area. She lives with him, sleeps with him, keeps him company, and spends his money. Sometimes he rationalizes his behavior by referring to his good intentions: "I want to help her kick the habit, she can do that better with me than with somebody who takes advantage." Neither has any illusions about the instrumental nature of the arrangement: each has something to offer that the other needs. They visit the scene regularly, she to do her shopping and he to foot the bill.

> Caroline appears at the street cafe on the Liesdelsluis with a man of about 60. He's called William. Caroline announces that she is living with William and strokes his hair. She asks if I would mind waiting, while she "hustles up" something, as she puts it. Turning to William for the money, she asks him for 25 guilders. He examines his wallet and mutters sorrowfully that he only has a 100 guilders note. "Oh, that'll do," answers Caroline gaily, and before poor William knows what's happening, she's off with the money.

The advantage of street prostitution in the red-light district over street-walking elsewhere is that protection is relatively good. The girls usually work independently and are not protected by a pimp. This observation is confirmed by research among this group of female addicts (van de Berg and Blom 1986). During our project, one of the girls put it like this: "Do I have a pimp? You mean a man? No, my pimp's called Dope." Protection comes from the crowds in the district and from the fact that the girls work in hotel rooms, where there is at least supervision of sorts. Those who work behind the Central Station are in very different position. They usually go off in the customer's car, devoid of any protection. Sometimes they try to arrange for some in other ways. One pair operated with a pair of "walkie-talkies." She took it in her bag, and he followed the car on his moped, the walkie-talkie pressed to his ear. In practice, he systematically lost the car and the experiment had to be abandoned as a failure. Personal risks can be reduced by asking a colleague, or paying a fellow addict, to note down the number of the car. But the scope of this measure is limited too: once in the car the prostitutes are at the mercy of their customer's whims and there is nobody to whom they can turn directly.

Although the classic "employer" (pimp)— "employee" (prostitute) relationship is relatively rare in this form of street prostitution, some pairs do try to arrive at some sort of division of labor. She receives customers and he does all sorts of little jobs. This sometimes means that the male partner does indeed try to protect the girl. Otherwise he takes care of the dope so that she needn't go out and can keep on working, he gets food in or arranges for clean needles; sometimes the customer pays him. His contribution is to provide the basics, while she does the actual work. However, the life histories of our respondents reveal that many of these symbiotic relationships end up with the man simply receiving the profits and spending them as he sees fit. After a while, this almost always results in the end of the relationship. It is obvious that this, in its turn, regularly leads to fights, in which, equally obviously, the woman is usually the victim. Nevertheless, she generally manages to go on working independently.

A "less uncomfortable" activity in the sex industry (if only because it takes place indoors) is working in clubs--both in brothels and in sex theaters. They have the advantage of offering protection to the prostitute and, compared to street work, good working conditions. Although the girls must give part of their earnings to the owner or manager of the club, it allows the girls to simply do their work, "without having to bother your head," as one respondent put it. But often an increasing dependence on drugs means the end of a girl's employment. Working in a sex theater, that is to say, participating in live shows, is generally on a contract basis. If the owner of the theater is satisfied, the contract is sometimes changed to fixed employment. Two respondents reported taking a dose of cocaine before going on stage in order to pep up their self-confidence and improve the show.

Up till now we have dealt only with the role of women in prostitution. However, a number of boys are known to be active in prostitution too. Their circle of clients is limited almost exclusively to homosexual men. Because most punters explicitly prefer (innocent-looking) youths, prostitution is only a solution for young, reasonably unscathed, addicts. In comparison with their female colleagues, male prostitutes are only able to earn a living in this way for a relatively short time.

Contacts between male prostitutes and clients are usually made in the hall of the Central Station. Anonymity here at this busy spot is guaranteed. After a while, some addicts have built up a network of connections and need no longer take to the streets to find a client. They operate as call boys, and are also active outside of town. One of our respondents, for example, worked the whole of the west of Holland. Finally, a few addicts work in clubs, but the same is true here as is true of the women: increasing drug use often leads to dismissal.

Most male prostitutes deny being homosexual themselves. In conversations with field-workers they would boast of their virility in their (sexual) dealings with women. Only three respondents confirmed being homosexual. Others stated explicitly that they had gone into prostitution in order to earn money as easily as possible. Some respondents said that they might act like a prostitute, but rarely allowed their customers to get as far as sex. These boys are out to rob the clients of their money as quickly as possible; they don't always mind a bit of violence either. This shows how the customers of male prostitutes are more at risk of becoming the victim of violent crime. Here too we see the difference between male and female prostitutes in physical strength: streetwalkers are sometimes roughed up by a customer, but as far as their male colleagues are concerned, the reverse is true and the victims of violent crime are likely to be the customers themselves.

In all, about one-third of our sample had been involved in deriving income from commercial sex in one of the above ways.

Miscellaneous

As well as the four main categories of income acquisition discussed above (social security, acquisitive crime, the drug market, and the sex industry) there are less important sources of income that are really sidelines, and that reveal how drug addicts are not only extremely ingenious in acquiring income, but also how they form a pool of readily available labor for all sorts of work and small jobs.

During the past few years, a large amount of research has been done on the Amsterdam scene. In almost every study, respondents were paid for participating. Inevitably such financial incentives lead to situations in which addicts try to obtain advance payment for an interview that has yet to take place. Sometimes a respondent would try to get around a researcher.

> I meet Chris on Nieuwmarkt Square. He has been making himself useful these past months by getting addicts enthusiastic about this study. It is natural to stop for a chat. After about half a minute he says confidentially: "Can I talk to you for a minute." At the same time he pulls me half behind a camper that

is parked there. "I'm thinking about a complete change. I have managed to rent an apartment and I'm going to put a stop to this life, I'm getting so tired of it. The only problem is that I have to put something down on the first month's rent and I haven't quite got it. Do you think I could have the 25 guilders for the next interview now, we can square up later." Remembering that we have agreed not to pay in advance, I answer: "No, I wouldn't dream of it. If I lent everybody who asked for it money, I would be bankrupt." "But you know that I'm different, that I stick to agreements and so on. If I can't get the money together, I won't get the house and I'll never get out of this life." Stubbornly I try to resist the temptation to give in just to be rid of him. He tries another tack and his persuasive tone becomes one of indignation: "And you know that this is my only chance, and yet you won't lend me the money? It'll be your fault if I'm still here years from now!" "No, I won't lend you the money," I say in a desperate attempt to hold firm. Now there are even tears in his eyes. "Well, please, let me have ten guilders. I'll find the rest somehow."

Eventually we agree—partly in order not to sour our relationship—that I shall lend him five guilders. As fate would have it, the only available banknote in my wallet is one of 25 guilders. Alas, having taken the wallet out, there is no going back, and at once Chris disappears with the money in a state of high contentment, calling back over his shoulder how grateful he is and how he will pay it back that very same week. During the days that follow, Chris never seems to have any money when we meet, but always says he will have it within the hour. Then he takes to avoiding me altogether for a couple of weeks. One must learn to live with one's losses, so I make a deal with Chris: he can keep the 25 guilders if he finds two new respondents. Chris makes a wide gesture to demonstrate his agreement with this arrangement: "Of course, man. Sure. But where were you last week? I was looking for you all week with your 25 guilders in my pocket."

Borrowing money, or at least attempting to do so, is one of the legitimate ways of acquiring money. Everybody has the same attitude.

> You have to try to borrow money whenever you get the chance. It doesn't often work, but when it does, borrowing is the same as getting. Everybody knows they're not going to get it back.

Dope addicts who have been more or less accepted are sometimes able to do small jobs for local shopkeepers: washing windows, doing shopping, helping to unload a van, sweeping the pavement, etc. Others make a habit of scouring the streets for interesting castoffs and then try to sell them to rag and bone men. Some are known to rent out their homes and live on the streets themselves. One of our respondents had a lot of trouble getting the tenants out of his home again when he wanted to live there himself. There is, in brief, a whole range of sidelines, of ingenious ways of acquiring money or drugs, including income in kind.

Income in Kind

One way of acquiring hidden income is by reducing expenditure on food, drink, shelter, etc. A number of organizations have created amenities where addicts can get a meal for (next to) nothing. Large-scale use is made of such organizations, each existing amenity swiftly becoming an integral part of life with drugs. But addicts don't only make use of such government or private initiatives. Their families and friends are also involved in attempts to keep expenses down. Some addicts still live at home, at least they go home if the occasion so demands. Usually they stay for a short time and then disappear again for longer into the scene. A variation on this is the addict who lives independently but goes back home to mother regularly for a meal. Activities on the market of white and brown are also partly paid in kind. For every five balls of dope sold, the intermediary usually receives one for personal use. If the intermediary has done well, that is to say, has earned enough to cover his own drug use, he may adulterate whatever dope he has left and sell it himself. Of course, most addicts know that this goes on, if only because they have done it themselves. This is also why they go through such trouble to find the right dealer. Although desperate and sick addicts might buy from these "dealers," newcomers to the scene, or addicts from outside Amsterdam, are usually easy victims.

If there is any threat of dealers being arrested, they always, at least if they have time, throw away any incriminating material. Other addicts have developed an instinct for these situations: they watch the scene from a distance and then, when it is all over, scour the street for the balls of white and brown that might have been thrown away. This observation is confirmed by Verbraeck (1988):

"(...)I [see](...) a black boy sprint past, followed by three policemen with their batons drawn(...)The boy must have had dope on him, because the whole procession is followed by a wave of addicts feverishly combing the ground for balls of dope." The story told with some satisfaction by Chris, whom we have already met, is typical for the alert and creative grasping of opportunities that goes on in the drug scene.

> At the corner of the Gelderse Kade I saw a dealer surrounded by a group of addicts, all pushing and shoving. I stood among them and put out my hand towards the dealer. And what I hoped happened. The dealer thought it was the hand of a junkie who had just paid him, and put a bag of white into it.

A QUANTITATIVE PICTURE OF INCOME

Different Sources of Income and Their Relationship.

The first sections of this chapter distinguish between categories of income. We shall make the same general distinctions here. Table 5-1 shows the different categories.

Together, our 148 respondents "earned" about $270,000 per month (not counting income in kind). On average, that is approximately $1,825 per respondent. This figure is higher than the separate means for the categories because many users have income from more than one source. In total most of the income derives from social security benefits, with acquisitive crime a "good" second. However, if we consider individual earnings, it appears that prostitution is the most profitable—for those who engage in it; and here too, acquisitive crime comes second. Most income from crime (about 80 percent) derives from the sale of stolen goods. Such goods bring in about 20 percent of their original value.
There are large differences in frequency and profit between the 53 percent of respondents who commit acquisitive crime. Frequency of offenses varies from two to eighty-five a month; profits from $5 to $11,500 a month. Respondents with at least one offense a week form 22 percent of the sample.

Income in kind represents a considerable sum of money, the size of which reconfirms the notion that drug users are highly proficient in tapping all possible sources of income.

TABLE 5-1
Monthly Amounts by Type of Income[1]

Category	Total Amount	Number of Respondents/ Percentage	Mean per Category
Social Security	$77,000	128/87	$600
Salary	$9,700	14/10	$690
Drug Market	$52,700	90/61	$585
Prostitution	$41,000	38/26	$1080
Acquisitive Crime	$65,700	79/53	$830
Other*	$21,000	117/79	$180
In Kind**	$50,000	131/88	$380
Total	$317,100		***

[1] The original Dutch guilders were converted to U.S. dollars by multiplying by 1.75.

* Jobs for shopkeepers, selling to rag and bone men, selling personal property, collecting empty bottles, support from family, begging, etc.
** One gram of heroin or cocaine was calculated at an average of $70, pharmaceutical drugs at $1 per pill. The respondents themselves were asked to estimate the value of, e.g., meals, clothing, and shelter.
*** It is not possible to calculate an overall mean, because the numbers per row differ.

Table 5-2 shows the contribution of each category to the total income.

Although in a strict sense dealings on the drug market should be counted as crime, we had two reasons for deciding to distinguish between income deriving from acquisitive crime and income as a result of activities on the drug market. The first is that there is a difference in the degree of victimization. Acquisitive crime inevitably results in the victimization of relative outsiders, for in order to commit acquisitive crime, addicts step outside the limited circles of the drug culture. On the other hand, transactions on the drug market are the result of agreement between both parties, dealer and addict, an economic agreement based on the same

TABLE 5–2
Percentage of Total Income by Type*

Category	Percentage
Social security	29
Acquisitive crime	24
Drug market	20
Prostitution	15
Salary	4
Other	8

*Cash only; income in kind excluded

rationality as that between greengrocer and customer. Viewed in this light, there is seldom a victim. The fact that, from a legal point of view, the transaction on the drug market is unlawful makes no difference.

The second reason for distinguishing between both sorts of crime is the difference in life-style between those who commit acquisitive crime and the addicts who deal in drugs. We shall return to this later in this chapter.

THE FIGURES FOR AMSTERDAM COMPARED WITH OTHER STUDIES

Not many studies deal with the income and expenditure of drug addicts in such a detailed and integrated way as does this one. Examples are Johnson et al. (1985), Parker et al. (1988), and Reuter et al. (1990); Dutch language research in which the subject is discussed was published by Korf (1986 1987, and 1990) and Hoekstra (1987). In itself, the relationship between heroin use and crime has always been the main focus of interest. But the relationship tends to be described in an isolated fashion, instead of as an element of the addict's life-style and of the total pattern of income acquisition. Numbers of offenses often form the basis of calculation, while the central question is one of causation: to what extent does drug use cause crime? The answers rarely agree. We are also unable to answer that question for once and for all. Results in themselves can never solve the question of causality. This study is no exception. The nature of our figures, however, allow us to make a comparison with other studies as to the relationship between the different sources of income. Table 5–3 shows general results of more or less comparable studies.

TABLE 5–3
Comparison of Sources of Addicts' Income as Revealed by Different Studies

	This Study	Johnson et al. (1985)	Parker et al. (1988)
Social Security	29%	11%	11%
Salary	4%	9%	7%
Drug Market	20%	17%	11%
Prostitution	15%	7%	4%
Acquisitive Crime	24%	43%	65%
Other	8%	12%	2%

The results from this study are very similar to those from another Dutch study by Korf et al. (1990).

Most interesting are the differences and similarities that appear between our study and the Johnson and Parker studies, conducted respectively in New York and Liverpool. Especially with regard to income from social security and from crime. There is a reverse ratio in these categories: in the Netherlands a relatively high percentage of income derives from social security, with relatively few criminal offenses. The foreign studies reveal the opposite. It should also be noted that the drug market itself as a source of income is less prominent in the two foreign studies than in ours. This could mean that the markets in New York and Liverpool are run relatively more often by nonusers. The pattern seems clear: in the Netherlands a large part of an addict's income is acquired in a way that is less socially injurious. By socially injurious we mean that Opium Act offenses (drug dealing) may be regarded as victimless crimes, while there are almost always victims in the case of acquisitive crime.

A Closer Look at the Different Offenses

On a monthly basis, the seventy-nine respondents who reported acquisitive crime committed 951 offenses. Shoplifting and bicycle theft score highest; breaking into cars is third (see table 5–4).

TABLE 5–4
Number of Offenses and Profit per Month, by Type of Offense

	N	Percentage	Total Profit	Profit per Offense
Shoplifting	415	44	$13,250	$32
Bicycle theft	218	23	$4,430	$20
Breaking into cars	98	10	$5,970	$60
Burglary	76	8	$16,225	$215
Fencing	37	4	$3,300	$90
Pickpocket Theft	25	3	$3,230	$130
Other	80	8	$19,315	$240
Totals	951	100	$65,720	*

*It is not possible to calculate an average, because the number of respondents per row differ.

Within the group reporting acquisitive crime, for the month referred to by these figures, a small group of nineteen persons (13 percent of the sample) is responsible for 60 percent of the 951 offenses. Shoplifting, breaking into cars, and stealing bicycles or mopeds is the domain of a small group of specialists. For example, only three respondents committed 60 percent of the car break-ins. One respondent reported thirty incidents of shoplifting in one week; another reported fifteen bicycle or moped thefts. These data confirm the widely held view that a small group is responsible for most of the acquisitive crime.

There is a fairly extensive category labeled "other." It contains offenses that were difficult to categorize. The questionnaire did not distinguish between ripping off a dealer, stealing a Rolex watch from a drunken pub crawler, a prostitute's grabbing a few hundred dollars, pinching a fur coat from the coathook in a high-class restaurant, stealing a whole car, and cashing a forged check. It is this category, which indeed contains the most serious offenses, that also provides the most profit; otherwise the gains are but small. A total income of slightly more than $57,000 earned by means of more than 900 offenses, amounts to about $60 per offense. If exceptionally large profits are deducted, we are left with about $40 per offense. This confirms the picture of opportunistic thieves and burglars making a small amount of money, but running considerable risks, and causing not only material but also, and perhaps equally importantly, immaterial damage to their victims.

Another important source of income is related to involvement in the drug trade. In Table 5–5 we distinguish among the different activities that contribute to the income from this source.

TABLE 5–5
Monthly Amounts for Activities on the Drug Market*

Activities	Total Amount
Drug Dealing	$24,800
Intermediary Activities	$10,000
Other	$18,000
Total	$52,800

*Drugs earned in kind are not included in these amounts.

As we have explained in the section on the market of white and brown, there is a large variety of activities on the drug market. We distinguish here between three main groups.

Direct drug dealing brings in the most money. It is not, however, the most frequent activity; a more or less equal number of addicts work as intermediaries. It probably pays more because those who deal independently enjoy a high degree of trust from their own sources of drugs. That trust has to be paid for.

Periods of Abstinence and Income from Crime

Chapter 2 mentions several studies (mainly from the Anglo-Saxon countries) that compare periods of drug use with periods of abstinence at an individual level in terms of crime committed. These studies invariably show that abstinence corresponds with a reduced level of crime. We too attempted to discover whether, and to what extent, a reduction in use of or abstinence from hard drugs (heroin and cocaine) is linked to a lower level of acquisitive crime.

We calculated the periods of abstinence or seriously reduced use for those respondents about whom all information was known over a whole year (n=85). We then compared the level of crime during these periods with that during periods in which they reported drug use (of more than 2 grams a week). We did this first for heroin and then for cocaine (see Table 5–6).

We were able to identify fifty-one respondents out of eighty-five (i.e., 60 percent) who had had at least one such period of abstinence in the course of the research project; that is to say that they reported during at least one interview that they had used much less heroin than during another week in which they were interviewed, or no heroin at all. For our analysis, we compared income from crime during the weeks to which the interviews referred by means of a t-test for paired samples.[1] In a week in which they used a lot of heroin, the fifty-one respondents who also experienced periods of abstinence generated four times as much income from crime as they did in a week in which they used little or no heroin. In the former case, average income from crime is $95, in the latter $20 (t=2.30; p=0.03). So this amounts to a highly significant difference.

If we repeat the exercise for cocaine, the picture is more or less identical. We have fifty-nine out of eighty-five (i.e., 69 percent) respondents with periods of abstinence or greatly reduced drug use. During such periods, income from crime for this group averages $30. During the period of intensive drug use, the average climbs to $85. The corresponding t-value (2.29) also has a level of significance of 0.03.

---

1. Paired samples means that we are not dealing with independent samples, but with a comparison of two values, namely income from crime during two different weeks for the same respondent. The differences between these values provide the so-called t-value, of which the significance can then be tested.

TABLE 5-6
Differences in Income from Acquisitive Crime During Periods of Drug Use and Abstinence for Both Heroin and Cocaine (N = 85)

	Average Income from Crime		
	During Abstinence	*During Use*	*p*
Heroin	$20	$95	<0.03
Cocaine	$30	$85	<0.03

Table 5-6 shows the results of our comparison. In general, there is little difference between heroin and cocaine. Indeed, any differences are so small that we must put them down to coincidence.

The conclusion will be obvious: during periods of abstinence, considerably less income is generated from acquisitive crime than during periods of drug use. These findings correspond to those of the aforementioned studies. However, finding a clear link between the use of hard drugs and the level of crime does not enable one to say anything about the actual meaning of that relationship. One cannot simply say that more drug use *therefore* leads to more crime.

The big difference between our study and other (foreign) research (Nurco et al. 1985; Dobinson 1989) is that drug users in other countries show a proportionately much larger decrease in criminal activities during periods of abstinence.[2] A possible explanation -apart from definitional problems- for the difference in results may be found in what was already discussed in the section on the figures from Amsterdam as compared with other studies: Dutch addicts are less dependent on crime as a source of income anyway; not only as far as a percentage of the total income is con-

---

2. This does not, however, seem consistent with the Dutch situation. In his study, Swierstra (1990) traces eleven abstainers. None of these ex-users had committed any crime after definitely breaking with being an addict. As is so often the case, this difference is probably due to the definition used. In our study we are talking about dope users who reported that they used much less dope— or none at at all—during one week. Swierstra's minimum period of abstinence is one year. This seems to confirm what we noted in chapter 2, namely that the duration of a period of abstinence is important in this connection.

cerned, but also with regard to the number of addicts who commit criminal offenses. It is likely that this is partly (or even mainly) due to social security. As dependence on crime decreases, there will be by definition smaller fluctuations.

AN ECONOMIC TYPOLOGY

The previous sections discussed extensively the ways in which respondents earn money and/or its equivalent in kind. This section is an attempt to construct a specific typology, based on the most important sources of income.

Construction of the Typology

In a study such as this, the obvious way of constructing a typology is on the basis of economic variables. We shall, therefore, start with a distinction according to the most dominant source of income compared to the others. Sources of income are acquisitive crime, activities on the drug market, and legal income. Table 5-7 shows the distribution according to frequency over these three sources.

TABLE 5-7
An Economic Typology

Sources of Income	N	Percentage
Mainly Legal	94	63
Mainly from Drug Market	22	15
Mainly from Crime	32	22

In this typology we do not have a type that earns money mainly through prostitution. The most important reason is that the number of respondents for whom prositution forms the most important source of income is too small (twelve). Moreover, when judged by other characteristics, this group is extremely heterogenic. Prostitutes are therefore represented in all three types.

Now that we have drawn the contours of the typology, we can proceed to fill it in. By crossing a number of background variables (shown in Table 5-8) with the types of Table 5-9, we can arrive at a rough character outline for each type. The result of this exercise is explained below.

TABLE 5–8
The Typology Completed

Characteristics	Normalized User	Dealing User	Criminal User
Methadone	Community Station	None/Bought	Bus
Heroin	+/-	++	++
Cocaine	-	++	++
Pills	+/-	+	++
Dealing	-	++	+/-
Crime	-	+	++
Age	+/-	+	-
Ethnic Background	Dutch/Surinam	Surinam	Dutch
Duration Career	+/-	++	+
Sex	male/female	male/female	Male

Note: A '-' indicates that the characteristic is not very common; '++' indicates that it is very much present; '+/-' indicates that it is evenly spread.

The following is an ideal-typical characterization of the addict whose income derives from mainly legal sources. He is registered at a community station for his daily dose of methadone, he uses a small amount of heroin (i.e., up to 4 grams a month) or none at all, and he uses even less cocaine. Fifty-two percent of this group use pills, but infrequently. For this addict, methadone has the function it was originally supposed to have: it is a "medicine" that helps break the habit. As far as age, sex, duration of drug use, and social-economic background are concerned, there are no special characteristics. We have called this type the *normalized user*.

The addict whose income derives predominantly from activities on the drug market uses many drugs: a large amount of heroin and cocaine (i.e., more than 8 grams a month), while 73 percent of this group take pills regularly. This addict is not registered with a methadone maintenance program, but he does buy methadone now and then on the black market if forced to by circumstances. There is a strong representation of Surinam addicts here, namely 55 percent, while they only account for 19 percent of the sample. Sixty-four percent of this group are older than thirty; 77 percent have been taking dope regularly for longer than eight years. Here too, sex and social-economic background are not significant. We have called this type the *dealing user*.

Finally there is the addict whose income derives mainly from acquisitive crime. He too uses many different drugs: his normal pattern of consumption includes heroin, cocaine, pharmaceutical drugs, and alcohol. He also takes methadone, for he is registered at one of the buses. For him, methadone has a fundamentally different function than for the normalized user. The majority of this type regard methadone as a cheap and easily available extra drug. They wouldn't dream of trying to kick the habit. Eighty-one percent of this group are Dutch. There are relatively more men than women and they are younger than the average addict in the sample: 69 percent are younger than thirty. Sixty-six percent have been taking drugs for more than eight years. We have called this type the *criminal user*.

Additional characteristics in Table 5–8 refer to different life-styles, all strongly linked to patterns of income acquisition. The normalized user has seen it all before and has really had enough; methadone may help him. The dealing user has found a career on the market of white and brown. These activities also give some structure to his life. Such addicts often enjoy a certain status among their fellow addicts. This is their reward. The criminal user is (still) hyperactive in many areas. He keeps going on cocaine. The excitement of this intensely deviant life-style may be particularly rewarding for this type of user.

Illustrations of the Typology

In order to bring the types we have described above to life, we shall give an example of each type.

> **The Normalized User** Ringo is a man in his late twenties. He has been taking heroin at a moderate level for a few years, that is to say, he uses about one gram a week spread out over about three days. This means that he takes about a $60 worth of her-

oin a week. He has his own home and he also looks after his own social benefit. He uses heroin because he likes its effects. He knows that he is physically dependent on it, but he does not want to take more than he is doing already. By controlling his habit, he attempts to preserve the pleasurable effects. In order to function normally during the periods in which he does not use dope, he obtains a dose of methadone via his general practitioner each week. He doesn't sell this opiate on the streets, rather he keeps it carefully in order to have enough to take at certain times. He doesn't look like a stereotype heroin addict either. There is nothing strange about him, except for his rather pale complexion and red-rimmed eyes. In general he is careful about looking well-groomed, and he is proud of it. He regularly buys new clothes, albeit usually through the Salvation Army or second hand. It is difficult, but he can manage on social security. Every so often he gathers enough courage to supplement his meals with an illegally obtained pork chop. But this is as far as his criminal activities go. He is rarely to be found in the scene and he gets his heroin from friends who live round the corner. They charge him less than normal. His level of dope use has been stable for years. The scene no longer attracts him; he's had enough of it, really. Ringo's life is actually rather dull and he spends a lot of his time in front of the television.

The Criminal User Zeke is 25 years old, an addict with a long career of drugs and delinquency behind him. He was already involved in serious crime by the time he was 12. He was a member of a street gang that, so he says, stole goods worth millions. His forced visits to the police station became more frequent. Eventually he was convicted by the juvenile judge when he was 13. At borstal he started experimenting with drugs. He tried almost everything at that time, including heroin. He was allowed back home when he was 16. Not long afterwards he tried intravenous use for the first time. In his own words, he stole anything worth having and he wasn't afraid of violence. Sometimes he made a big haul. Like the time he stole a briefcase from a doctor's waiting room, that had $48,000 in it. Sometimes his criminal ingenuity presented him with peculiar problems. One day we found him rather down outside a methadone bus. That afternoon he had stolen an expensive foreign language course, with tapes and a luxury edition book. He had just found out which language it was, and he was wondering who in heaven's name would be interested in a course in Swahili. Zeke has had a lengthy career with the different forms of methadone distribution. He has never seriously intended to give up drugs. He is terrified of the 'black hole' that awaits the addict who is 'clean': "you can say what you like about a junkie's life, but there's something to do all day long. I enjoy visiting the bus, I know everybody there. And hustling, and scoring, it all takes time, make no mistake." According to Zeke he has been arrested by the police 76 times and has seen nine different prisons from the inside during sentences of varying lengths. Both Zeke and his -non-using—girlfriend are HIV-positive. They have both been in hospital for some time.

The Dealing User Roberto and Frankie are practically inseparable. Both are of Surinam extraction (39 and 43 years old) and both are highly experienced junkies. Besides their Surinam background, they share a number of other characteristics. Both are from reasonably affluent backgrounds, they have had some education and are from big families. Their drug career differs on a number of points. Frankie did not start on heroin until he was 35. By that time he had already had an impressive career as a drug dealer. He married young and had a number of children. A jack of all trades, but master of none, he was barely able to earn enough to keep his family. He left them in Surinam and moved to Holland. His brother, already a heroin dealer, brought him into contact with big money. Most lucrative were transports to Germany. His biggest problem was laundering all this money. At that time he was living in a big house on a canal. He remembers there being "a hundred grand in every cupboard." Roberto was his bodyguard and chauffeur. Every morning they drove to between ten and fifteen drug cafes to deliver the dope. Their turnover was between $12,000 and $25,000 a day. They were looked upon as charitable figures. 'Sick' and destitute junkies could count on help from Frankie and Roberto. They were everybody's darlings. At that time, Frankie was not taking heroin. "I knew the name, but not the stuff.." He did not start until the stress of large-scale drug-dealing became too much: heroin allowed him to relax in his approach to life. He was arrested during one of his trips to Germany, and he spent some time in prison. "That was when I found out I was a junk." Back in Amsterdam, he discovered he had lost the trade. Roberto was still there, and now they move around the scene together. Intermediary here, little deal there, ripping off a dealer or selling bad dope if they have the guts. If neither has enough money, they put their cash together to be able to buy some dope. At present Roberto seems to be getting on better than his ex-boss Frankie. For

128   A WORLD OF OPPORTUNITIES

Roberto also has a window prostitute who gives him a percentage of her takings. Frankie is bitter about the scene and the people in it. "They always used to be able to come to me if they were in trouble, but if I need some brown now they laugh at me, they're shits, rats." They don't want methadone because it doesn't solve anything and they think that the distribution of methadone is hypocritical, anyway: doling out liters of the addictive substance methadone to junkies, but not allowing heroin. Neither have a fixed address and they sleep in doorways or under a bridge at the Central Station. Frankie is the prototype of the addict at the mercy of the changing odds of drug-dealing. At the end of this year he will take stock of his life. A positive result, and he will go back to Surinam, negative and he will stay here "and probably die on the job."[3]

The Typology in Time

The economic typology in the previous section is based on aggregate monthly data and represents a fixed moment in time. That makes it rather static and this is unsatisfactory in a study based on a career perspective. In chapter 3 we discussed how an addict's life is full of ups and downs and how his perception of that life changes during the different stages of his career. A drug career is capricious, and it is, therefore, necessary to reexamine our respondents at a later date in order to see whether they still belong to the same type. The longitudinal nature of this study made such reexamination possible.

We analyzed the data from the last interview in an identical way as the aggregate data from the first three interviews. Because some of our respondents did not complete the full research cycle, we had to make do with eighty-nine respondents. The results of that analysis are shown in Table 5-9.

There are some pitfalls in comparing both points in time. To start with, the "original" typology was constructed on the basis of a series of several interviews. This means that it applies to a longer period of time, namely one month. The typology "a year later" is restricted to data over one week. There is more chance that a respondent would be categorized as a criminal or dealing user in the original typology than a year later, for the simple reason that

---

3. Some time after we had completed our fieldwork, Roberto told us that Frankie had gone back to Surinam—and died shortly afterwards.

addicts with less frequent criminal or drug-dealing affinities have had more time in the original typology to acquire income in that way, while social security and salary remain stable during that period. Secondly we have lost a number of respondents. Of the 148 with whom we started, there are 89 left—a loss of 40 percent. The most important effect of this would be on dealing users: in our percentage of loss, respondents of Surinam extraction are overrepresented. The original typology revealed that they are also overrepresented in the category dealing users. We must not lose sight of this in comparing the two typologies.

TABLE 5-9
Typology of Addicts at Two Points in Time

Typology One Year Later	Original Typology			
	Normalized User	Criminal User	Dealing User	Total
Normalized User	59	3	6	68 (76%)
Criminal User	1	9	3	13 (15%)
Dealing User	2	3	3	8 (9%)
Total	62 (70%)	15 (17%)	12 (13%)	89 (100%)

It is immediately apparent that the number of normalized addicts has increased (from 70 percent to 76 percent), that the number of criminal users is more or less stable (17 percent and 15 percent) and that there is a relatively large decrease in the number of dealing users (from 13 percent to 9 percent). This could be the effect of our dropout percentage. We also see that 80 percent of our respondents are still in the same category as the original typology a year later (59+9+3)/89*100). This is also expressed in the correlation coefficient that is .71 and significant at 0.001 percent. The most important shift is to be seen in the top row, where three criminal and six dealing users have become normalized a year later; the reverse is true for only three respondents. There is a balanced exchange between criminal users and dealing users: three to three.

Considering the aforementioned restrictions, and therefore with some degree of circumspection, it must be said that there seems to be a tendency towards a reduction of the number of addicts that could be labeled socially problematic.

Finally, we shall examine the extent to which the typology is related to the point in time when any acquisitive crime started: before or after the first use of opiates. This is an interesting question, because it could throw some light on the continuity of deviant careers. If respondents who commit acquisitive crime at an early stage continue to do so during their drug career, it would mean that they had opted for this specific illegal means of income acquisition at an early age (see chapter 3).

TABLE 5–10
Types of Addict and Time of First Acquisitive Crime

Time of First Acquisitive Crime	Normalized User	Dealing User	Criminal User	Total
Before Hard Drugs	35(43%)	10(63%)	18(69%)	63(51%)
After Hard Drugs	26(32%)	1(6%)	8(31%)	35(29%)
No Crime	20(25%)	5(31%)	0	25(20%)
Total	81 (100%)	16 (100%)	26 (100%)	123*(100%)

*This information is not available for twenty-five respondents; chi-square=11; df=4;p,<0.05.

Table 5–10 shows our three types in relation to a number of other categories: the first contains respondents who were already criminal before starting to use hard drugs, the second contains those who became criminal on starting to use drugs, or afterwards, and the third contains respondents who never committed criminal offenses.

There is a significant relationship between current ways of income acquisition and the question of whether respondents committed offenses before they started taking drugs. In general, the data confirm our suspicion that those who were criminal before starting on drugs remain so afterwards. Some 70 percent of current criminal users were committing offenses before ever taking drugs. We have already said that, to a certain extent, the dealing user is comparable to the criminal user. Here too we see a large percentage of addicts who mainly operate on the drug market also committing criminal offenses before they started taking drugs. This is not surprising, for we have already seen that a large number of the addicts that belong to this type have criminal activities besides those on the drug market. At the same time, however, we see that 31 percent of the dealing users do not commit acquisitive crime, or have never committed such offenses, and stick strictly to drug dealing. In general it may be said that many of the respondents who set out on a criminal career at an early age persevere with it during their drug career. Eventually, however, many slow down, sometimes to the extent that their life-style transforms to "normalized addiction."

SUMMARY AND CONCLUSIONS

In studying the drug user's economy, the picture one gets is very much that of a busy existence and taking advantage of every opportunity available. The scene is full of hurrying addicts, on their way either to get or to spend money. This pattern repeats itself many times a day: cycles of earning money, spending, and consuming with but little space to breathe. Only a few make time to hang about, eat, chat, and the like. The behavior that accompanies income acquisition is characteristically opportunistic. Although most addicts have eveloped some sort of specialism, a main hustle, in practice almost no one lets an opportunity to earn money in whatever way slip by. This means that one may find an addict acting as an intermediary on the Zeedijk one day, and then selling stolen goods in the Damstraat another, only to leave the scene again to collect his weekly pocket money from social security, and finally returning to the Gelderse Kade to sell the clean needles he has just obtained. The route from Nieuwmarkt to Gelderse Kade to Stormsteeg to Liesdelsluis and so on round to the Zeedijk and back is covered many times a day. Sometimes shortcuts can be taken. But always looking for ways of making money or for the right dealer with whom to spend it.

Although it is true that the average addict has his work cut out just being an addict, it is a myth to suppose that most of his income typically comes from acquisitive crime. The group of hard drug addicts is indeed more criminal (in terms of both profits and frequency) than almost any other group in Dutch society, but only a few are highly criminal. One of our most important conclusions is that the percentage of total income that derives from acquisitive crime is smaller than is generally assumed. Fifty-three percent of our respondents report having acquired some income from such offenses, 20 percnet of whom can be regarded as highly criminal. In total, acquisitive crime accounts for 24 percent of the total income. The most important source of income is social security. A third important source is drug dealing and intermediary activities on the drug market. This picture is confirmed by other Dutch studies (i.e., Korf 1990). When we compare these with British and American research, we see that income in the Netherlands is usually acquired in a less socially injurious way. Acquisitive crime is partly replaced by trading on the market of white and brown. Although it is difficult to point to direct causes, at least two factors are at work here. Compared to Britain and the United States, the extensive social security network of the Netherlands provides a means of subsisting that prevents individual addicts from having to resort to acquisitive crime. Secondly—and we shall return to this in chapter 7—the relatively easily accessible drug market means that a large group can maintain their pattern of spending thanks to dealing in drugs or intermediary activities on the drug market. One of the reasons is that possession of drugs for personal use, and therefore also small-scale drug dealing, is not a police priority. A fairly large group would rather earn money or drugs this way than by committing acquisitive crime. The fact that the Public Prosecution Office and the police are reluctant to interfere with addicts just for possession or use of drugs is an important factor.

Hoekstra (1987) reaches a similar conclusion. She calculated the effects of several policy alternatives using simulation models. Halving police repression of small-scale drug dealing, together with extending front line aid and therapy to addicts, was seen to reduce acquisitive crime by 55 percent. We have, therefore, an at-first-sight paradoxical situation in which a lower level of action by police and prosecution results in a smaller group of hard drug addicts committing acquisitive crime.

Patterns in income acquisition allow us to construct a triple distinction: users with mainly legal income, users who are active on the drug market, and users whose income derives mainly from acquisitive crime. This typology is related to a number of other characteristics. Closer investigation reveals that these characteristics refer to clearly different life-styles. The two different functions that methadone may fulfill are important here. Originally it was intended as an aid to overcoming hard drug addiction, but it also serves as a cheap and easily obtainable extra drug. In the latter case methadone programs have become a fully integrated part of being a deviant drug user.

Analysis aimed at testing the stability of our typology in time revealed that there is a tendency towards less socially problematic behavior. In other words: income is generated less frequently from acquisitive crime. At the same time we saw that respondents who committed criminal offenses before they started taking drugs have crime as a main source of income during the period in which they are on drugs. There is a certain continuity in manner of income acquisition if the addict's deviant career started with criminal behavior.

CHAPTER 6

Spending and Drug Use

We have arrived at the question of how the income -described in the previous chapter- is spent. First we shall outline the different items of expenditure and determine their relationship to each other. We shall then delve more deeply into the most important item: drugs. In the section on drug use we determine the amounts taken of each drug separately. The next section deals with the functions that the different drugs fulfill according to the addicts themselves. Finally, in the last section we shall be examining patterns of drug use, looking first at the use of combinations of drugs (so-called polydrug use) and then at the (in)variability of drug consumption.

This chapter is mainly about illegal drugs. The different functions and effects of methadone and its distribution will be discussed in chapter 7. Nevertheless, methadone also appears in this chapter now and then, especially where it plays a part in explaining certain results.

SPENDING

Categories of Expenditure

It is inevitable that a description of the patterns of expenditure of a group so specific as compulsive heroin users will provide a rather one-sided picture. Precisely because being an addict is compulsive, and is accompanied by ever-repeating rituals, by far the largest percentage of an addict's income will be spent on dope. This does not mean that he will spend everything at once. In general, an addict spends small amounts at a time, but frequently. This is mainly due to the fact that the average addict simply does not have large sums of money at his/her disposal. Let us take the "garbage men" from the previous chapter as an example. It is immediately apparent that their income is spread out over the day: and so is their need for drugs. As soon as they have earned enough, they buy a ball of dope and withdraw from the scene for a while. This pattern not only applies to the garbage men, but to all addicts who are active on the market, at least in so far as they earn ready cash. If they are paid in kind, they spend little cash on drugs. However, there is a group of addicts with a different pattern. They are not particularly involved in the life of the street scene. They usually buy their dope from house dealers. If they come to the Zeedijk or the "pill bridge" to satisfy their needs, they make their stay as short as possible. This is not to say that they also spend less on drugs. They often buy more at once, so that they need not return to the market of white and brown so often.

A striking feature is that many respondents pay a monthly rent and therefore have fixed lodgings. Besides the rent—in some cases paid on behalf of the tenant by the foundation that administers social benefits—there are also the costs of the gas bill and (sometimes) telephone. 70 percent of our respondents have such fixed items of expenditure. Others are quick to arrange a temporary stay in a (small) hotel if their financial situation is favorable and it is less desirable to be away from the scene because of certain activities. And there are others who make use of the habit prevalent in the scene, of allowing one's home to be used for a small fee as an overnight shelter for homeless addicts.

A third category of expenditure is related to food and drink and takes up considerably more income than the fixed items referred to above. A daily meal often consists of a liter of custard, eaten on the move and sometimes a roll, and hamburger or some other form of fast food from the snack bar at the Liesdelsluis. Such snacks, eaten in passing, are relatively expensive. As we can see from Table 6-1, the relative amount the respondents spend on such food and drink is quite large. Some respondents make use of the hot meals provided for a small sum by the Salvation Army.

And finally there is a category of miscellaneous items of expenditure. It includes such things as tobacco and cigarettes—almost without exception they smoke—but also packs of chewing gum, and perhaps a T-shirt bought cheaply from a fellow addict.

Expenditure in Figures

As is to be expected, the item drugs by far exceeds all other items. In the month to which these figures refer, there were three respondents who spent nothing at all on drugs. That is not, however, to say that they did not take any. It may well be that they were given dope, or paid in kind.

Least is spent on fixed items, although on average still a sum of $175.

TABLE 6–1
Monthly Sums for Different Categories of Expenditure

Category Item	Total Amount	Number of Respondents/ Percentage	Mean Expenditure
Drugs*	$197,000	145/98	$1,360
Fixed Items**	$18,000	102/69	$175
Food/Drink	$43,750	148/100	$295
Misc.***	$29,500	148/100	$200
Total	$288,250	****	

* including cannabis and alcohol
** rent, gas and electricity, telephone
*** tobacco, overnight shelter, gambling, public transportation, clothing, etc.
**** It is not possible to calculate a general mean, because the number of respondents per row differs.

A comparison of the total income from Table 5–1 ($270,000) with total expenditure as shown by Table 6–1 ($288,250), reveals that $18,250 more was spent than was acquired as income (about $125 per person per month); during this month, in other words, expenditure was 7 percent higher than income. That is not a very big percentage, especially since respondents were asked to go over their income and expenses retrospectively in one week. Everybody's memory fails sometimes and not necessarily intentionally. It is quite likely that the difference arose mainly from slight mistakes during that process of reproduction.

As we compared the relationship between different items of income, so we also examined the relationship between items of expenditure (see Table 6–2).

Table 6–3 shows the result of breaking down the most important in terms of expenditure into its different components.

TABLE 6–2
Percentages of Total Expenditure by Item

Category	Percentage
Drugs	68
Fixed items	6
Food/Drink	15
Miscellaneous	11

TABLE 6–3
Monthly Expenditure per Drug

	Total	Mean
Heroin	$95,350	$700
Cocaine	$86,000	$850
Psychopharmaca*	$1,750	$20
Alcohol	$8,450	$95
Cannabis	$4,000	$50
Methadone (bought)	$1,400	$60
Miscellaneous	$285	$28
Total	$197,235	$1,330

*Two-thirds of this item is comprised of Rohypnol

DRUG USE

The average amount spent on different sorts of drugs need not correspond to actual use of those drugs. For example, buying drugs does not automatically imply that the buyer will immediately consume them himself: he may give some away, share some, buy a lot at once but spread the taking of them over several days, etc. On the other hand, it is possible to consume drugs that one has not bought, but has been given, or earned in kind. In short, if we would like to know more about actual use of the different drugs, we must move to a more detailed level. In doing so, we shall concentrate on the drugs most commonly found on the Amsterdam scene.

Heroin and Cocaine

Heroin and cocaine are the drugs most often used. Table 6–4 shows monthly consumption. The cells show the percentages of addicts taking either drug. The rows should be read independently of each other: for example, the 33 percentage of heroin users from the second column are not necessarily represented in the 34 percentage of cocaine users from the second column. A person may well use more than 2 grams of heroin, but no cocaine at all, or only half a gram. We shall take a closer look at the combined use of heroin and cocaine later.

TABLE 6–4
Monthly Use of Heroin and Cocaine by Percentage (N = 148)

Monthly Use	Nothing	0.05–4g	4–8g	>8g
heroin	9	33	32	26
cocaine	32	34	10	24

Nine percent (n=13) took no heroin at all during this month. They were all registered with a methadone program. The table shows that 65 percent restricted their intake to a maximum of 8 grams a month, while 26 percent took more than 8 grams. On average, our respondents took 7 grams of heroin a month. If we leave the abstainers out, then the average rises to 7.7 grams; that is, on average, a quarter of a gram per day. Maximum consumption was 40 grams per month (one respondent).

There are fewer cocaine users than heroin users; the difference is especially apparent in the category of moderate consumers (4–8 grams per month). On average, our respondents took 10 grams of cocaine per month; if we calculate this for *cocaine users only*, it works out at an average of 14.6 grams. We may therefore conclude that those who take cocaine take almost twice as much as those who take heroin (on average half a gram a day). This higher average is due to the fact that one or two addicts take extreme amounts, with maximum consumption in the group reaching 140 grams a month!

Psychopharmaca, Alcohol, and Cannabis

Psychopharmaca Many other drugs are also used regularly besides heroin and cocaine. Many of these belong to the group of psychopharmaca, of which there are many kinds. There are sleeping tablets, tranquilizers, antidepressants and antihistamines. Some antiepileptic and antipsychotic drugs are also taken as dope.

For the sake of not becoming too involved in details, only Rohypnol is mentioned separately in Table 6–5: other drugs are divided into two categories. The data show that Rohypnol is the most popular pill. It may well be, however, that by now things have changed, for the use of such drugs is very much subject to trends and ups and downs in patterns are inherent. At the beginning of the eighties, everyone swore by Vesparax and Mandrax; after a few years Rohypnol increased considerably in popularity and, accordingly, in price. The price of this pill also rose, however, because GPs became more reluctant to prescribe it. Rohypnol went up from $1.50 per pill during the week to $2.50 and even to $4 on Saturday and Sunday nights. This later ebbed away again, and Tuinal partly replaced Rohypnol. According to stories that grew greatly in the telling, this pill was said to be ten times as strong as Rohypnol and possessed of fantastic qualities. However, Tuinal didn't last very long. Unlike Rohypnol, no drug mythology grew up around it.

Addicts are usually well informed about what the different drugs are supposed to do. This is illustrated by one addict who regularly bought the antiepileptic drug Haldol on the "pill bridge" and also used it. It had side effects not unlike Parkinson's disease: uncontrollable shaking of head and limbs. In order to suppress these side effects—that he found unpleasant—he always took a dose of Tremblex at the same time, also for sale on the "pill bridge." The net result of this combination was a relatively cheap but long-lasting high, to which he sometimes contributed by means of alcohol.

TABLE 6–5
Monthly Use of Psychopharmaca in Percentage

	Rohypnol	Tranquilizers	Others	Total
None	59	70	80	46 (N=68)
1–15 Pills	32	15	10	26 (N=39)
15–30 Pills	3	6	5	8 (N=12)
30–60 Pills	3	3	3	10 (N=14)
60 or More	3	5	1	10 (N=15)

Alcohol Eighty-eight (60 percent) of our respondents are regular drinkers: thirty-five drink moderately (on average two glasses a day during one month), thirteen are heavy drinkers (more than eight glasses a day), and the rest (forty respondents) are somewhere in the middle. The heavy drinkers are most likely to drink in the street. Half-liter bottles of beer and cheap fruit wine are very popular. Some carry a flask of Dutch gin (jenever) in order to be able to make chasers whenever they fancy. Although we have yet to discuss the use of combinations of drugs, we can say now that there are relatively many pill takers among the heavy drinkers. Subjects themselves say that alcohol is likely to increase the effect of many psychopharmaceutical drugs and that this is why they combine the two.

Cannabis Cannabis is consumed on a fairly wide scale. Of our 148 respondents, 80 take amounts varying between 1 and 96 grams a month.

Little-Used Drugs

It is perhaps just as interesting to discover which drugs are not, or hardly, used by the addict population in our study. Of the older drugs, LSD (trips) and speed are no longer in fashion among indigenous drug addicts in Amsterdam. Not one respondent had taken LSD during the month in which the first three interviews were conducted. The most important market for LSD is among Germans and Italians. Only six respondents had taken speed (pervitine) during the month to which these data refer. Most of those who took it say that they prefer cocaine, but that they were reduced to taking speed for lack of money.

The media regularly carry stories about new drugs being consumed on a large scale or ("no doubt") becoming the drug of the future. They cite examples such as crack, XTC or ecstasy, ice, and other "designer drugs." XTC is used on a small scale, mostly recreationally (De Loor 1989). Our respondents use neither XTC nor ice. Apparently these drugs do not attract the hard core of addicts. The result seems to be separate markets; indeed, when asked, even the oldest hand in the Amsterdam scene was not sure where to get such drugs.

We met no addicts who took crack during this study, at least not in the form in which it is available on the American market. However, something is rumored to have appeared near the Central Station in Rotterdam that sounds like crack. There one can buy processed, that is, boiled, cocaine in small amounts (Grund et al. 1991). This Dutch variation of crack is sold to marginalized street junkies who are no longer welcome at the different shelter organizations in Rotterdam. The authors pinpoint a number of factors that have led to this development. The most important is the fact that it is so busy at the Central Station and the police presence so strong, that addicts there are unable to make preparations themselves. The big advantage of processed cocaine is that it can be taken immediately and reasonably inconspicuously. These data, and of course, developments in the United States, seem to justify the conclusion that the crack problem grows as repression of the *use* of hard drugs increases. As far as this is concerned, the pragmatic approach in Holland, aimed at normalization of drug use, is unlikely to lead to an explosive crack epidemic. Two other factors provide some support for this assumption. In the first place, many addicts appear to attach special value to the preparatory rituals that accompany the taking of drugs (cf. chapter 3). With crack or processed coke, the charm of the rituals is lost. And then there is the fact that the cocaine (and heroin) for sale in the Netherlands has a high level of purity.[1] This means that there is no

---

1. The most recent figures on the purity of cocaine on the Amsterdam market are provided by Cohen (1990). His conclusion is an average purity of 65 percent. Grapendaal and Aidala (1991) report an average purity of 85 percent for Arnhem.

necessity to experiment with different ways of administering drugs on a large scale in order to increase their effect. This may also be the reason why intravenous use in the Netherlands is much less widespread than in other countries. In the United States, for example, heroin is used intravenously almost to the exclusion of other techniques, such as "chasing the dragon." Indeed, such techniques would lose their effect because of the impurity of the heroin in the United States. But although intravenous use is not so popular as in many other countries, it is nevertheless, among the many different methods, still one of the most prevalent ways of taking drugs.

Methods of Drug Taking

The most frequently used methods of taking heroin and cocaine are "chasing the dragon" and intravenously, known as shooting. Chasing the dragon involves sprinkling a small amount of powder—of either drug or in combination—onto a strip of tin foil. This is then heated from below with a lighter and the smoke from the evaporating drug is inhaled through a straw or a small piece of paper rolled up. Junkies with an eye for status sometimes use a bank note. For intravenous use, the powder is dissolved in a spoonful of water -sometimes with lemon juice added- which is boiled by means of lighter. It is then drawn up through cotton wool or a fluffed-out cigarette filter into a hypodermic needle and injected into a vein. The heavily addicted may inject five to ten times a day, often in unhygienic circumstances. A "speedball" taken in this way (a combination of equal parts of heroin and cocaine) takes effect and reaches its peak immediately. Chasing the dragon with either drug has a slower and more leveled effect. The latter method is also more expensive; some of the drug is lost through evaporation. A less frequently used technique of taking cocaine is free-basing (cf. chapter 3). This method is very expensive, but it has a stronger effect than chasing the dragon.

In our sample, forty-two (28 percent) of the respondents take their drugs intravenously only, fifty-four (36 percent) restrict themselves to chasing the dragon, and twelve use both methods. Thirty-two respondents use a wide range of techniques, such as smoking (with tobacco), free-basing, sniffing, and eating; ten of them also inject now and then. Finally, ten respondents took no drugs at all during this month. In general, addicts of Surinam extraction prefer chasing the dragon. About half of the Dutch respondents inject. Of course, those who use drugs intravenously run an extra risk of being infected with the HIV virus. This applies to sixty-four addicts (43 percent) in this sample. Table 6–6 shows possible changes in methods of taking drugs in the course of our research (perhaps as a result of prevention strategies). It is based on a comparison of the answers given during the first and last interview. For many different reasons (see the Appendix) we were only able to compare answers from eighty-nine respondents.

TABLE 6–6
Intravenous Use at the Beginning of the Study and One Year Later

1 Year Later	Intravenous Only	Intravenous + Other	Nonintravenous	Total (absolute numbers)
Intravenous Only	22%	5%	2%	29% (26)
Intravenous + Other	—	3%	2%	6% (5)
Nonintravenous	8%	7%	51%	65% (58)
Total	30% (27)	15% (13)	55% (49)	100% (89)

Beginning Study

Intravenous users did not drop out of the project systematically, so we are able to compare them on this point. Of the respondents who injected drugs at the beginning of the study (n=40), thirteen had stopped a year later. On the other hand, there were four respondents who did not inject at the beginning, but who had started to in the course of the year. The size of the group at risk therefore decreased from 43 percent (of 148 addicts) to 35 percent (of 89 addicts), a reduction of about 19 percent. The percentage of addicts who inject only also decreased. Korf reports similar findings (1986 and 1987) with regard to foreign addicts in Amsterdam. So the number of drug users taking drugs intravenously seems to be decreasing. We got the impression that addicts know very well the dangers that accompany intravenous drug use. For some, this is enough reason to stop certain dangerous behavior.

THE FUNCTIONS OF THE DIFFERENT DRUGS IN THE SCENE

Within the drug subculture, the different drugs all have their own value, meaning, and significance. We shall now examine the (development of the) functions of heroin, cocaine, and psychopharmaca for the lives of drug users.

The Function of Heroin

The function of heroin for heavy users seems to be changing. This opiate was originally used for the "rush" or "high" that heroin causes. Many experienced addicts now report continuing with heroin in order to be able to function "normally." The development of tolerance reduces the "rush," "kick," "flash," or "high" that is experienced in the beginning. What is left is "being sick" through abstinence. "Being sick" prevents one from functioning normally. Heroin no longer drugs the addict, but makes him feel able to function normally. Because of this effect, the use of heroin has shifted from hedonistic pleasure to self-medication. Its dampening effect on cocaine is also reported as a motive for continued use.

The following opinions of addicts about the opiate heroin illustrate its changing significance. Many addicts would probably agree with these statements.

> Heroin used to be much more part of my life. It had more effect, I liked it much more. Now I only use it to stop feeling sick and to keep going normally; and, of course, to slow myself down if I take coke.

> When I had just started on horse, it was much easier to be satisfied. If I was stoned I didn't feel like taking more. It only made me sleepy, and I dropped everything. That feeling, being stoned, I haven't had it for ages now.

Only a small minority of addicts report still liking heroin. These are mainly addicts whose drug careers started at the end of the sixties or the beginning of the seventies. In the age of love and peace, people were interested in drugs that made one feel sleepy or afloat. Although the ideals of those years have now mostly disappeared, some older addicts still prefer drugs with a sedative effect. They are less keen on cocaine, and the action and speed that is inevitably linked to it.

> I've seen so many people go wrong with cocaine. By definition it leads to immoderate use and in the end you go crazy. Some people like that, I don't. I always preferred dope that makes you relaxed and easy.

The heroin that is referred to in the scene as "brown" comes from Turkey or Pakistan. This is almost the only sort that is to be bought on the street, although some house dealers offer white Chinese powder for sale. Opinions on this Chinese product differ. Many think it a weak version of the real thing, others swear by it. David loves Chinese heroin, making it quite clear that he still really enjoys the drug.

> That pleasurable feeling of a flash, I still get that, even after all these years. If you say that a lot of people don't like heroin any more, you have to look at two things. First, at the quality of the stuff on the market. There is a lot of shit for sale on the street, it can really mess you up. I'm ok with my Chinese powder, so I needn't complain. And then you should look at the circumstances people are taking it in. I mean, if you're on the street, and it's freezing, you can take it till you're blue in the face, but you won't really like it. All you're really doing is taking it to keep warm. But if you have a home, and the fire's on, then you can really enjoy it: a shot of good horse, that gives you a real flash; there's nothing like good quality.

The link David makes here between using opiates and the weather seems fairly general. As soon as it gets colder outside, heroin functions more and more as a "warm blanket." Addicts are highly sensitive to drops in temperature, probably because most associate shivering with withdrawal symptoms. One respondent said:

> This morning when I woke up, I was cold. Junkies always think that sort of thing comes from the lack of dope. Maybe other people are cold too when they wake up, but if you're an addict, the first thing you think is that you need dope.

Those who use heroin to keep warm are often unable to gage just how cold it is outside, and their clothes are sometimes too thin for the time of year. It is obvious that this increases the risk of pneumonia or some other serious complaint.

Besides providing medication, warmth, and—for a small number of addicts—enjoyment, heroin is most widely used as a suppresser of emotions, more especially certain feelings of disquiet.

> I feel much surer of myself with heroin. I'm rather shy and dope makes it easier to be with people. When I take heroin, all my troubles melt away. Unpleasant emotions are pushed aside and I calm down.

And a respondent who had resolved to stop taking it:

> The day after I've taken drugs, I could kick myself. I know I'm really pulling the wool over my own eyes, because the problems come back twice as hard later, but I've never yet been able to take a sober look at a bad experience. I always choose the easy way: drugs, and I think that's true of most addicts.

This remark is illustrative of the fact that many addicts suffer from a very negative self-image. In order not to have to face themselves too often, they would rather take a "forgetting" drug.

Heroin also appears to be the favorite drug for compensating for lack of affection and intimacy. According to some addicts, consumption of heroin is even a substitute for sex. Heroin is not particularly good for the libido and indeed a number of addicts report—without being asked—that they have not been sexually active for some time. In this connection, one female respondent made the following remark.

> Methadone replaces heroin, and heroin replaces a person's sexual needs; it might suppress sexual hunger, but nevertheless it gives you a sort of psychological orgasm.

Addicts who are professionally involved in sex use heroin for a different reason. To start with, the drug allows male and female prostitutes to be more free and easy with other people, a characteristic that is quite important if potential customers are to be approached. The opiate also ensures that prostitutes are less aware of what they are doing when providing their sexual services. Eventually many end up in the vicious circle of streetwalking to be able to take heroin, and taking heroin to be able to streetwalk.

The Function of Cocaine

> If God ever invented anything better, He must have kept it for Himself.

So declared a respondent, trying to describe the effect of a speedball. Other addicts also wax lyrical about the combination of heroin and cocaine, and it is by far the most popular with most dope users. As we have said, cocaine is regarded as a means of enjoyment, heroin as a medicine to prevent the user from going too far.

> The coke is best by far, but I don't want to become paranoid, so I always take it with a bit of brown.

The preference of a number of addicts for cocaine reflects their life-style, which inclines to adventure, action, and speed. The stimulating properties of the drug are regularly used to allow the addict to continue his hyperactive existence for days and nights on end. Other than is the case with heroin, which has a certain maximum dose depending on the individual, with cocaine there is no danger of taking an overdose—with possibly fatal results. From a physiological point of view, very large doses of cocaine (remember the maximum of 140 grams a month reported in the section on heroin and cocaine) can be taken without directly disastrous effects. At a psychological level, however, immoderate consumption of this stimulant may well lead to serious problems (cf. Cohen 1990). It appears to be difficult for cocaine users to find their saturation point. The effects of the drug are ultrashort and, according to those who use it, it creates an insatiable hunger for more: "the bottomless pit," many call it.

> You just go on and on with white. It's never enough. The more you take, the more you want it.

Cocaine is always a "forbidden fruit" to any addict wishing to slow down his hectic and deviant existence. He knows from his own experience that one cannot keep cocaine consumption in hand and that taking it runs counter to attempts to calm down.

> White sucks you dry. You would have to steal for ever more to keep up a life on coke. I am managing now messing about a bit, but I daren't think of what would happen if I went back onto coke. The stuff has no brakes.

From this we may conclude that addicts deliberately choose to give up cocaine (temporarily). Unlike heroin, no compulsion arises from the pharmaceutical properties of cocaine itself. Addicts use cocaine for as long as it brings certain rewards and is functional for a certain style of life. They stop using it if, in a manner of speaking, the costs outweigh the gains.

The Functions of Psychopharmaca

The kick that users of a psychopharmaceutical drug are looking for is mainly the self-assured feeling they think it gives them. One respondent put this—rather histrionically—in words as follows.

> If I take pills I feel better inside and I think I could take on the world. For me, pills are a combination of guts and pleasure. I get a different kind of kick than from horse; with horse I could always lose myself in relaxation.

Several respondents report "feeling above themselves" after taking medicinal drugs, and they refer surprisingly often to the comic hero Superman. Some addicts report using certain medicines in order to feel less afraid when committing criminal offenses. Medicinal drugs help some addicts over the threshold if they are involved in crime that needs any daring. We should however note that only very few actually use drugs for this purpose. It is also important to realize that the drug itself does not incite crime, but that the decision to commit the offense has already been taken and the drug then swallowed out of purely instrumental considerations.

We have already remarked that some prostitutes take heroin in order to be able to make contact with punters more easily and to narrow their awareness during the provision of sexual services. Because several pharmaceutical drugs have the same effect and are, moreover, cheaper than heroin, they are popular among prostitutes.

While experimenting with different medicines is an attractive option for some addicts, proceeding to use such drugs excessively is certainly not. In order to maintain at least some status, any association with the so-called "pill-freaks" must be avoided at all costs. The scene is condescending about excessive pill swallowers and they are at the very bottom of the hierarchy.

> The pill-freaks lose themselves completely in a few years, and then they go about town like zombies. I want to keep myself under control a bit. Now and then a Valium or a Seresta, ok, but not a handful every day. I don't want to be a loser like the guys on the "pill-bridge."

To a relative outsider, the number of pills some of these addicts can put away is astounding: sometimes one of them comes up with a handful of colored pills out of his coat pocket. Gazing at this assortment thoughtfully, he pushes pills this way and that with the index finger of his other hand, turning them over and looking for the most attractive one. Confronted by so many, and unable to choose, he eventually puts his whole hand to his mouth.

PATTERNS OF USE

The previous sections have shown how many different drugs are used, but we have not looked at whether that use shows any pattern. This paragraph addresses that question. It can be answered in different ways. We shall approach the subject from two different directions: the use of several drugs at once and the (in)variability of drug consumption.

Polydrug Use

Only a few addicts in the Amsterdam scene restrict themselves to one type of drug. Most take several types. Maybe not every day, but at least a few times a week they sample something from the range of drugs we have outlined as well as heroin. Countless combinations are possible. Table 6-7 shows the most usual. The column of figures represents monthly prevalence in terms of number of respondents who has "taken sometime last month" the combination mentioned (regardless of amount or frequency). Methadone includes methadone bought on the street.

The most usual combination of illegal drugs is heroin and cocaine. It should be noted that *every* respondent on cocaine also takes heroin; there are 101 respondents on cocaine, and 101 addicts who use both heroin and cocaine. So within this population, cocaine is not a drug that is taken separately. Table 6-8 shows the combined amounts. Both the chi-square and the correlation coefficient (r) are highly significant. This means that there is a strong link between the use of heroin and the use of cocaine. If both drugs are used, the preference is for equal amounts, as can be seen from the figures on the diagonal from top left to bottom right (or vice versa); in general it is here that we find the highest figures.

Heroin and cocaine are not the only drugs to be used in combination; methadone is another one. Almost all addicts on metha-

TABLE 6–7
Monthly Prevalence of Polydrug Use

Combinations	Number of Respndents Who Have Taken Combination This Month
Heroin	135
Cocaine	101
Methadone	125
Heroin and Cocaine	101
Heroin and Methadone	119
Cocaine and Methadone (and Heroin)	81
Heroin, Cocaine, and Pills	57
Heroin, Cocaine, Methadone, and Pills	49
Heroin, Cocaine, Methadone, Pills, and Alcohol	35
Heroin, Cocaine, Methadone, Pills, Alcohol, and cannabis	27
Heroin, Pills, and Alcohol	45
Heroin and Alcohol	82

TABLE 6–8
Combined Monthly Use of Heroin and Cocaine

		Cocaine			
Heroin	None	0.05–4g	4–8g	>8g	Total
None	13	0	0	0	13
0.05–4g	17	30	2	0	49
4–8g	11	18	10	8	47
>8g	6	3	3	27	39
Total	47	51	15	35	148

chi-square =105.37; df=9; p<0.001; r=0.64

done also take heroin: 135 methadone users and 119 respondents who use both drugs; 81 respondents use cocaine as well.

In previous sections we discussed the functions that the different drugs may have. In order to confirm these impressionistic observations, we examined whether these drugs can be significantly distinguished in factors, to which end factor analysis was performed on seven types of drugs: heroin, cocaine, methadone, psychopharmaca, speed, cannabis, and alcohol. The results of that analysis (Table 6–9) fit the general picture that we already have of the different sorts of drugs.

TABLE 6–9
Factor Analysis of Seven Psychotropic Drugs

	Factor 1	Factor 2	Factor 3
Heroin	0.87	-0.04	0.01
Cocaine	0.80	-0.10	-0.04
Methadone	-0.34	0.73	0.06
Psychopharmaca	-0.02	0.70	0.20
Speed	0.10	0.53	-0.43
Cannabis	-0.11	0.02	0.80
Alcohol	0.21	0.37	0.55
Eigenvalue	1.8	1.3	1.1
Explained Variance	25.8%	18.8%	15.3%

Heroin and cocaine are the drugs that count in the scene: the illegal "hard" drugs (factor 1). Methadone and psychopharmaca are mainly replacement drugs; speed is somewhat out of place, but it does play a (limited) role in replacing cocaine (factor 2). Cannabis and alcohol are the socially integrated, more recreational, and accepted drugs (factor 3). This model of three factors is satisfactory here, considering the total 60 percent of variance explained.

Our respondents' drug use is mainly polydrug use. There is a certain connection in the use of drugs that corresponds with their different functions.

Variability in Consumption

There is a widespread idea that drug addicts need a physiologically fixed amount of heroin each day. In other words, opiate use is said to be invariable. The idea is that the use of (in this case) heroin over a long period of time causes physical tolerance of the drug to increase until an individually determined maximum has been reached. That maximum is necessary each day in order to prevent withdrawal symptoms.

Figures from this study reveal that the consumption of drugs varies widely. We developed a method of measuring the extent to which drug use varies. We calculated for each respondent what his daily average was for all of the days in the first cycle during which he was interviewed. We then calculated the standard deviation: variability in consumption expressed as a deviation from the average. As the standard deviation increases, so does variability in consumption. The advantage of a standard deviation above variance is that it is expressed in the same measure as the original variable—in this case grams. There is also a disadvantage to using the standard deviation: the standard deviation for those who use small amounts of drugs will never be very big and therefore never comparable to someone using a lot of drugs. We solved this problem by expressing the standard deviation as a percentage of the daily average (variability=s/m*100).

Table 6–10 shows the frequency of deviation percentages of heroin use.

TABLE 6–10
Deviations as a Percentage of Average Drug Use

		N	Percentage
Constant*		23	16
Deviation	1– 25%	25	17
	26– 50%	18	12
	51– 75%	19	13
	76–265%	63	43
Total		148	100

*No use (n=13) or constant use (n=10)

The results are quite remarkable. Forty-three percent (!) of all respondents have deviations from their average use (in either direction) that (far) exceed 75 percent. In other words, in the case of a deviation of 80 percent, an addict taking on average 10 grams may vary his use from 2–18 grams, with a range of 8 grams.[2] As the percentage increases, so too does variability in use. Only thirty-five addicts show a more or less constant level of intake, that is to say, deviations are no more than 25 percent of their average use. Relatively moderate users display the greatest variability.

There is a connection between these variations and other important elements within the drug world. There is, for example, a strong link with the use of methadone ($p<0.001$). As the deviation increase, there is a greater chance that the person concerned is a participant in a methadone program. Very small deviations are found mainly among those who are not registered with a methadone program. It is quite likely that this group has relatively simple access to the street market and even plays an active part in it, as couriers, intermediaries, etc. (cf. chapters 5 and 7). For these small dealers and hustlers, the availability of dope is more constant. An addict, therefore, may well take 2 grams one day, and nothing at all the next. In the latter case, methadone ensures that no withdrawal symptoms occur.

One may, however, wonder whether such large variability in consumption of the illegal drug heroin is proof of the elasticity in the *demand for opiates* and therefore a refutal of the view that there is a physiologically determined maximum amount that the body "requires" every day (the habit). A relatively easily accessible distribution network for methadone in Amsterdam offers drug users a way of replenishing opiate deficiencies on "bad days" with this synthetic opiate. Addicts do indeed cut their coats according to their cloth, but this is far more likely to be the result of the limits they set on activities they are prepared to undertake in order to obtain heroin. The fact that the respondents with the greatest variability in heroin consumption are registered with methadone pro-

---

2. Our method does not show whether deviations are higher or lower than average. In practice the distribution is probably even, so that in this example drug use will vary between 6 and 14 grams. Use is between 2 and 10 grams if the deviation is consistently lower. If the deviation is more than 100 percent, then the surplus can, by definition, only be found in a level of consumprion above the average.

grams confirms this. In this sense, a favorable effect of methadone distribution on crime may not necessarily be a lower individual level, but a reinforcement of individual limits to criminal behavior. "Everybody," including the drug addict, has his own (moral) restrictions for his own (criminal) behavior.

> I do break into cars, but always properly. I never kick the window in and mess up the dashboard for one shitty radio.

> I only break into shops and offices if I know there is nobody there. I always avoid violence.

The pharmacologically determined opiate habit to which we refer above acquires a whole different meaning in the light of results of urban ethnographic research into the daily activities of drug addicts. As we have said, the inelasticity of the need for heroin means that an addict will acquire about the same dose of opiates every day, whatever the price. However, the illegal drug market is not known for its reliable prices and neither is there legislation to ensure the purity of the heroin that changes hands on the street. Inelastic demand should imply that junkies produce more income as the relationship between price and quality of street heroin deteriorates.

Goldman (1981) has developed a theory that an addict's daily activities are not so much controlled by the relatively constant product of pharmacological quantity and quality of heroin, but rather by the "habit size," expressed in relatively constant money value. This is turning the microrelationship between drugs and crime—often thought of as self-evident—upside down. Perhaps crime is not a function of drug use, perhaps the level of drug use is a function of income produced. This is to assume that the junkie does not steal to the value of the drugs he needs to take, but that he takes drugs to the value of what he has stolen or earned. Addicts who wish to cut down should perhaps start by reducing their income: "The reason I don't do much crime is, I'm trying to cut down on my drugs" (Johnson et al. 1985).

We made many such observations during our study in Amsterdam. Many respondents divide the week into "good" days and "bad" days. On the days that a lot of money or dope has been earned, a lot of drugs can be consumed. A drop in earnings means a proportionate drop in drugs. Sandra, a heroin hooker, told a newspaper reporter in 1989: "What do I need every day? It depends on how much I earn." So, like his conventional counterpart, the opiate addict lives according to his earnings. This seems to adequately refute the assertion that "every junk has to steal to get his daily dose of heroin."

According to Goldman, the market and individual patterns of consumption adapt to the fluctuating price of heroin. The amount of quality controlled-heroin per unit sold varies. If the market price of pure heroin goes up, the packages get smaller, or the drug is adulterated further. In practice this would mean that the number of units ("$15 worth") would remain relatively constant with the amount of actually effective heroin varying with the price. In other words, the junkie's habit may not be a drug habit, but a "money" or "activities" habit. The latter expresses the individual junkie's characteristic competence to acquire (criminal) income. As is the case in the respectable world, drug addicts may attain more or less profitable positions, depending on their capacities, connections, and diligence. In this connection, ethnographic research refers to the "main hustle," a "professional" specialization, such as forging signatures, shoplifting, drug dealing,. or prostitution (Haverkamp 1984; Faupel 1986). The world of drugs may be just like the conventional world, with level of income dependent on personal competence and socially determined opportunities, while income level itself determines the level and style of (drug) consumption. The dope user confronts the same hard economic constraints as the respectable citizen. Both live according to their purse. If the price of petrol goes down, the car owner does not earn less, he simply spends his normal income on something else. Drug users may well be the same as bank clerks in that they dream of being able to let their consumptive needs take precedence.

Variations in patterns of heroin and methadone consumption led us to conclude that the function of methadone is to compensate. Despite the fact that there is no replacement drug for cocaine, cocaine and heroin use display similar variations. These similarities could be interpreted as follows. If necessary, methadone can fulfil an addict's primary need, namely avoiding being sick. Besides that, he also has a certain scope for taking drugs for pleasure, within which he may take, depending on the vagaries of income acquisition, more or less heroin, but also more or less cocaine. The level of income acquisition depends on individual characteristics (such as competence, normative limits, degree of involvement in being a junkie).

According to this interpretation, an addict's social behavior is not governed by a pharmacologically determined addiction, but rather his social behavior determines his consumption of drugs. Within this perspective, the distribution of methadone probably has a wide variety of meanings and possible functions. We shall return to this in chapter 7.

SUMMARY AND CONCLUSIONS

This chapter brought several important facts and conclusions to light. In chapter 5 we concluded that addicts can and do tap a great variety of sources of income, but as far as expenditure is concerned, the picture is very much more one-sided. Only 6 percent of income is spent on fixed items such as rent and gas and electricity; 15 percent goes on food and drink, and 11 percent on miscellaneous things (such as clothing, tobacco, etc.). As was to be expected, the greatest part of an addict's income is spent on (illegal) drugs and almost 70 percent on acquiring drugs. Of these, the most frequently used is heroin. It should be noted that this opiate is used increasingly as a drug that allows those who take it to function "normally": as a "cure" for withdrawal symptoms. As a means of enjoyment, heroin has been replaced by cocaine. Sixty-eight percent of the heroin users also consume cocaine, although for both drugs in lesser quantities than is often assumed. There are regular rumors that the level of consumption is several grams a day. On average, actual daily use of heroin and cocaine is between a quarter and half a gram respectively. The difference between these drugs is mainly due to the existence of a small number of excessive cocaine users. Besides these two substances, psychopharmaca also play an important part as drugs. Fifty-four percent of our respondents take a large variety of medicinal drugs. At the time of our research Rohypnol was especially popular. The use of such drugs is subject to trends. One day Rohypnol is popular, the next day Vesparax or Tuinal. Popularity grows as expectations of a certain drug reach mythological proportions.

Other frequently used combinations are: heroin and alcohol; heroin, cocaine, and psychopharmaca; heroin and methadone.

In the course of this study, intravenous use decreased by about 20 percent; maybe thanks to informative advertisement campaigns by the health authorities, addicts seem to have realized that injecting carries great risks. This is a favorable development, especially with an eye to preventing the spread of HIV.

Each drug is different, both with regards to its properties and its functions for the addict. Both quantitative analyses and qualitative observations reveal that there are three main groups: the drugs that are all important to being an addict: heroin and cocaine; replacement drugs: methadone, psychopharmaca, and speed; and the more socially accepted and recreational drugs such as cannabis and alcohol.

However, our most important conclusion is that the use of heroin and cocaine is highly variable. Such variability may deviate from the average by as much as 200 percent. Addicts set limits to the activities they are willing to undertake in order to procure dope. On "bad" days they stay off cocaine and use the methadone programs in order to supplement their opiate deficiency. In this sense, methadone programs act as a brake on the amount of crime an addict will commit. Like his conventional counterpart, a drug addict cuts his coat according to his cloth. If he has had a "good" day he will take a lot of heroin and cocaine, if his day was "bad" he may not take any. The level of consumption of illegal drugs depends on the amount of money earned. In this sense junkies might be said to have a "money" habit, or an "activities" habit, rather than an "unlimited" need for cocaine or heroin, or an unlimited willingness to do "anything" to get it. There is little support in this study for the widespread notion that every junkie must steal to obtain his invariable daily dose of drugs.

CHAPTER 7

Methadone Maintenance, Illegal Drug Use, and Acquisitive Crime

Since its introduction as a "therapeutic" drug, the synthetic opiate methadone has played a prominent part in institutional reactions to the problem of illegal drugs. The first methadone maintenance programs were set up in the sixties in the United States by Dole and Nyswander, both educated and employed in the medical profession (1967). Since then, the distribution of methadone has become quite commonplace in a number of Western countries. Remarkably, this remains the case, despite the strongly fluctuating circumstances surrounding the nature and size of the problem of illegal drug use. Moreover, this development has occurred in countries with significant social-cultural differences, such as the United States and the Netherlands. In these countries, methadone maintenance programs provide an important policy instrument in the field of drugs, although the two countries are miles apart as far as both the nature of the drug problem and the basic assumptions and goals of drug policy are concerned.

In the Netherlands, social control is an explicit argument for distributing methadone (Gemeente Amsterdam 1985 and 1988). The social reality of illegal drugs entails risks to the addict's health and his psychological and social functioning. It also adversely affects security and well-being in society as a whole and in the addict's more direct environment. It is for this reason especially that methadone maintenance programs cannot be detached from the policy goal of achieving a decrease in drug-related crime. Because the distribution of methadone must serve the interests of both the addicted individual and society, contradiction and ambiguity are inevitable. A certain tension exists between the goals of social control and (medical) aid. To what extent is it possible to both improve the fate (health) of the addict and protect society from the social effects of addiction by providing a synthetic opiate? The contradictions inherent in these goals become clear if we take a closer look at two extreme but existing points of view. In black political emancipation movements in the United States, methadone maintenance programs are sometimes regarded as a way of neutralizing the tensions that arise from social-economic and racist injustice. One even hears the term "genocide" in this connection (Kaplan 1983 p.219). Troublesome heroin addicts are rendered "harmless" by catching them in a system of control based on a drug that is "worse" than heroin itself. According to this view, methadone maintenance allows the addiction to continue for longer than is probably necessary in order to remove the threat that is associated with illegal drug use. "Methadone scares me. It's a government plot to control people. Once they hook you on it, they never let you go. You can't leave town. They've got records. I'd rather have a $100 a day habit than go on methadone" (Rosenbaum 1981 p.117). The criticism that control prevails above therapy and aid is also expressed in the far less polarized situation of the Netherlands. Like their American counterparts, Dutch addicts also feel that it is far more difficult to kick a methadone habit than a heroin addiction (Hunt et al. 1985; Verbraeck and van de Wijngaart 1989; Visser 1989; Reijneveld 1990).

On the other hand we find the ideological opposite in the criticism that the unconditional distribution of methadone is based on a naive therapy goal, so that heroin addicts are given too much support for their morally abject and socially injurious life-style. On the basis of this point of view, methadone maintenance is/was rejected as a matter of principle in Germany.[1] Earlier it led to methadone maintenance programs in the United States being regarded as strictly within a social control framework. We shall be returning to the significance of this for the effects of methadone maintenance later.

In the Netherlands, too, the distribution of methadone constitutes one of the most prominent institutional reactions to illegal drug addiction. And here too, the problem of combining different

---

1. Nowadays some states/cities cautiously incline towards a model of methadone maintenance programs based on the Dutch example, but the federal government in Bonn is still strongly opposed to such experiments.

goals is as relevant as it is anywhere else. For all of these reasons this project centered around the possible effects of methadone maintenance on the addict's ways of income acquisition. First we shall be looking at the major theoretical expectations concerning this relationship. From the second section onwards we shall be examining the empirical material.

METHADONE MAINTENANCE PROGRAMS AND CRIME: THE THEORY

Methadone and Crime According to the Orthodox Theory of Methadone Maintenance

In a certain sense, methadone maintenance programs have a lot in common with other institutionalized solutions to social problems, such as imprisonment and psychotherapy. These social systems of reaction are often based on historically coherent justifications, while expectations based on such justifications usually far exceed practical results. But such solutions, though doomed to fail, remain in place for lack of alternatives. Alas, "it should help, it doesn't help, but it's the best we have" is the pervasive reality of therapy and punishment. This is even more obvious when we examine borderline areas between therapy and control, of which methadone maintenance is one.

In answer to such fundamental inadequacies of the system of solutions, expectations may be lowered. For example, in the seventies the ambitious goal of achieving a prisoner's rehabilitation by means of imprisonment was replaced by the much more modest aim of keeping the adverse effects of imprisonment to a minimum. The inherent contradictions of methadone maintenance programs can be solved by more explicit emphasis on the one or the other goal (control or therapy). Traditionally in the United States the emphasis has been on the former, in the Netherlands on the latter. But disillusionment, ritualism, and cynicism may overpower all participants in the system of solutions (both objects and subjects). In the Netherlands, both distributors and clients regularly express doubts and ambivalences about the aims of official methadone distribution (Hubert and Noorlander 1987; Sengers 1987).

The theoretical justification of methadone as a good and "proper" means of improving an addict's social behavior (and achieving a decrease in crime) fits perfectly with a biological theory of heroin addiction. The orthodoxy of methadone maintenance, as founded by Dole and Nyswander and their first followers, provides a perfect construction of coherent ideas in which methadone forms a simple and effective remedy for drug problems. Within this construction, methadone transforms heroin addiction into a medically controlled, socially and psychologically indifferent metabolic disease. Here is the classic imagery of the socially and psychologically malfunctioning addict coming to depend on methadone as a diabetic depends on a daily dose of insulin, but leading an otherwise "normal" life. "Methadone, when properly prescribed, acts as a normalizer rather than as a narcotic. In this respect the treatment is similar to other maintenance therapies used in medical practice for treatment of patients with chronic metabolic disorders. The medical analogies are numerous—insulin for the diabetic, digitalis for the cardiac patient, cortisone for the arthritic(. . .) The methadone patient who is also dependent on the daily dose of his medication for his normal functioning, is in the same medical status" (quotation from Dole 1965, source: Schoone 1989). In 1988, the founder of methadone maintenance again testified to his undiminished faith in a purely medical solution to many social problems, including drug addiction: "(. . .) all diseases, including disorders of behavior, might ultimately be reduced to biochemical terms" (Dole 1988).

The original biological theory upon which methadone maintenance programs are based maintains that (heroin) addicts are motivated by pharmacologically produced principles of pleasure and pain. The addicted heroin user experiences painful withdrawal symptoms about six hours after last using heroin, and these are acute, disease-like symptoms. The avoidance of these unpleasant experiences is an elementary and universal biological motive to specific behavior. Under certain circumstances (depending on the manner of use and the level of addiction), heroin offers a short moment of pleasure that has been called orgastic. This "flash" constitutes, positively formulated, the attraction of heroin. Moreover, this physical experience of pleasure provides an obvious biological basis for the psychological component of addiction. The psychological dependence on drugs is most adequately expressed by the word craving. Addicted heroin users crave the renewed experience of pleasure that occurs immediately after taking the drug. Addicts of long standing sometimes crave in vain, because the "flash" may be lost in the (physiological) routine of drug use (cf. chapters 3 and 6). This does not mean that the craving will be weaker, but it will perhaps become insatiable.

The biologically based theory of methadone maintenance assumes that methadone is an effective drug that, in solving contradictory aims, serves both addict and society. The salutary effect that the synthetic opiate can and will have on the social behavior of drug addicts is described as follows: "(. . .) the methadone stabilized addict is no longer pressured into constant criminal activity so as to maintain his supply of heroin and is, thus, free to engage in such constructive pursuits as working or attending school regularly" (Ausubel 1983). In this train of thought, this can all be achieved on the basis of the same imperative principles that are said to govern the criminality of drug addicts. Methadone removes the heroin addict's withdrawal symptoms, so that he no longer "needs" heroin for that reason. (In fact, of course, this merely means that methadone is an addictive drug, pharmacologically similar to heroin.) The effect of methadone lasts longer than that of heroin, about twenty-four hours instead of six, so that in principle drug metabolism controls the addict to a lesser extent. Moreover, in the correct dosage (i.e., not too low), methadone is said to block the "flash," so that it no longer constitutes the reward for heroin use. The latter justification of methadone maintenance therefore fails to take into account the possibility outlined above, that addicts of long standing are not motivated by the sensation itself, but rather that they seek the illusion of heroin-induced euphoria.

A more essential failing of orthodox maintenance theory, however, is that it takes no account of the social reality of deviant drug use. We refer here especially to two elements that seriously undermine all too optimistic expectations with regard to the possible effectiveness of methadone maintenance. What can we expect of methadone, if an addict's addiction fulfils important social and psychological functions? Methadone helps to keep withdrawal symptoms at bay, but does it also help fill the void of existence (Hunt et al. 1985)? Neither can one ignore the reality of poly drug use. How effective can methadone be in a deviant life with drugs that need not be centered around heroin? What can be expected of methadone if addicts turn to cocaine?

The foregoing implies that methadone maintenance may have a decisive influence on the way an addict functions *if and in so far as* addiction depends on the pharmacology of the drug. This gives orthodox maintenance theory such a link with the causal-deterministic explanations of the relationship between drug use and crime that methadone distribution may, to a large extent, be regarded as a "natural experiment." If it can be proved that methadone maintenance *results* in a decrease in crime committed by drug addicts, this will provide an indication that such crime was *caused* by the addiction. We can reformulate the same problem as a question that is undoubtedly more relevant for practical drug policy: to what extent and under what conditions can methadone maintenance programs contribute to a decrease in drug-related crime? Later in this chapter we shall return to this aspect in the light of our empirical findings. However, first we shall briefly analyze, on the basis of existing literature, the possible effects of methadone distribution on crime. We shall be looking at two theoretical possibilities: methadone maintenance is linked and methadone maintenance is not linked to a decrease in crime.

Methadone Maintenance and a Reduction in Crime

After methadone maintenance programs had been running for about twenty years in the United States, one author summarized the state of affairs as follows: "Methadone has been used in hundreds of thousands of patients, in disparate social, economic, cultural and geographic situations; it has been evaluated in scores of studies. The large majority of evaluations demonstrate that opiate use, criminality and general health status are affected positively in many addicts" (Senay 1985). During the first years of methadone maintenance programs in the United States, spectacular successes were claimed. Clients were said to improve dramatically. Not only did abstinence or a serious reduction of illegal drug intake occur in most clients of methadone maintenance programs, it was also estimated that between 50 percent and 85 percent showed marked progress in social functioning. On the basis of ethnographic research, Preble maintains that these seemingly fantastic results were probably due to the naivety of the distributing institutions, that simply accepted (and not without a degree of self-interest) the information provided by the clients. Somewhat cynically the researcher provides his own observations at and around methadone maintenance programs: "The most typical drug scene on the streets today is two or three methadone users sitting on a stoop or standing on a street corner with pints of wine in paper bags, panhandling for change to get more wine" (Preble 1977).

In later years news from America on methadone maintenance was more moderate, but there remained a relatively strong consensus that methadone maintenance programs lead to a reduction in the use of illegal drugs and to a (connected) reduction in illegal income acquisition (Edwards 1979; Sechrest 1979; Anglin et al. 1981). The aforementioned article by Senay reports the results of a large number of evaluation studies on methadone distribution, the majority, though not all, of which are favorable. According to this article, the results of a large-scale follow-up study involving 44,000 clients of methadone maintenance programs are typical. Random samples from this group were followed during a period of six years. This research concluded that: "(...) the rates of illicit opiate use and criminality decreased sharply in comparison to pretreatment rates. Employment rates improved in methadone maintenance clients; 39% were employed before treatment and 62% were employed in the year after leaving treatment" (Senay 1985).

A more detailed look at the results of a number of individual evaluation studies on methadone maintenance reveals the same positive picture. A comparison between matched groups of heroin addicts, on methadone treatment and not on methadone treatment, shows that the group undergoing treatment committed less frequent and less serious crimes. Sixty-eight percent of the group on methadone reported not having committed acquisitive crime during the previous two weeks, as compared to 50 percent of the group not undergoing treatment. The researchers reach the following conclusion, which shows, in any event, that they do not assume that the distribution of methadone has a monocausal effect on crime: "When the need for money for drugs is removed, one of a larger set of interacting factors generating crime has been removed, but only one" (Faupel 1981).

The positive effects of methadone maintenance programs on drug-related crime in the United States should be approached with a certain degree of caution. It is important to consider two points. Firstly, the reliability of the research results, and secondly the question of the extent to which the population of heroin addicts, admitted to and kept in methadone maintenance programs, can be generalized.

One could ask whether the dominant ideology of methadone maintenance in the United States does not create a certain blindness to shortcomings in such seemingly brilliant results. We have already pointed to the ease and naivety with which success stories about methadone were presented during the early years of maintenance programs in the United States. Undoubtedly we may still question the reliability of (self-report) data on illegal drug use and crime, now that they were obtained within the context of (criminal justice) maintenance programs that attach severe penalties to illegal drug use and undesirable social behavior. A critical article on methadone distribution in the United States places a large question mark beside the reliability of data on the use of illegal drugs during methadone maintenance programs: "Failure to find evidence of these drugs in the urine does not in the least confirm the absence of abuse inasmuch as urine tests are typically neither randomized nor supervised (. . .) Similarly denials of abuse made to interviewers employed by official evaluating agencies are also little better than worthless" (Ausubel 1983). We could add that the prevention of crime is, in principle, even more difficult to measure, in the absence of a urine test for theft.

The success of methadone maintenance in the United States also fades somewhat if the question of double selectivity is taken into account. By this we mean both the admittance criteria to, and the requirements addicts must meet to stay in, the methadone maintenance programs. Certainly in comparison to the situation in the Netherlands (Amsterdam), methadone maintenance programs in the United States have a high threshold and impose a large number of conditions. For example, one of the most important programs in Baltimore only takes clients who have been employed for at least two years (information obtained from Richard Lane, executive director of this program). The use of illegal drugs besides methadone and committing criminal offenses usually constitute reasons for refusing admittance to or for removal from the program. This means, therefore, that to a certain extent a decrease in crime rates should be regarded as an artifact of the strict criminal justice context of many maintenance programs.

It would be going too far to draw the conclusion from all of this that the reduction in crime reported for the American clients of methadone programs has no meaning at all. But the results do imply a more specific interpretation of the relationship between methadone and crime. There is no reason to assume that there must be a biological-causal effect; the effects of methadone on crime can be understood in the context of the usual process of development of deviant drug addiction. The American experience indicates that methadone can be a stabilizing factor in an addict's social functioning, depending on the course of his drug career.

Methadone Maintenance and Nonreduction in Crime

From the large number of available American evaluation studies on methadone maintenance we may deduce that, under certain circumstances, the distribution of methadone allows a degree of regulation of a heroin addict's social behavior. Caution with regard to overoptimistic expectations of methadone maintenance automatically brings us to the conditions under which a positive effect of methadone maintenance on social behavior (namely criminality) need not be expected at all. From a social point of view, this is an equally important question. We shall examine some of its theoretical aspects.

In the foregoing pages, we pictured the chance of a reduction of crime as a result of methadone maintenance as a function of the degree of the addict's involvement in his life with drugs. As that involvement increases, so we must expect less from the effectiveness of methadone as far as crime reduction is concerned. Some research indicates that characteristics of the social position of the different types of addicts influence the effectiveness of methadone. This is especially true of highly marginal segments of the population, who show a smaller reduction in crime in relation to methadone maintenance (Ausubel 1983). It seems, therefore, that regulation of social behavior by means of methadone has a greater probability if the addicts are "middle-class drop-outs," than when we are dealing with addicts who originate from and are living in deprived minority groups and marginal lower social-economic groups. A plausible explanation for this could be that in the latter case deviant drug use is strongly linked to a life-style that is deviant in more ways than one. It is difficult to unravel the worlds of addiction, illegal income acquisition, and unconventional pastimes in socially marginal groups. The distribution of methadone affects one aspect of this deviant existence only. How big a reduction in crime rates may we expect from methadone maintenance involving addicts from a neighborhood where both crime and deviant drug use are regular henomena; addicts who, moreover, have come to regard the illegal drug market as one of the few effective ways of acquiring income, and spending that income on the illegal drug market as one of the few obvious ways of immediately satisfying their needs?

In this connection we should take a closer look at the concept of "heroin structure." This refers to the degree in which illegal drugs (heroin) are integrated into a social system and have a function for the structure of social-economic opportunity within that system (Kaplan 1977). As drug use comes to be more closely connected to such a structure, crime becomes a phenomenon that has many functions and is rooted in various psychological and social conditions. In that case, an addict's addiction would merely be one of many factors in the development and continuation of delinquent behavior. Almost by definition then, methadone will have but a very slight influence.

According to Kaplan, the heroin structure (in the United States) is usually more strongly developed in black addict populations than in white populations. This suggests that in the latter case there is a relatively more autonomous relationship between drug use and crime. In the United States, black drug addicts are more likely to grow up in delinquent opportunity structures, within which drug use occurs as a matter of course, contributing (through positions in the illegal distribution system) to the development of delinquent status and career. The following summarizing conclusion confirms that we need not expect much from the rehabilitating effect of methadone distribution to addicts whose characteristics include multiple deviancy and marginality: "The vast majority of minority-group ghetto addicts, exhibit no significant improvement in the area of drug use, criminal involvement or vocational and family functioning" (Ausubel 1983).

Such research is predominantly concerned with methadone maintenance programs in cities of the United States. To what extent are the conclusions relevant for the distribution of methadone in Amsterdam? The results of this study will help answer that question. Before taking a look at those results, we shall briefly outline the methadone distribution network in Amsterdam.

METHADONE MAINTENANCE PROGRAMS IN AMSTERDAM

The distribution of methadone in Amsterdam is mainly in the hands of the drug department of the local public health authorities (GG&GD). In principle, the service is not available to aliens; methadone is only provided for addicts who are residents in Amsterdam.

There are several different modalities of distribution, each with its own character. To start with, there are the methadone buses. Originally, old public transportation buses that had been adapted were used, but in the spring of 1989, new purpose-built buses were put into service. Seven days a week, two of these buses follow a fixed route through the city, stopping at special bus stops at set times. The buses are divided into two compartments. One is for the staff, the other is accessible to clients. Data are kept on the clients, including information of the daily (free) dose of methadone. After the information provided has been verified, liquid methadone is handed through a window in the bus. On the bus not only methadone is distributed, but there is also the possibility to exchange used needles and syringes for sterile ones.

The buses provide a service that has the lowest threshold in Amsterdam. There are barely any requirements that a client has to meet in advance to be able to register with a methadone bus program: there are no urine tests for illegal drugs, addicts do not have to turn up every day, and they are not expected to fundamentally change their life-style. If a client at one of the buses is "functioning well," he may be promoted to a community station. The three community stations are situated at the edge of the old city center. They are open on working days; clients are given pills for the weekend. The community stations differ essentially from the buses. Their explicit aim is abstinence from illegal drugs. To that end, urine tests are conducted twice a week, contact with doctors and social workers is obligatory, and active support is available wherever possible. Although the clients of the community stations are, in general, the more regulated addicts, some problematic users have been admitted for a while now. The aim is to keep a closer watch on them. A client may not only be promoted, but also demoted from community station to bus if he misbehaves too often (in terms of illegal drug use). Most clients of methadone maintenance programs visit either the buses or the community stations.

The public health authorities also provide methadone to specific categories of addicts: the so-called extremely problematic cases, prostitutes, and, at police stations, addicts under arrest. As well as a regular dose of methadone, extremely problematic cases also receive other support, such as food, shelter, and administration of their social benefit. Experimental distribution of morphine was also tried on this group (see Derks 1990, for an evaluation).

As well as the GG&GD, some general practitioners (GPs) in Amsterdam also provide methadone. The family doctor occupies the highest rung on the promotion ladder in the world of methadone maintenance: addicts may be promoted from bus to community station, and from community station to GP. Doctors give prescriptions that addicts can take to the chemist in order to obtain methadone pills. In general, a client may collect a prescription every two weeks. A lot is expected of the client's own responsibility, for on the street two week's worth of methadone fetches between $110 and $170. Although this form of methadone distribution is highest on the promotion ladder, it is nevertheless very similar to the buses. The doctor does not test for illegal drugs, neither does he provide further support. Moreover, clients often use the same arguments to justify their choice of doctor or bus.

> They leave you alone, nobody wants you to do anything. They just give you the methadone or the prescription, and nobody bothers you.

The difference between doctor and bus is that addicts are usually not able to obtain a prescription from the doctor unless the community station recommends it. This prevents problem users from gaining access to the doctors too easily, so that the GP can stay at the top of the promotional ladder.

Finally, the Consultation Bureaus for Alcohol and Drugs (CAD) also distribute methadone, decreasing the dose within the framework of drug therapy. The CADs also test for illegal drug use and are stricter than the community stations. Addicts caught using illegal drugs as well as methadone are removed from the therapy program immediately.

The structure of methadone distribution described above means that some of the methadone (especially the pills) flows into the street market. Most of it is traded on the "pill bridge" (see chapter 4). The price of a pill varies, depending on supply, from $1 to $2. Most of the methadone that is sold on the street comes from the doctors.

Of the forty-five respondents who participated in this study and who were not registered with a methadone program, twelve used methadone bought on the street; not every day, but if circumstances so required, for example if they had had a "bad" day. This phenomenon of the black methadone market may be regarded as an undesired side effect of the system. On the other hand it also can be viewed as an informal extension of the methadone supply to heroin addicts who, for whatever reason, do not want to participate in a regular program.

The characteristics of the methadone distribution system will be used in forthcoming analyses of empirical data. The main distinctions will concern the requirements that clients have to meet: these may vary from almost none to obligatory abstinence from illegal drugs.[2]

METHADONE USE AND THE USE OF ILLEGAL DRUGS

Methadone Use

When they were included in the sample, 105 of our 150 respondents were registered with a methadone program, 80 were on methadone maintenance, while 25 reported that they were gradually cutting down. The average duration of participation in the

---

2. Of late, the system of distribution has been changed drastically. Urine tests at the community stations have been stopped. This means that the health authorities have moved away from the promotional model almost entirely. Community stations are now meant to cater for addicts who need extra attention, the extremely problematic cases. The special station for these cases has been done away with. In principle, clients of both buses and community stations must submit to a (social-)medical examination once every three months. Because the data for this study were collected at a time when the health authorities still adhered to the promotion system, the results should be viewed in that context.

present methadone program is twenty-one months. This average is high, and it is determined mainly by a relatively small number of very faithful participants: 30 respondents have been receiving their methadone at the same location for three years or more. The median (the value that divides the sample exactly in half) is eight months. Table 7–1 shows the number of respondents who have ever participated in some form of methadone program.

TABLE 7–1
(Previous) Participation in Methadone Program

	Present in Program		
Previous in Program	Yes	No	Total
Yes	86	27	113
No	19	18	37
Total	105	45	150

Eighteen respondents (12 percent) have never participated in a methadone program. This means that 88 percent of our respondents have been registered with such a program in the past or are registered now. Nonparticipation is usually a conscious choice and not the result of unawareness of the existence of methadone programs. Of the forty-five nonparticipants, twenty-seven no longer have any contact with methadone programs. Some stopped methadone deliberately. The most frequent arguments for doing so are the following: dislike of any form of registration, fear of becoming addicted to two drugs at once, and/or the feeling that a methadone habit will be much more difficult to kick than a heroin habit. These motives reflect something of the resistance to methadone programs in the black emancipation movement in the United States mentioned earlier. Although the Dutch situation is far less polarized, here too a number of addicts—mainly of Surinam extraction—perceive methadone maintenance as a system of control. They seriously object to any interference in their lives and reject methadone programs on principle for that reason. Others are not guided by moral objections at all. They no longer use the facilities offered by the methadone programs because they are no longer welcome there. For example, having once taken their frustration out on the furniture in the bus or the community station, they were—to use their own words—"kicked out." This has happened to relatively few addicts.

Table 7–2 shows for how many days a month methadone was used, regardless of whether this was regular or street-market methadone. Leaving the twenty-three nonusers aside, 56 percent use methadone on a daily basis. With the exception of two respondents, all of these daily users are registered with a methadone program. Although not apparent from the table, thirty-nine respondents (26 percent) buy methadone on the street; of these, 77 percent do not do so more than four times a month.

TABLE 7–2
Frequency of Methadone Use per Month

Frequency of Use	Number of Respondents
Every day	70
Up to 7 Days	11
7–14 Days	9
14–21 Days	10
21–30 Days	25
Did Not Use	23
Total	148

Table 7–3 gives a picture of the modalities that distribute the most methadone, that is, that have the heaviest users amongst their clients. The methadone programs run by the health authorities (community stations and buses) have the clients with the highest doses, with most visiting the buses. GPs and the CAD prescribe relatively low doses.

Methadone and the (Illegal) Use of Heroin and Cocaine

Chapter 6 describes, among other things, polydrug use. Although we did refer to methadone, we did not pay special attention to it; we were more interested in illegal drugs. In this section we shall try to determine whether and how the use of methadone is linked

TABLE 7-3
Amount of Methadone per Week per Modality

modality	methadone <150mg	150–300mg	300–450mg	>450mg	Total
Community Station	15	17	10	2	44
Buses	8	13	17	3	41
GP	7	7	1	-	15
CAD	2	2	1	-	5
Total	32	39	29	5	105

to consumption levels of heroin and cocaine. We shall first look at how the use of methadone is linked to those levels in general. We shall then examine how this picture changes if we differentiate according to the type of methadone program. The importance of the latter exercise derives from the promotion model of methadone maintenance programs in Amsterdam. We shall also include the existence of the street market for methadone in our analysis, because the market allows hard drug users to take methadone while they have no obligation to register with a regular methadone program. One could even say that it is the methadone program with the lowest threshold in the city; the price of the methadone pills is not really a barrier.

We examined the relationship between the use of heroin and the distribution of methadone in both the above-mentioned ways. Table 7–4 shows that 93 percent of the nonmethadone users use more than 4 grams of heroin a month; this percentage is 43 for the methadone users. Less heroin is consumed if the addict is also on methadone. The relationship remains if we examine not only those *registered* with a methadone program, but also add the addicts who *take* methadone bought on the street market as a variable. A word of warning is necessary here: such relationships are all too easily interpreted as causal, ignoring other factors that are more significant for explaining the result. In this case, for example, one simply cannot say that methadone is the cause of a

TABLE 7-4
Level of Heroin and Methadone Use

| | \multicolumn{5}{c}{Monthly Heroin Use} |
Program	None N=13	0.05–4g N=49	4–8g N=47	>8g N=39	Total N=148
Yes	13%	44%	26%	17%	104
No	0%	7%	45%	48%	44

chi-square=14;df=3;p<0.01

reduction in heroin use. Respondents who decide to take methadone may do so in order to minimize withdrawal symptoms if, for whatever reason, they are unwilling or unable to take (as much) heroin. In terms of causality, it is not the use of methadone that causes decreased heroin use, but rather the respondent's motivation to give up or cut down on heroin.

There is support for this view if we differentiate within the group of methadone clients according to the threshold of the program in which they are participants. One group consists of the clients at community stations, GPs, and CAD (high threshold). The other represents the low threshold programs: the methadone buses and the distribution of methadone to extremely problematic cases. Our third category consists of respondents who are not registered with a methadone program. Table 7-5 shows the monthly use of heroin for these three categories.

The results shown in this table are significant. Compared to the other two groups, not many moderate and heavy users (more than 4 grams a month) can be found at the community station or the general practitioner. If this group does take heroin as well as methadone, it is not likely to be more than 4 grams a month, which boils down to chasing the dragon a few times a week. We also see that 62 percent of the bus clients and 93 percent of the nonmethadone users take more than 4 grams a month. Our previous conclusion that there is a significant relationship between methadone programs and a reduction in the use of heroin needs reexamining: any reduction in the use of heroin is mainly due to the clients who frequent the community stations, the doctors, and the CAD.

TABLE 7-5
Type of Program and Monthly Heroin Use

Type Program	None N=13	0–4g N=49	4–8g N=47	>8g N=39	Total N=148
Not Registered	0%	7%	46%	47%	44
High Threshold	18%	52%	15%	16%	62
Low Threshold	5%	33%	43%	19%	42

chi-square=46; df=6; p<0.01

Tables 7-6 and 7-7 show the same exercise, but now for cocaine. We see the same relationship, although it is not as strong as in the case of heroin.

TABLE 7-6
Level of Cocaine and Methadone Use

Program	None N=47	0.05–4g N=51	4–8g N=15	>8g N=35	Total N=148
Yes	39%	35%	9%	17%	104
No	14%	34%	14%	39%	44

chi-square=8; df=3; p=0.05

TABLE 7-7
Type of Program and Monthly Use of Cocaine

Type Program	None N=47	0–4g N=51	4–8g N=15	>8g N=35	Total N=148
Not Registered	14%	34%	14%	38%	44
High Threshold	52%	31%	7%	10%	62
Low Threshold	21%	41%	12%	26%	42

chi-square=24.2; df=6; p<0.01

Respondents registered with a methadone program use less cocaine or none at all; 74 percent as opposed to 48 percent of the nonregistered respondents. As was the case with heroin, there is no change in this relationship if we add the respondents who are not registered with a regular program, but who obtain (irregular) doses of methadone on the street market. Table 7-7 differentiates again according to the different types of programs. Although the relationship with a reduction in cocaine use is, again, less strong than in the case of heroin (chi-square is lower in Table 7-7 than in Table 7-5), we nevertheless see that a reduction in cocaine consumption is linked to the high threshold programs and is caused, to a large extent, by the 52 percent (n=32) in the first column that use no cocaine at all. This result is similar to that for heroin and, again, the similarity also applies to nonregistered respondents using methadone bought on the street.

Although the synthetic opiate methadone is primarily meant to replace heroin, we see a strong relationship with a decrease in the use of cocaine. This result contradicts orthodox methadone maintenance theory, that predicts that methadone will only influence heroin consumption. Once again our data show that the essence of drug addiction is not so much the pharmacological consistence of the different psychotropic substances, but rather the functionality of being an addict. In order to explain our results, one must look primarily for the reasons why drug addicts should present themselves at methadone maintenance programs at regular intervals at all.

The fact that the clients of high threshold programs use significantly fewer illegal drugs than other addicts, is mainly, if not exclusively, connected to the fact that these are addicts who have calmed down: "retired junks." They no longer desire, nor are they able to lead, a busy and successful life as an addict and methadone allows them to continue their deviant life-style, but at a lower pitch. Addicts who turn to low threshold programs have entirely different reasons for doing so. For them, methadone is a basic amenity in a hectic life with drugs that also brings other rewards. These addicts regard methadone as a sort of insurance against hard times. If all goes well, and enough is scored to be able to buy the desired drugs, methadone either provides an extra dose or can be sold for extra cash.

Methadone has become integrated into the drug scene, but it does not stop or "cure" addiction. In some cases it has become a necessary condition for leading a life of addiction; in others it provides a comfortable basis for being an addict.

The fact that it makes no difference to our results if we include those who use street-market methadone supports the view that this market fulfils the same functions as the official distribution of methadone. It is probable that street methadone is used mainly as an emergency solution for withdrawal symptoms. The figures confirm this notion. Apparently methadone not only functions for those who are registered with a methadone program, but also for those who are, for whatever reason, unable or unwilling to use regular distribution sources.

THE DISTRIBUTION OF METHADONE AND CRIME

An important question that this study must attempt to answer is the extent to which the distribution of methadone contributes to reducing acquisitive crime committed by drug addicts. We shall approach this question in different ways.

First, we shall examine the significance of methadone programs for acquisitive crime in the light of other addict-related variables, that, for several reasons, may be regarded as relevant to such crime. These are: *age, sex, the receipt of social benefit, participation in a methadone program, level of heroin and cocaine consumption, and the total duration of opiate use*. In order to examine the relationship between these variables and the rate of acquisitive crime, multiple regression analysis was performed on this group of variables. Such analysis reveals the relationship between a number of background or independent variables on the one hand, and one dependent variable on the other. As a measure of criminality (the dependent variable), we took individual gain from acquisitive crime because this study is mainly concerned with income and expenditure. Table 7-8 shows the result of this analysis.

Although the comparison can be used as a predictor of crime, the percentage of explained variance is small. However, the analysis was not meant to predict crime, but to show the influence of methadone programs in relation to other variables that could influence the crime rate. We see that 20 percent of the explained variance in individual gain from acquisitive crime is explained by

TABLE 7-8
Gain from Acquisitive Crime and Seven Background Variables

	Mult-R	R^2	R^2-increase	ß	p
Level of Cocaine Use	0.34	0.12	0.12	0.26	0.00
Sex	0.38	0.14	0.02	-0.20	0.01
Age	0.43	0.18	0.04	-0.18	0.07
Level of Heroin Use	0.45	0.20	0.02	0.16	0.08
Duration of Use	0.45	0.20	0	-0.05	>0.1
Social Benefit	0.45	0.20	0	-0.02	>0.1
Regular Methadone	0.45	0.20	0	-0.01	>0.1

p for F<0.001; i.e., the comparison as a whole can be used as a significant predictor of crime.

four variables. This percentage does not increase after the variable heroin consumption has been added. Neither do registration with a methadone program, duration of opiate use, or the receipt of social benefit make any difference to the prediction of the level of gain from acquisitive crime.[3] Only four out of eight variables are significant (two at the 10 percent level): in order of importance these are: *cocaine consumption* (the more cocaine, the higher the gain), *sex* (men commit more crimes than women), *age* (the younger, the higher the gain; the—coefficient is negative), and *level of heroin use* (the higher the level, the more crime). The use of cocaine correlates most strongly with the level of crime.

In general then, and in the midst of other variables, participation in a methadone program does not seem to influence the level of criminality. This is confirmed if the first-order correlation between criminal gain and methadone distribution is brought into consideration: it is -0.08. Although the relationship is in the expected direction (negative), it is very weak. But we cannot be absolutely sure about this conclusion. Further analysis is needed to examine whether participation in a methadone program under

---

3. An increase in explained variance of 0.001 percent may be interpreted as nil.

certain circumstances may be related to a decrease in level of criminality.

The classic or orthodox approach to methadone maintenance implies that methadone has an unconditional effect on crime, while the circumstances of methadone distribution or the type of addict are regarded as merely (perhaps) influencing the extent of that effect. Indeed, the pharmacological properties of the substance, together with the physiologically determined "essence" of addiction, are seen as the main ingredients of the metabolic effect of methadone. Falsification of this reduction-in-crime hypothesis is an important indication that the orthodox theory of methadone maintenance is untenable. Conversely, orthodox methadone theory would not be falsified if no difference in crime levels were found to exist between the different types of methadone programs. Again we distinguish between high and low threshold programs as an operationalization of the conditions under which methadone is distributed.

Table 7–9 again shows the respondents divided into three groups. These are then compared as to criminality.

TABLE 7–9
Acquisitive Crime and Different Types of Methadone Programs

	Aquisitive Crime		
	Yes	No	Total
Type of Program	N=79	N=69	N=148
Not Registered	59%	41%	44
High Threshold	40%	60%	62
Low Threshold	67%	33%	42

chi-square=7.8;df=2;p<0.05

The results in this table are significant ($p<0.05$): there is a clear relationship between the type of methadone program and acquisitive crime. It should especially be noted that, both absolutely and in percentages, more clients from the low threshold programs (the buses) commit criminal offenses than the other two groups. In other words, not only has the hypothesis that methadone maintenance always leads to a reduction in crime been falsified, those who obtain methadone from the buses even commit more crime than those not on methadone maintenance. We may view this phenomenon as an important indication that the most relevant factor is not the methadone, but the addict's life-style. Here we see the same sort of mechanism at work as that already described in connection with the striking "successes" of methadone distribution in the United States. Distribution itself does not explain a reduction in crime, but (self)selection for the different types of programs, on the basis of motivation and life-style.

Under these conditions, the results of Table 7–11 may simply be regarded as an artifact of the way in which the distribution of methadone in Amsterdam was organized when we conducted our research. Regular tests for and sanctions on the use of illegal drugs at the community stations and the CAD resulted in those who regularly took illegal drugs being taken off the program and "sent down" to the buses. As a result, the community stations and the CAD retained only clients who did not use illegal drugs, or only rarely. In the knowledge that there is a strong connection between the use of cocaine and crime (Table 7–8), we may conclude that most criminal addicts registered with methadone programs end up on the buses. Now, this explains why clients from the buses are more criminal than those from the community stations, but not why addicts from low threshold programs should be more criminal than those not registered at all with a methadone program. We shall try to arrive at such an explanation in the following section.

Up till now we have made use of a rough measure, looking only at whether crime had been committed, and not at how much. We shall now compare the three groups of respondents as to their average income from crime. To this end, we conducted t-tests for differences in averages and obtained the following result. Not surprisingly, there is a big difference in criminal gain between the nonregistered respondents and those attending a high threshold program: an average of $775 per month as against $150 ($p<0.05$).

There is a difference in average gain between the nonregistered and low threshold groups ($775 and $500 respectively), but it is not significant and should primarily be put down to coincidence. The other difference in average gain from crime (between high and low threshold groups) is also significant ($p=0.01$). Table 7–10 summarizes the results.

TABLE 7-10
Tests for Differences in Average Gain from Crime Between Three Groups of Respondents

	LowThreshold (average $500)		High Threshold (average $150)	
	t-value	p	t-value	p
Not Registered (av.$775)	0.76	0.45	2.1	0.04
High Threshold (av.$150)	-2.8	0.01	—	—

By and large, this confirms the results from Table 7–9. There is, however, one big difference. Although more clients from the methadone buses commit criminal offenses, their average gain is less than that of the nonregistered group. In other words: (a substantial) number of clients from the buses commit "less serious" acquisitive crime, while the criminal respondents who are not registered with a methadone program, commit the more serious offenses.

Although the average gain from crime for bus clients is lower than for the nonregistered group, this still does not explain why they should head the league in terms of number of offenders. In seeking to explain this phenomenon, we shall also use the economic typology.

THE DISTRIBUTION OF METHADONE AND THE ECONOMIC TYPOLOGY

The figures presented above show that the relationship between level of criminality and distribution of methadone is not as unambiguous as one might think at first sight. An addict's motivation and options play an important part here. How can the links we have uncovered be explained? In chapter 5, we developed a typology, by means of which we distinguished three types of addicts on the basis of dominant-income generating activities: the normalized user who usually acquires his income legally, the criminal user whose income—as the name suggests—is generally acquired through crime, and the dealing user whose activities are concentrated on the market of white and brown. This typology is related to a large number of variables concerning the addict, and together they indicate that categorization in one of the three types depends on an addict's style of life. We shall examine these three types in relation to the function fulfilled by methadone in that life-style (see Table 7–11). We divided our respondents into the same groups as before, only now we compared them according to their dominant source of income. We see a clear link between dominant source of income and the conditions under which methadone is distributed. A very high level of significance merely serves to emphasize this point.

TABLE 7–11
Three Types of Users and the Distribution of Methadone

	Normalized User N=94	Dealing User N=22	Criminal User N=32	Total N=148
Not Registered	23%	56%	31%	44
High Threshold	52%	22%	25%	62
Low Threshold	25%	22%	44%	42

chi-square=15.7; df=4; p<0.005

On the one hand, normalized users are motivated to put an end to their existence with drugs; on the other, they use the methadone facilities in order to keep their deviant existence going, be it at a much lower pitch. Of these addicts, 52 percent (percentage determined vertically) receive their methadone from the GP, the CAD, or the community station. Apparently these addicts want to take it easy and they are no longer (much) involved in a deviant career. They too regard drug use and crime as problematic elements of this way of life. At the same time, however, they realize that they will probably not be able to manage on their own. In giving up being an addict, they need support and supervision. This is what a high threshold methadone program provides. The clients use methadone as a medicine to combat possible withdrawal symptoms.

However, for the (ex) heroin users who visit the community stations, the use of methadone does not merely fulfill the classic role described by Dole and Nyswander (1967 and 1976). The significance of methadone maintenance also lies in its social-psychological context. The client is expected at the community station every day; this regulates his life and provides him with a reason for getting up in the morning. He meets friends and acquaintances there; he often hangs around for a chat and often too his relationship with the staff is good. If there are difficulties, he can always appeal to social workers, nurses, or doctors at the post. The clients of GPs form a somewhat different category. Although methadone fulfils a similar function for these addicts, they have more self-confidence and they feel less need for regular supervision. Some of the doctors' clients make use of the lack of supervision to earn some extra cash by selling their methadone.

These descriptions are, of course, of ideal types and not every addict at a community station will fit the bill. Some clients—albeit a minority—manage to continue their hectic life with drugs, despite urine tests. At one point there was a rumor on the Zeedijk that bottles of clean urine were for sale. One had to take care—so the story went—to warm them up to body temperature before handing them in, to which end the armpit could be used. Deceiving the staff is exciting, and if it works it confirms an addict's ability to "survive." So not all of the clients an the community stations fit our description. This is also true of the extremely problematic cases to which the section on metadone maintence programs in Amsterdam refers and who are deliberately sent to the community stations so that the authorities can keep an eye on them. However, the main thing is that the method of methadone distribution at the community stations attracts a certain type of addict, motivated to a certain degree to change a life-style of involvement in drugs into something more conventional.

To a certain extent, the dealing user is comparable to the criminal user. He is a polydrug user, his drug related activities occupy his day entirely and he frequently commits criminal offenses. The difference, however, is that acquisitive crime occupies a less important place in his total pattern of income generation. The dealing user's main activities are on the illegal drug market. Of this group, 56 percent are not registered with a methadone maintenance program. They have no need to be, for they have easy access to the desired drugs. As well as cash, the dealing user's income also consists of drugs. The high-frequency pattern of crime characteristic of the criminal user does not fit the dealing user's style of life that is, in a certain sense, more structured than that of the criminal user. In order to stay in the running for a job as lookout, courier, dealer, etc., he must spend most of his time hanging around the Zeedijk. If he goes off too often to commit acquisitive crime, he risks losing his connections among the big dealers. If anything goes wrong, for whatever reason, he can always fall back on street-market methadone. The relative ease with which addicts can trade on the market of illegal drugs is partly the result of criminal policy. As mentioned in chapter 1, possession of drugs for personal use will not be prosecuted and is, therefore, no police priority. Big dealers make use of this by putting out small amounts of drugs to intermediaries who sell them as small dealers. In this way, pragmatic drug policy in the Netherlands contributes to the fact that a substantial number of addicts generate their income on the drug market. As a result, these addicts are able to live a life of involvement in drugs, without resorting to (much) acquisitive crime.

Criminal users prefer to get their methadone from one of the buses; of this group, 44 percent are bus clients. They differ from community station clients in many ways. They are irregular customers. They take their methadone and disappear immediately. The greatest part of their income comes from acquisitive crime. Most lack the time to hang around; they have "work to do." Sometimes the bus provides a meeting point for addicts who take their methadone and then "go to work" together. In Amsterdam, the availability of methadone *allows* addicts who are highly involved in drugs to spend more money on cocaine. For these addicts, who need a deviant existence in order to fill their hectic days, a reduction in (criminal) income is, by definition, not an interesting option. A Dutch writer with personal experience, expresses it as follows: "Most bus-customers start the day with their dose of methadone, then they score some horse, and then the optional part of the day begins: how do I get some coke?" (Visser 1989). The criminal addict keeps going on a lot of cocaine; there are periods in which he keeps going all night and every night. This drug helps him to keep his "full-time job" and to remain alert and self-confident. For these addicts, methadone is a multifunctional drug and its use is opportunistic: it replaces heroin on bad days, it acts as one of many drugs, or it provides extra income. It is not unimportant that this drug can be obtained by doing practically nothing. It cannot be ruled out that this group might lay off methadone if the buses were to have the same rules as the community stations. They take whatever they can lay their hands on, legal or illegal; their deviant career is what matters most.

While many clients of the community stations use methadone as a medicine that enables them to lead the uneventful life associated with the receipt of social benefit, many bus clients regard the same drug as a facility that allows them to balance on the edge of the enticing big-city ravine, the most significant elements of which are polydrug use and crime. It is of course also true of the buses that they do not cater exclusively for criminal addicts. Other types also make use of them. Table 7–11 shows that for a quarter of bus clients their main source of income is legal.

The important point to make, however, is that for the majority of bus addicts, methadone fulfills a different function than for the clients registered with high threshold programs.

SUMMARY AND CONCLUSIONS

During our study, the structure of methadone maintenance programs in Amsterdam was such that it allowed us to differentiate between addicts in two ways. One way is the so-called promotion model. Addicts could be promoted (for good behavior) via the different types of methadone programs to the highest level in the model: the GP. This presumed that they were more or less able to manage on their own. The second way is the threshold to the different programs. The methadone buses had the lowest threshold, the community stations and the GPs the highest. That is to say that urine tests for the use of heroin and cocaine were mainly carried out at the community stations. This difference in threshold, or in the conditions under which methadone was distributed, is of decisive importance in explaining many of our results. At the same time, methadone in tablet form (and also the methadone that the community stations provide for the weekend) has contributed to the development of a street market for the drug. Although, at first sight, this would appear to be an undesirable situation, one could also argue that the street market succeeds in reaching people who do not otherwise make use of methadone distribution. Of the addicts who are not registered with a methadone program, 29 percent nevertheless take methadone. Perhaps not every day, but in any event when they need it most.

Another question answered in this chapter concerns the prevalence of methadone use. On a yearly basis, 65 percent of the known addicts in Amsterdam are registered with a methadone program. Of our respondents, 88 percent had participated in or were at that moment participating in such programs. Methadone programs have therefore a very wide coverage.

The following question concerns the effects of methadone on the levels of consumption of illegal drugs. *In general* there is a strong link between participation in a methadone program and a reduced level of both heroin and cocaine consumption. However, a closer look reveals that this result is almost entirely due to the high threshold programs: the community stations run by the public health authorities, the CAD, and the GPs. The low threshold programs (the buses) show no reduction in illegal drug use. We found similar results with regard to levels of criminality. A comparison between two groups of respondents (participation in a methadone program and nonparticipation) reveals no differences in crime. From a straightforward point of view at least, methadone has no influence on acquisitive crime. This no longer applies if we divide the group of methadone users into visitors to high and low threshold programs. We now see that the clients of high threshold programs commit significantly less crime than those registered with low threshold programs—the latter even committing offenses in greater numbers than those not registered with methadone programs at all.

Both results can be explained by means of the concept of lifestyle. The three groups—high threshold, low threshold, not registered—demonstrate the characteristics of three different life-styles. Within those life-styles, the function of methadone differs. In a normalized life-style, methadone is used as a medicine. Both the consumption of illegal drugs and income-generating crime are greatly reduced. In a criminal life-style, methadone is just one of many (free) drugs, or it forms an emergency solution should the addict fall on hard times. Methadone is effortlessly fitted into a highly deviant, criminal career. Finally, the most salient feature of an dealing user's life-style is easy access to drugs. This type of addict does not need methadone, because he is partly paid in kind. These addicts also commit less crime. Their career and daily activities are concentrated on the market of white and brown. It is most likely that this group would have more "need" to resort to criminal behavior if police repression of the drug market were to increase. In this connection, it should not be forgotten that the very possibility of shaping one's life as an addict in this way is partly due to the fact that police and prosecutors are reluctant to interfere too much in the small-scale market of white and brown. In chapter 6 we noted the paradoxical situation that moderate police tactics lead to less acquisitive crimes by a certain group of addicts.

These results clearly show that addiction not only has a physical, pharmacological, or medical component, but also that an addict's options, motivation, and competence, and some policy measures, may, to a great extent, determine his life-style. This is especially apparent from the fact that methadone has two opposite functions. In one case it is a necessary condition for building a normal (or at least more normal) existence; in the other it is part of being an addict.

Why then, one could ask, should low threshold programs remain available if they contribute neither to a reduction in illegal drug use nor in levels of criminality; indeed, for some addicts methadone is a necessary condition for being an addict. We cannot discuss the general health of the addict population here. Experience during this study provides us with the following, tentative, answer: the distribution of methadone without far-reaching conditions helps to keep some addicts in contact with social institutions and within the scope of policy reality. Ties with society have not been completely cut. It goes without saying that close contact with a group that can be regarded as at risk in many different ways guarantees that developments within that group will be noticed at an early stage and that—in the most favourable case—policy can be brought up to date and implemented sooner and more adequately; the necessary infra-structure is already there. Low threshold programs may also provide a "stepping stone": addicts who are "not ready" to kick the habit may find it easier—once they find the motivation—to move to a type of methadone maintenance program that requires them, for example, to stay "clean."

CHAPTER 8

Conclusions, Theoretical Implications, and Possible Policy Consequences

Now that we have presented both relevant theory and research results, the time has come to examine those results in the light of that theory and to consider the possible consequences of this study for future policy. However, the results of this research are not all equally important for synthesizing theory and empirical data into policy alternatives. We shall, therefore, limit ourselves to the findings that we consider to have the most obvious implications, referring to the final sections of the empirical chapters (3–7) for more detailed summaries.

The role of crime in the addict's economy was central to this study. We have looked at the nature and amount of crime, as well as its functionality. At a theoretical level, we have dealt not only with the relationship between drug use and crime (chapter 2), but also with the possible effects of methadone maintenance programs on drug-related crime (chapter 7). This final chapter has three themes:

1. A summary of the amount and nature of drug-related crime and a description of different patterns of criminality. It is important to realize that the word crime refers here to acquisitive crime. Although infringements of the Opium Act also constitute crime, they are dealt with as a separate category.
2. The significance of the relationship between crime and drug use in the light of the results of this study. This centers around the three models described in chapter 2.
    - *Model 1: Drug use causes crime.* The emphasis is on the drug and the addiction. Crime is simply a function of the psychopharmacological (physical dependence) and

economic (price) properties of the drug and in that sense it is an inevitable consequence of drug use.
- *Model 2: Crime causes drug use.* Here the primary concern is a criminal style of life, in which drug use is inevitable. Drug use is regarded as a secondary effect of socialization within a criminal subculture.
- *Model 3: Crime and drug use are both equally significant and functional patterns of behavior that allow realization of a deviant life-style.* Both phenomena are considered from a deviant career perspective. They influence each other and are mutually reinforcing. Both crime and drug use are based on common conditions and processes.

3. Possible policy alternatives in terms of crime control based on the themes sub 1 and 2. We shall examine the extent to which findings from this study necessitate two quite different models of policy adaptation. The first is based on the necessity and possibility of basically changing current drug policy. In the second, changes entail little more than adaptations.

THE MOST IMPORTANT RESULTS

The use of drugs was a possible determining factor in the development of criminal behavior for only a relative small minority of the problematic addicts who figure in this study. This could apply to the 20 percent who began to commit criminal offenses *after* the use of heroin became an important element in their lives. A smaller number (8 percent) began committing crimes more or less at the same time as they started using heroin. There is also a group of 21 percent who report not committing any crime, neither in the past nor during the research project. By far the largest group (51 percent) is comprised of respondents who were already committing criminal offenses before they started on heroin. The development of illegal drug use, addiction, and delinquency often occurs against a common social background. The results of this study again provide little indication that one single element, addiction to dangerous and forbidden drugs, plays a decisive role in the development of a criminal way of life.

Certainly not all of our respondents commit criminal offenses frequently or regularly. Calculated over one month, 53 percent of the respondents committed (acquisitive) crimes. For more than half of these, crime provided a (limited) addition to legal income. "Only" 22 percent of the respondents report having acquisitive crime as a main source of income. These addicts—together with the respondents active on the (street) market of illegal drugs—belong to the group with the highest levels of consumption of both heroin and cocaine. However, this result does not necessarily mean that intensive crime is the inevitable result of an apparently serious addiction. In the light of our findings, the opposite is more likely to apply. People who earn a lot by conventional means either invest for the future or take to immoderate consumption. There is no essential difference if one is an addict, but in this case the first option is purely theoretical. A large degree of (criminal) competence and vitality and an established position in a deviant subculture make earning a lot possible. Addicts who earn a lot buy a lot of dope.

Most respondents demonstrate great variability in their use of drugs, and this is a primary indication that an addict's day-to-day behavior is not simply determined by pharmacological addiction. Only ten respondents report stable drug use during a period of one month. The rest (with the exception of a number of respondents who take methadone on prescription only) show deviations from average use that vary from 25 percent to 265 percent. The level of consumption of illegal drugs depends on earnings. Deviant drug addicts also cut their coat according to their cloth. On days of economic good fortune, they consume a lot; on "bad" days they cut back on cocaine and heroin.

Most drug-related income-generating crime consists of petty opportunistic theft. In general, the offender has no contact with the victim. This sort of crime is a nuisance and it also causes financial loss, but it does not form a direct threat to the (objective) security of city dwellers. A lot of the loss is processed through conventional economic channels and is included in the price of goods in shops and in insurance premiums. Of all offenses, shoplifting is most popular; 44 percent of all offenses reported during one month (N=951) concern shoplifting. Large department stores are the most popular victims. Almost a quarter of all offenses (23 percent) concern bicycle theft. This result shows "the other side" of what many young students in Amsterdam already know and practice. If one cycles a lot in town but does not possess $60 for a sturdy bicycle lock, one's bicycle is bound to disappear (sooner rather than later). However, $15 will buy a new bicycle that same evening at a student cafe or simply on the street.

More serious (more injurious or threatening) forms of crime were reported less frequently by our respondents: breaking into cars (10 percent), burglary (8 percent), fencing (4 percent), pickpocketing (3 percent), and other offenses (8 percent). There is every reason to consider whether special deterrent measures are conceivable, directed towards this specific group of addicts, for the more serious forms of income-generating crime in which an element of contact between offender and victim or violence could be involved. We shall return to this matter later.

In general, crime rates do not go down as a result of methadone maintenance programs. On average, the group of addicts not registered with such programs, commit the same amount of crime as those who are. The use of cocaine, gender, age, and the use of heroin (in this order) are more important correlations of crime.

However, differences in crime rates can be traced if the participation in different methadone maintenance programs is taken into account. Addicts registered at a *community station* (high threshold program) commit significantly less acquisitive crime than other addicts. Those *not* registered at a methadone program come second as far as this aspect is concerned, while the addicts who are regular visitors of the buses (low threshold program) commit the most crime. The latter result should not be interpreted as a paradoxical criminogenic effect of the drug methadone. Rather, the explanation lies in the fact that different programs attract addicts that differ in their orientation towards a deviant and criminal life-style.

Although we did not find any direct reduction of crime resulting from methadone maintenance, the programs do allow addicts to set a limit to the activities (crime) they are prepared to undertake in order to acquire income. The knowledge that methadone is relatively easy to come by (via regular maintenance programs or on the street) takes the sting out of the threat of the withdrawal symptoms that would occur if an addict lacks the money to buy heroin. It becomes easier to respect the moral boundaries that hard drug addicts also draw.

We divided the research group into three types, on the basis of different economic activities: the normalized user (63 percent of the sample), the dealing user (15 percent) and the criminal user (22 percent). For the first type a pattern of income acquisition obtains that is predominantly based on legal means. Addicts from the second category earn their money—and often drugs in kind—mainly by means of activities on the street market, while acquisitive crime forms the most dominant source of income for the third type. We found connections between this economic typology and a number of other characteristics which, together, can be traced to different life-styles. A normalized user leads a more or less stable life, helped by methadone maintenance from the community station or general practitioner. He is often still part of the scene, where he finds contacts, activities, and numerous little material advantages. But his use of expensive hard drugs is moderate and often incidental. The more chronic craving for intoxication that such addicts sometimes experience can be satisfied with less expensive drugs such as pills and alcohol. However, the hassle and turmoil of living with illegal drugs has usually disappeared. If such addicts use expensive drugs, they finance the habit from (predominantly) noncriminal sources of income by drastically cutting back spending on ("normal") costs of living, something an addict is able to do thanks to his identity and his dependent social position as an addict. Many of them can count on receiving free meals from family, or from a facility for street people in the red-light district. He doesn't pay for public transport as nobody expects him to have a ticket. And finally, his knowledge of and contacts in the scene ensure that he can lay his hands on cheap clothing or consumer goods.

The dealing user has his own place on the drug market, which is often that of small intermediary between the real dealers and the addicts. Much of his payment is in kind, thus he has relatively easy access to dope and therefore a high level of consumption. Because heroin is so easily available, he has less reason to register with a methadone program. He is fully occupied by his work on the small scale drug market. Although he also commits acquisitive crime, this is less important for his income than dealing in drugs.

The respondents who belong to the category of criminal users are hyperactive in many fields. These are the opportunists, active and alert and ready to seize any opportunity, especially as far as acquisitive crime is concerned. It is the excitement that goes with this aggressive survival strategy that makes being an addict especially attractive. On average, the criminal user also has a high level of consumption, but it is more variable than that of the addict-dealer, because it depends more on his changing fortunes. It is certainly no coincidence that these addicts are to be found on the methadone buses. The low threshold programs on the buses are functional for and easily adapted to an existence in which good fortune and bad luck follow each other around. Indeed, the criminal user does not regard methadone as an aid to kicking the habit. Rather, it is a sort of insurance against a rainy day and sometimes a (somewhat inferior) drug for getting kicks. Cocaine is important to these addicts. Their most basic opiate is (prescribed) methadone; their lust and most of their money is for cocaine. This stimulant, with its ultrashort pharmacological cycle of effects, is probably best suited to the impatient and energy-consuming hassle of being an addict.

The strong connections between criminal income acquisition and drug use that were also found in this study are most directly apparent in differences in crime between periods of abstinence and periods of drug use. During periods of abstinence, significantly less income is generated from crime than during periods of drug use. Calculated for the whole of the research group, income derived from crime during periods of abstinence is three to four times less. If we consider criminal addicts only, we find that they commit half the amount of crime during periods of abstinence.

As we have indicated in chapter 5, the difference in crime rates between Dutch addicts and addicts from Great Britain or the United States is considerable. Dutch addicts commit relatively less acquisitive crime. This picture is fairly consistent and also holds true for Korf's earlier study (1990). It is partly due to the more favorable social welfare situation in the Netherlands. Undoubtedly it is also the result of Dutch drug policy, regarded as tolerant from an international perspective. There are two important effects of the lack of repression and the readily available (therapy) amenities for addicts. The first concerns moral/social control, which also affects drug addicts. The second concerns the greater options for income acquisition available to addicts in the Netherlands. To a certain extent, Dutch social and criminal policy on drugs prevents extreme stigmatization and marginalization. Dutch junkies (at least in Amsterdam) are not forced back entirely into an anomic underworld where desperate and revengeful antisocial behavior is more or less a matter of course and easily legitimated (in one's own circle). The more pragmatic side of the fact that Dutch addicts are less "dependent" on all sorts of theft is the relatively easy accessibility of the illegal drug (street) market. A relative lack of repression by police and criminal justice authorities has meant that certain groups of addicts are able to acquire income through activities on this public hard drug market. If there are realistic behavioral alternatives, stealing and robbing are not the inevitabilities that some authors seem to suggest.

THE RELATIONSHIP BETWEEN DRUG USE AND CRIME

In chapter 2, we approached the relationship between drug use and crime in three different ways. The first two models (drug use causes crime and crime causes drug use) are highly deterministic. Both reduce the drug user to a "black box" with variations in input and output. Either the addictive drug goes in (in the most literal sense) and crime comes out or it is the other way round. The third model of explanation, however, is primarily concerned with the rationality and functionality of the deviant behavioral complex that both illegal drug use and crime form. Here the addict as a person is the central figure. An individual who is addicted to illegal drugs reacts to his situation and aspires to solutions that are determined neither by the biological conditions of addiction alone, nor by a supposedly coercive deviant socialization.

Causal explanations have the advantage of a strong internal consistency. This virtue, however, only exists at the expense of leaving aside the intentional and subjective nature of a deviant life with drugs. In turn this will easily result in generalizations about the relationship between crime and drug use that have little meaning for the social reality of the drug problem. Most of the results of this study run counter to the basic assumptions that underlie deterministic models of explanation. For example, the first model implies that methadone maintenance should lead to a reduction in crime. This study shows that only the clients of relatively high threshold methadone programs actually commit less crime than others. Clients of low threshold programs are even more criminal than addicts who are not registered at a methadone program at all. Another assumption upon which this model is based is that drug use and crime are inevitably connected. However, a substantial number of addicts do not commit criminal offenses and have never done so. It is in no way *inevitable* that drug use should lead to crime. Nevertheless, we found that a large part of the income acquired by criminal means is spent on drugs. There are many reasons why drugs have a high priority in an addict's pattern of expenditure. Orientation towards taking drugs (and perhaps towards intoxication) may even be so pervasive during the most involved phase of a drug career that it becomes the most explicit motive for (criminal) income acquisition. In this sense we may assume that a certain subgroup commits crime in order to be able to pay for drugs. As far as a limited group of addicts is concerned, and during a limited phase of their lives, drugs may provide the dominant and "manifest" reason for crime. But this does not justify the conclusion that there would be no crime in this case if there were no addiction to illegal drugs. Within another deviant style of life, a preoccupation with expensive entertainment (visits to gambling halls and discos) fulfills the same role.

The second model, in which the causal order is reversed, also contains both unjustified reductions and elements that may contribute to a usable analysis of the strong connections between drug use and crime. According to this explanation, that is based on the aetiology of drug use, the use of drugs is the (self-evident) result of socialization in a criminal environment in which drug use is seen as a "normal" form of behavior. The logical consequence of this very sociological reduction is that drug use need not have more significance than tattoos, more often seen inside than outside of prisons. We would maintain that the use of drugs does have independent functions and a significance and development of its own and that these may be disconnected from criminal socialization. This study has also uncovered a group of problematic addicts with conventional (middle-class) histories of socialization. In such cases, the development of drug use is more easily explained by personal or family pathologies than by psychologically "normal" deviant socialization. Some addicts from such backgrounds do end up (via drugs) with a highly criminal style of life, for others the limits and nature of their criminality during the whole of their career of addiction is strongly determined by their conventional socialization. On the other hand, however, this study also shows that many drug careers are indeed rooted in delinquent subcultures in which both parental environment and adolescent peer groups play a part.

At best, the validity of both causal models is limited. Individual needs, motivations, options, competence, and the presence or absence of alternatives form the restrictive conditions of validity. This study shows that hard drug users should not be regarded as the mindless victims of some white or brown powder, neither are they the mindless victims of their environment and social circumstances. They are extremely active, they make choices, and sometimes they do the unexpected. A life with drugs, of which crime is often an integral part, allows them to shape and make sense of their lives in a radical way.

Contrary to the aforementioned approaches, the career approach to the relationship between crime and drug use does not place both forms of behavior in an inevitable sequence. The significance of (individual differences in) the development, continuation, and end of a life with drugs and the possible part played by crime are considered within the more general framework of deviant life-styles. The way in which individual addicts shape their lives varies enormously, and depends on competence, ambition, motivation, external circumstances, etc.. It is impossible to explain the diversity and variability within the group of hard drug users that formed our sample, solely on the basis of the causal models. The deviant career perspective is more suitable in this respect. It fits both the hassle of junkie life as tradesmen or customers in the Amsterdam drug scene, the risky business of being a shoplifter, burglar, and heroin prostitute, but also the tired and "retired" junk, who spends his days watching television like any other citizen on the dole, and who differs from the average only in a somewhat unusual pattern of consumption. In the case of retired junkies, it is as if a conventional life-style has been transformed into a variation of living with drugs. Essentially, the same applies to the dealing user, although he really is more like a workaholic. His career is at its zenith and is situated almost entirely within the subculture of drugs. He hangs around the red-light district day and night; his working hours rarely amount to less than eighteen. He aspires to success and recognition. He certainly finds satisfaction in more than drug use alone; it also comes from his competence and from the social contacts that are inherent in his profession. The functionality of a life with drugs is similar in the case of the intensely criminal user. However, the consequences of his behavior are the most problematic for society. This is why measures aimed at deterrence are most relevant as far as this specific style of life is concerned. This is a specific group of addicts at a specific stage in their career. We shall return to this point at the end of the chapter.

In chapters 4 and 7 we reported that many addicts have periods that are more hectic, but also calmer than average and in chapter 5 we drew attention to the periods of abstinence that may occur within a drug career. There are often several such periods. A drug career may be regarded as a development over a long period of time, gradually rising towards its zenith and then decreasing again. Within this development there are phases, shorter cycles, during which an addict may be more or less involved in his career. On average, the career curve covers a period of between fifteen and twenty years, while the length of the more rapidly varying phase curve is much less regular and is influenced by a variety of external circumstances: prison sentences, illness, admittance to a therapeutic community, entering into or breaking off a relationship, the death of a friend or acquaintance, scarcity or abundance on the drug market, etc.

If dramatic events (an overdose, for example) do not lead to the career's being broken off abruptly, three options are open at the end of a "normal" career. The first is the tired, domesticated, and more or less stabilized junkie, who has seen it all before and now provides for a moderate consumption of drugs through his friends, the liquor store, the "pill bridge," and methadone maintenance: the Dutch variation on the "methadone, wine and welfare junkie" described by Preble (1977). Secondly, the ex-addict, who has put a definite stop to his career, now lives in a council house and maintains a conventional life-style. Thirdly, the socially and psychologically decrepit junk, who spends his days searching the gutter for the dope lost or hastily discarded by other people; if he fails to find enough, he will seek refuge in excessive alcohol or medicinal drug use. These junkies have ended up at the bottom of the ladder and their ability to generate income has been reduced to a minimum. Although they are the most 'visible' junks, in terms of crime control they are not the most serious problem.

POSSIBLE POLICY CONSEQUENCES

Having seen our results and conclusions, we must now turn to the possible consequences for policy that arise from them. According to the basic tenets of the Dutch drug policy, the goals of crime control should be considered within the wider context of a public health and welfare policy. The primal question would be whether the results warrant a fundamental change of current drug policy. Such a change could take one of two directions, both of which would mean radicalization: on the one hand an increase in police repression and control by means of criminal law, and on the other decriminalization and legalization of hard drugs. A third option is to stick to the essentials of current Dutch (i.e., Amsterdam) drug policy and to introduce a number of adaptations: reformation, therefore, of drug policy.

In this section we will have a closer look at these three options without any pretence at dealing with all the pros and cons imaginable.

Two Radical Policy Models

Current drug policy in the Netherlands is a compromise between prohibition and legalization (ISAD 1985). Although there seems to be a gradual change in favor of the Dutch model, there has been, and sometimes still is, harsh criticism of it to some extent in the Netherlands itself, and much more abroad. The critics occupy two contrary positions. On the one hand, (criminal justice) policy in the field of drugs is seen as too soft, defeatist, diffident, and providing implicit legitimation for the use of dangerous drugs. The result of this assumed lack of energetic action is said to be a "Mecca" for international trade, a "paradise" for addicts, "deteriorating" public order and "flourishing" crime. These critics regard a radical increase in police and criminal justice activities as self-evident improvements to policy.

Criticism from the opposite side maintain that it is the illegality of a life with drugs that is decisive in leading to decay, far-reaching marginalization, and crime. In this notion, the drug problem is not so much a matter of drugs, as a matter of policy. The solution is simple: somehow or other, hard drugs must be legalized. The Netherlands even have a promising precedent. Cannabis use as a social problem, a great worry to many twenty years ago, was simply solved by normalizing and integrating the consumption market within the regular economic order (Jansen 1989) and doing away with criminal justice repression (except for the wholesalers). Cohen (1987) has argued that there is no reason why this same cannabis policy should not be extended to include cocaine.

Legalization does not imply that heroin and cocaine will "be found on the shelves in the supermarket." There are many other forms of regulation that would provide an alternative to penal prohibition. Moreover, in the light of a comparison between the alcohol and drug problem, it seems obvious that legalization would remove an incentive to income-generating crime and would also reduce social and health risks to *addicts*. What can this study tell us about such opposite radicalizations of drug policy?

Inevitably, increasing drug law enforcement would have repercussions for the way in which addicts lead their lives with drugs. Increasing criminal justice pressure would cause addicts to continue their activities underground, as is the case in countries where criminalization and law enforcement are prominent features. They will go underground for fear of being arrested. The street market, currently fairly accessible, will partly disappear and partly change character. The result may well be that public order problems in what is now drug territory will decrease. But violence and paranoia on the drug market will undoubtedly increase, while we must expect the market to spread out over the city. We must also expect an increase in acquisitive crime as a result of criminal justice repression. Addicts who are now able to provide for their addiction by providing (intermediary) services on the drug market, will have to "fall back on" acquisitive crime in order to be able to exist. Simulation research based on empirical data by Hoekstra (1987) has shown that increasing police pressure on the hard drug retail market would result in more acquisitive crime. From a social point of view, a shift from small-scale dealing to stealing hardly seems an improvement. Dealing drugs is, of course, a criminal offense, but there is no "innocent" victim in the usual sense of the word. Transactions on the drug market are agreed to by both parties: dealer and addicts. They are economic agreements, with the same rationality and lack of damage to third party interests as an agreement between punter and prostitute. In the Netherlands, the criminal justice system has a tradition of minimal moralization, and such "victimless" crime is regulated predominantly from a public order perspective.

Another result will be that addicts will be less accessible to organizations for public health and or social welfare. In practice, Dutch policy has developed a degree of coordination between the executives of criminal and social drug policy. Because this policy gives priority to aspects of public health and social welfare, it is important that penal repression does not interfere too much with welfare and therapy activities. There is, for example, an arrangement in Amsterdam between the police and the methadone maintenance programs that there will be no police activity (arrests) in the immediate vicinity of distribution points. In practice, public health and welfare agencies are involved with individual addicts, while the criminal justice authorities refrain from interfering with possession of drugs for personal use. Dutch drug addicts are much more prosecuted for crimes under the criminal code (i.e., more traditional felonies) than for infringements of the Opium Act (Rook and Essers 1988; Rüter 1988; de Beaufort 1989).

During the past decades, a concentration on low threshold programs for drug addicts has created a relatively easily accessible addict population. On a yearly basis, about 60 percent of the addicts in Amsterdam are known at methadone maintenance programs (Buning 1990). Nationally, this statistic 75 percent (Driessen 1990). A policy that is more heavily oriented to enforcing the Opium Act will threaten the link between addict population and regular society. This means that *maximization* of law enforcement will inevitably and adversely affect a policy oriented towards public health goals and the solution of the secondary problems arising from drug addiction (Mol and Trautmann 1990). The following example serves to demonstrate the actual effects of penal repression. In New York City alone there are an estimated 200,000 heroin addicts (2.5 percent of the total population), of whom the great majority take heroin intravenously, while about 50 percent are HIV-positive (Wever 1990). As a comparison: there are about 6,300 heroin addicts in Amsterdam (0.8 percent of the total population), of whom about 40 percent inject, while about 15 percent of the total heroin population are HIV-positive (Buning 1992).

Thus, the prevention of crime is not to be achieved without endangering the relatively benign social and health consequences of illegal drug addiction in the Netherlands. And viewed from a separate perspective of criminal justice interests, one should also not underestimate a number of administrative effects. If police and penal repression and a move towards prohibition are to be real policy alternatives, the police force will have to be reinforced, with regard to both manpower and powers of investigation. And if such penal policies are to succeed, penitentiary capacity must be increased. The net result of such measures at an administrative level is an increase in workload and (personnel) costs that is difficult to estimate.

The other radical alternative involves the further decriminalization and eventually the legalization of hard drugs. We shall examine this option as if it were possible for the Netherlands to take such measures without coming up against international agreements and treaties. To that extent, this is an academic question. Nevertheless, it is worth looking into here. Considering our research aims, we shall restrict ourselves to the demand side of the problem. Three themes keep occurring in the debate on legalization. They concern addicts' crime rates, the number of those addicted to hard drugs, and public health risks.

We shall consider the possible effects of legalization on crime committed by addicts in the light of the deviant career perspective that we found to be the most plausible explanation for the results of this study. The perspective implies that hard drug users play a certain active role in setting out on and continuing a life with drugs, that they make choices, and that they are usually well aware of the (direct) consequences of such choices. Chapters 2 and 3 show that there are both theoretical and empirical reasons for maintaining that, in a sense, they aspire to a deviant existence, because it provides a solution to individual problems that concern both social position and personal development. The illegality of the drugs used, and the illegality that therefore surrounds a life with drugs, is not a coincidental property of a drug that is sought after solely for its pharmacological effects. In other words, people who are attracted to illegal drugs are looking not only for dope, but also for illegality.

Logically, of course, this is a strong argument in favour of *minimizing* penal repression. However, for precisely the same reason, it is not a compelling argument for totally doing away with penal repression. Legalization may remove one of the elements of a deviant life-style, but it will not influence the "search" for, the motivation for, and the (social) conditions that underlie that lifestyle. An interest in deviance may be fulfilled by taking drugs, thanks to legislation, moral codes, and fashion. In this sense, being an addict is no more, nor less, than a historical form of deviance, a bed along which a river of delinquent behavior, among other things, flows. A change in fashion or legislation may change the course of the stream, but this is not to say that it will also run dry.

The results of this study, among others, show that addicts, at a certain stage in their development, are able to live "quiet" lives, despite the current illegal status of hard drugs. It seems that an optimal reduction of drug-related crime can be achieved if the criminalization of drug addicts is as moderate as possible. From the point of view of crime prevention, legalization is not necessary for those who have had enough of an illegal existence, and not enough for those for whom that existence still fulfills many functions. The assumption that legalization would immediately reduce drug-related crime derives from the same causal assumption underlying the (falsified) hypothesis that methadone maintenance will lead to a reduction in crime rates.

As far as the problem of drug-related crime is concerned, legalization would be much more effective with regard to the supply side of the problem. This study did not aim to examine that aspect. The most relevant arguments for and against legalization concern the tension between primary and secondary prevention of drug addiction. This theme is especially relevant to social drug policy and only partially affects penal policy. For that reason we shall deal with it very briefly. Social drug policy aims on the one hand at restricting the spread of drug taking as such, and on the other at limiting the adverse effects of drug taking that is already established. It is highly likely that legalization would have contradictory effects on these important policy goals. Lifting the prohibition on drugs will reduce the taboo on drug taking and increase the availability of drugs through different channels. One need only look at the (pseudo) legalization of pornography and cannabis. They are offered for consumption very much more frequently than they were in the days when they were still banned and the ban enforced. There is no reason at all to suppose that things would be different in the case of heroin and cocaine.

As well as probably increasing the availability of drugs, legalization would also lead to changes in the attraction and significance of hard drugs. It is difficult to estimate what changes in the functions of hard drug use would take place and to what extent these would result in changes and increases in the consumer population. At least two important factors are at work here. On the one hand drugs would be less attractive as an expression of a deviant style of life, and this could mean that the number of users would decrease. Or, as Nadelmann (1991) puts it with regard to Dutch cannabis policy: "The policy has succeeded (...) in making drug use boring." On the other hand, greater accessibility could lead to more experimental users. However, experimental use need not become problematic use (Zinberg 1984; Cohen 1990). The greatest social (public health) risk attached to legalization may well be the greatly lowered threshold (both practical and psychological) for "normal" populations. We do not really want adolescents, at odds with school, their parents, and themselves, to be able to escape too easily to a pharmacologically created other world. The "coffee shops" are already a place of asylum for some of these kids. The question of whether horse and coke would figure there on the menu after legalization is not just a figment of the imagination.

On the other hand, it is indisputable that the problems attached to hard drug users would be greatly diminished after legalization. The illegality and marginality of being an addict would largely disappear. The significance of drug scenes would be greatly diminished. The quality of drugs would be controllable, the conditions in which they are taken more hygienic, and developments around infectious "drug diseases" such as hepatitis B and AIDS more easily monitored.

On the demand side, the social problem of drugs can be defined as the product of two variables, the *number* of drug users and the *extent* of the problems per user. The question then arises as to the necessity of making concessions to the primary prevention of hard drug use for the sake of the secondary prevention of risk. There are many reasons for assuming that there is no great need to legalize drugs in the Netherlands. From an epidemiological point of view, problematic drug use is a reasonably restricted and stable phenomenon. Pragmatic Dutch drug policy allows a variety of control strategies. Legalization is the obvious option if the "war on drugs" is lost. Contrary to the United States, there is, fortunately, no such war in the Netherlands.

Reformation of Drug Policy

As has been explained before, current Dutch drug policy -with regard to the demand side of the problem is meant to be pragmatic, rational, and normalizing (Engelsman 1988; van de Wijngaart 1991; Leuw 1991). Its central aim is to control the problems associated with drugs in terms of public health, the "livability" of the city and public order, and not primarily minimize the use of illegal drugs absolutely by all possible means, as is the case under traditonal prohibitionistic regimes (MacCoun 1993). However, one cannot pretend that the problem of drugs and drug-related crime (the major drug problem element of this study) in the Netherlands is really under control.

This study has shown that the most concrete and central policy measure—methadone maintenance—only leads to a reduction in crime rates under certain conditions and for a certain category of addicts. These conditions include urine tests, obligatory contacts with social workers from the public health services, and daily visits to a methadone program. Such conditions are to be found at the community stations. According to this study, addicts in another category (the clients of the methadone buses) are even more criminal than addicts who are not registered with a methadone program. The above-mentioned conditions do not apply on the buses, where the threshold is lower and there are no obligations attached to methadone distribution.[1]

The easiest, but also most deceptive, reaction would be to simply make the regime on the buses stricter. Unfortunately, in that case we may not expect the results to be more similar to those of the community stations. The relative success of methadone programs at the community stations is determined not by their regime, but by their clients' motivation. This study shows that different types of methadone programs attract different types of addicts for whom methadone fulfills different functions.

Assuming the aforegoing, a stricter regime on the buses would probably merely result in them becoming less accessible to the category of junkies who originally visited them, rather than substantially affecting the clients' criminal style of life. The most impor-

---

1. The differentiation in types of methadone programs has almost disappeared since 1991 (see chapter 7), but our reasoning still holds true.

tant function of low threshold programs is to allow practically all addicts, despite their deviant lives, some form of voluntary contact with institutions from conventional society. The ties with society have not been cut entirely. This makes it easier to exchange a deviant career for a more accepted existence whenever the individual course of drug addiction allows for such improvement.

In order to promote the most basic public health aims of drug policy, perhaps we shall just have to accept that methadone maintenance does not necessarily lead to a reduction in crime rates. In this view, the methadone bus is merely a stepping-stone towards a more regulated way of life. Something has to be offered if one wishes to establish and maintain contact with addicts who are not (yet) willing to give up drugs. That something is methadone. An invitation to come and have a chat every week is not enough.

This is not to say that low threshold methadone programs may not also have a certain effect in reducing crime. Although it is difficult to prove with this kind of study, it is not unlikely that relatively easily available methadone allows the criminal addict to stay within his own (moral) boundaries, so that he will be less quick to push his attempts to generate income beyond them.

Our results, especially those pertaining to the community stations, show that methadone maintenance does have a role to play in regulating a life with drugs. A direct crime-reducing effect of methadone maintenance is highly unlikely. Methadone is more likely to offer a welcome opportunity to anybody wishing (for whatever reason) to lead a different sort of life (for a while). Without this alternative, it would be more difficult, and sometimes impossible, to make the change to a calmer life with drugs.

All in all, the most obvious course is to look at methadone maintenance from a public health perspective, and not to expect too much as far as crime control is concerned. And yet, there is no reason why one should not also think about ways of providing methadone that would enhance its social-regulatory effects. Before we look into this question further, let us first examine the matter of providing the drug (heroin) itself in a social-medical context, instead of its substitute methadone.

The history of the official distribution of heroin or another natural opiate such as morphine, goes back a long way. During the sixties, a certain group of progressive politicians in the United States saw heroin distribution as a way of dealing with an increasing drug problem. However, there were unusually sharp protests against the plans, especially from the black community: "homicidal (...) a plan to enslave the ghetto youth" (Derks 1990). As a result of this controversy, heroin was distributed on a very limited experimental scale only. Other examples of heroin distribution are Great Britain and Italy (van Dijk 1984; Derks 1990; Pearson 1991).

Heroin was never provided officially in the Netherlands. There was, however, a lot of heated discussion about it—especially in Amsterdam. The plans centered around a regulated heroin maintenance program for a limited group of highly problematic addicts. The aim of such programs was explicitly not to be crime control. The main issues were those of public health. Only heroin was to be provided, because this opiate leads to physical dependence. Research in Utrecht showed that more than 30 percent of the heroin users interviewed had no desire to make use of heroin distribution. They had not yet given up hope of ever giving up drugs and were afraid that this would be more difficult if heroin were to be so easily available (Elzakker and Steinbusch 1982). The Amsterdam plans for heroin prescription faded away after the government in the Hague had forbidden heroin distribution (but not before there had been heated protests from the Federal Republic of Germany and Sweden).

The main reason for taking a renewed look at the medical distribution of heroin is the more recent identification of intravenous drug users as one of the factors in the spread of the HIV virus. Our discussion of the course of drug careers showed, among other things, that in any event one scenario leads to a deterioration in psychological, social, and medical respects. This relatively small group of addicts also demonstrates risky behavior in relation to HIV infection. Because their ability to generate income has decreased to a minimum, they search the streets for what others have left. They use, for example, syringes that have been used before. Because they are especially fixed on heroin, supervised distribution of the drug could perhaps mean that such behavior would become less "necessary." This specific purpose of heroin distribution only concerns a limited group of addicts at the extreme fringe of the population of hard drug users.

As a means of dealing with the whole range of problems arising from hard drug use, however, there is sufficient reason to refute large-scale distribution of heroin. This study has confirmed that the (Amsterdam) drug problem is a polydrug problem; a majority of addicts consume not only heroin, but also cocaine, to a smaller extent this is also true for medicinal drugs and alcohol. Although cocaine scarcely leads to physical dependence in a pharmacological sense, even more than heroin it is suited to a deviant life-style. It would, therefore, be quite irrational to distribute heroin on a large scale, but not cocaine. But this would mean that medical motives would no longer provide the legitimation for distribution. The state would be providing the kicks. At the very least, this would open up a whole new dimension of the welfare state.

Leaving aside this social-philosophical aspect of prescription, considering the results of this study it does not seem likely that the distribution of heroin and cocaine would contribute substantially to crime control. There is no reason to assume that the conclusion that a reduction in crime rates has more to do with the type of addict and his motivation than with the availability and distribution of replacement drugs would not hold true for the distribution of the drugs themselves.

We are still left with the question of whether, and to what extent, existing low threshold methadone programs could contribute more significantly to the prevention of crime, without detriment to the (primary) aims of social drug policy. Because our study was not aimed at evaluation of the sociomedical programs for drug addicts, we are unable to make detailed suggestions here. However, what we can do is debate some of the points of principle.

One of the explicit aims of the two-pronged approach in Amsterdam is the prevention of nuisance and crime by drug addicts (Gemeente Amsterdam 1985). However, contrary to public health goals, this aim is only implicitly present in the daily practice of methadone maintenance programs. There is an implicit assumption, and hope, that the distribution of methadone will also favorably influence an addict's social behavior. However, in practice many a methadone client has knocked back his daily swig for years and then left, sometimes after a chat with a colleague in the back of the bus, for an unknown destination in town. Officially the program provides for contact between each client and one of its social workers once in every three months. It would perhaps be possible to create conditions under which these methadone maintenance programs would become less freewheeling. The basis could be twofold: more explicit reciprocity between the program and the client and an extension of the options attached to the program and aimed at promoting integration. These basic requirements derive directly from the explicit aims of Dutch drug policy (ISAD 1985). However, reciprocal relationships in current low threshold methadone programs are few and far between.

At the same time, it is important to safeguard the fundamental accessibility of methadone maintenance programs. The threshold for registration with such programs must not be raised. As they become attached to the program, suitable clients should be provided with help to adjust socially. An alternative approach could be developed within the current social-medical practice that dominates methadone maintenance programs, with more elements of social casework and social therapy. What we are suggesting here is a separate project, for those addicts who are expected to be able to follow such a program reasonably successfully. The other programs would then act as "institutions of reference." Social work would have more significance than it has at present in methadone maintenance programs: more frequent contact with addicts and a more active role in tracing potential candidates, with special attention paid to their social functioning and motivation (or possibilities for motivating them). Possibly this approach is most suited to addicts who have passed the climax of involvement in a life with drugs and are aware of more conventional options with regard to their style of life.

Proceeding on the principle of reciprocity, it will probably be necessary to "persuade" addicts who are considered suitable to take part in such a project. This (experimental) project will, of course, require the creation of material, institutional, and organizational conditions; in other words, it will cost more money.

The following idea may serve as an illustration. The client can opt for a program of six months, with a flexible package of activities that take up a total of about twenty hours a week. Whoever opts for this program is bound to follow it, perhaps contractually. Failure to cooperate will have consequences. A standard package of activities would be made up of four parts: work, development, individual therapy, and sport/recreation. Whoever finishes the program can then enroll in an extension to it. Whoever drops out without good reason (or can no longer be tolerated) loses the right to free methadone. However, the dropouts will still be able to obtain methadone from the methadone program at an affordable price. This "punishment period" will last until the end of the program, but a maximum period could be set.

The work project that is part of the Drug Related Crime project in Rotterdam provides an actual example of a conscious attempt to reintegrate drug users. The program has three parts: work, training, and development. It takes one and a half years. The evaluation of the project (Intraval 1990) shows that 27 percent of the participants who started actually went through the whole program; a large number of these have found steady jobs.

The above is mainly based on a drug-therapy approach. Clients are asked to respond to the fact that they have approached a methadone maintenance program of their own accord and are receiving help free of charge. The criminal justice system, however, has its own claims, responsibilities, and options when dealing with drug addicts who have committed criminal offenses. Consistency in a drug policy that aspires to a mimimum of moral or criminal stigmatization of drug use requires that drug-related crime be approached in the same way as any other crime. Drug users are not being punished for using drugs; but neither does the fact that they are addicted excuse their crimes. On the other hand, there is little reason to regard the most frequent types of crime committed by drug addicts, as the results of this study show, as an exceptional threat to legal order. Shoplifting is an everyday occurrence and is certainly not only committed by drug addicts. The same applies to breaking into cars, usually thought of as a typical junkie offense, but probably commited most by nonaddicts (Bureau regionaal coördinator voorkoming misdrijven 1985).

On the basis of our data, we would estimate that about 40 percent of drug-related crime is frequent, opportunistic theft. In this case, deterrence policy should concentrate on offenses more than on offenders. It is important to develop effective measures for the prevention of the phenomenon of shoplifting. It is less relevant whether such offenses are committed by shop personnel, middle-class school kids, housewives, or junkies. By far the most adequate social reaction for controlling this crime problem is shop security. The other half of drug-related crime consists generally of Opium Act offenses (illegal dealing) and of relatively more serious and intensive forms of crime, committed by a highly criminal subgroup of the addict population. From the point of view of deterrence, to our mind this latter group deserves most attention.

Acquisitive crime is the most important source of income for about 20 percent of drug addicts. Slightly more than half of this group (13 percent of the total sample) are very active in this field. On average, they commit twenty-nine offenses a month with a minimum gain of $571, and a median gain of $1,543. Our data reveal that this small subgroup (in total 19 of the 148 persons) is responsible for the greatest number of offenses committed by the sample. For this intensely criminal segment of the addict population, an offender approach to deterrence is the more obvious choice. Empirical and theoretical findings from this study lead us to the conclusion that we are dealing here with a limited number of addicts in what is normally a limited phase in their career. If such intensely criminal addicts could be identified *as such* by the police and if they could then be adequately held responsible for their criminal behavior *pattern*, this would have the effect of importantly reducing crime rates.

One may well argue that in the Dutch case of generally short-term imprisonment,[2] longer prison sentences are an adequate reaction for the relatively small group of addicts whose life with drugs is distinctly antisocial. At the height of a drug career, the deterrent effect of detention on crime is considerable: people who are in prison cannot commit crimes. It has even been suggested that the apparently uninhibited criminal behavior displayed by this category of addicts, whose life with drugs may become psychopathic, might warrant coercive admission to a mental hospital, also known as detainment at the government's pleasure (Leuw 1991). A danger criterion would be important here. However, this study did not produce much in the way of violent crime by drug addicts.[3]

Because of the great diversity of the population of problematic drug users, policy that differentiates according to the sort and type of user is probably more effective than policy that claims to have found a ready-made solution to the drug problem. Policy modifi-

---

2. In 1990 more than 80 percent of the prison sentences where not exceeding one year of imprisonment.
3. It should be noted that our respondents were thought to be reluctant to admit to offenses involving an element of violence (see Appendix).

cations should be applicable to extreme groups within the addict population. Such differentiated policy can provide measures that keep up with individual or social injuriousness. That is to say, addicts who primarily both run and pose risks in terms of public health (the addicts who are in a state of psychological, social, and medical deterioration) should also be approached within that framework. One way would be to distribute the drugs themselves, as well as or instead of methadone. At the other extreme of the addict population we find frequent and uninhibited crime. The approach to this group should be less forthcoming. If criminal offenses are found to have been committed, a longer prison sentence is worth considering. A large middle of the road group lives a relatively innocent life with drugs. A policy of differentiation based on the different life-styles and the nature and development of the drug careers linked to them should leave these relatively innocent illegal drug users enough room to carry on as usual, or perhaps even give them more.

EPILOGUE

SOME CONSIDERATIONS FOR THE INTERNATIONAL PROHIBITIONISTIC POLICY PERSPECTIVE

More than is true for any other social and public health problem, drug policy has become a highly internationalized issue. Supranational conventions and agreements on practical drug policy leave little room for an independent and truly national response to the use and trafficking of illegal drugs. Significantly, this limitation of autonomy of single nations is much more typical for "international security" issues than for the kind of problems, which at least within the Dutch perspective, is first and foremost an issue of public health and welfare.

Within a unifying Europe a drug-political coalition has developed under the historically strong ideological (prohibitionist) leadership of the United States. This international system constrains the drug policies of single nations in a similar way as foreign policy options were constrained during the Cold War era. In this sense the United States has exerted an extremely successful leadership in coining the societal response to drug problems as "WAR" instead as normal, peaceful means to ameliorate inevitable adversities. Unfortunately the United States has been considerably less effective in reversing the trend of escalating violence, health damage, and social damage of the illegal drug phenomenon. This combination of American drug-political (ideological) preeminence on the one hand and a dramatic failure in actual problem solving on the other makes it inevitable that questions about the possible applicability of the Dutch approach will first of all pertain to the United States.

In a more general sense this book has highlighted a prominent and universal harmful secondary effect of illegal drug use, drug-related criminality, within the accommodating Dutch social context. For obvious reasons it does not make any sense to comparatively evaluate drug-related criminality as just one isolated element of the drug problem. Judging the importance of more or less income-generating delinquency of drug addicts will be strongly dependent on several other outcome indicators. To name just the most obvious: the violence of illegal drug trafficking, the nuisance and turmoil of drug taking and drug dealing for city communities, the level of social and health devastation connected to illegal drug addiction, the epidemiology of (dangerous) drug use, the level of social conflict and anxiety, and finally the moral significance connected to the drug phenomenon. Judging the desirability of (drug) policy results should, at least in our view, be decided on a national level. This means that for the United States there will be nothing to learn from the Dutch drug policy experiment if clear moral proscriptions against drug indulgence and "respect for the law" have strong priority. In this case social devastation and the rate of HIV infection among drug users is the price that has to be paid to maintain the clear (moral) standards of conventionality.

The decline of drug addicts might (sadly or grimly) even be accepted as a functional deterrent of addiction and a reinforcer of conventionality. If fundamental prohibitionism, that is, the reduction of the amount of drugs available and level of drug use, remains the bottom line in the American policy debate (Maccoun 1993), the effects of the Dutch approach explicitly aiming at harm reduction will scarcely be relevant for the United States. Recently, however, skepticism with law enforcement as the prevailing instrument for controlling illegal drug use may be increasing. Consequently, there may be more scope for compromising tactics. Essentially these entail some acceptance of the primary risks of drug use (the psychopharmacological hazards for public health) for the sake of a reduction of secondary risks such as drug-related crime, marginality, and violence. This shift in policy orientation has been noticed to occur both nationally within the United States, as within the international drug policy institutions (Reuter 1993; Pearson 1993; Kaplan et al. 1994; NeVIV 1993).

If on a drug-philosophical and drug-political level a shift to less law enforcement and more harm reduction becomes feasible, the consequences of the "Dutch experiment," which in a profound sense have been the theme of this study, may become increasingly relevant for the United States. The results of this study allow us to assume that in the Netherlands illegal drug use, drug addiction, and drug trading is comparatively less punishing for drug users as well as for the community. At the same time the Dutch illegal drug phenomenon is clearly more insolent and provocative to conventional principles of sanity and decency. Dutch drug users are comparatively less likely to be highly criminal, alienated, and antagonistic and to perish under their unwise habits. The Dutch consumers' market for illegal drugs is open, visible, and unabashed, as well as relatively quiet and peaceful. These assumedly objective blessings of the Dutch approach come at a price which, depending on views on public health and morals, may be deemed more or less acceptable. The utter consequence of the accommodating Dutch approach is the presence of "pseudo-legal" cannabis cafe's all over Amsterdam and other Dutch towns, and Amsterdam junkies who candidly prepare their treat of cocaine or heroin in the midst of a "normal" Amsterdam street car, with its "normal" passengers and the intransigence of annoying concentrations of junkie crowds in downtown areas.

No drug policy can be shaped or redirected without taking into account the possibilities and the limitations of a given society. Assuming their acceptability in principle, the feasibility of Dutch ways of drug control will be limited, relative to unyielding structural and cultural conditions which exist in the United States. The highly sociomedicalized approach to deviant drug addicts in the Netherlands is based on a comprehensive public system of health insurance, a vast and publicly funded system of welfare (social work, drug assistance) facilities, and the availability of substantial welfare allowances for any adult citizen without regular sources of income. If, such as seems to be the case in the United States, poverty is the inevitable condition in "drug-addicted communities," while structural increases of public welfare and health resources are politically inexpedient, there will be less room for the appeasing tactics of the Dutch approach. In the American case the eventual abolition of all penal drug legislation may turn out to be a more realistic alternative to the "War on Drugs." As the (recent) normative development against problematic use of alcohol and tobacco in the United States has shown, if repression fails, unhealthy habits can be effectively restrained by different means.

APPENDIX

METHODOLOGY

Nature of the Data

The quantitative data derive mainly from interviews according to a standardized questionnaire, completed in principle seven times by each respondent. Every interview provided information on his economic behavior during the seven days prior to the interview. During the following two weeks, the questionnaire was repeated twice. Thereafter less frequently, namely four times during a whole year (once every quarter).

During the quarterly interviews both the standard questionnaire and an intake list were used. The latter was designed to register developments in the field of social benefits, housing, work, and methadone maintenance.

Each respondent was also interviewed about his/her life history. Together with our field observations, this interview played an important part in putting our "hard" data into perspective.

Weekly Questionnaire

The weekly questionnaire provided the most important quantitative information. It was structured so as to provide information from all respondents on spending, income, and drug use.

Spending There is a differentiation in this category between expenditure for drugs and for other items, such as housing, food, transport, recreation, etc. Expenditure for drugs covers the sum of money per day spent on each drug used and the amount bought. Drugs included were: heroin, cocaine, Rohypnol (flunitrazepam), other sleeping tablets, and tranquilizers. As far as alcohol is concerned, respondents were asked about the sum spent weekly and the amount used weekly, while only the sum spent was noted with regard to cannabis and "other drugs" (such as amphetamines and trips).

The purchase of drugs does not automatically imply that the purchaser will consume them himself. It may well be that some will be passed on to a fellow user. Again, drugs that have been bought may not always reach the bloodstream for other reasons: lost, stolen, impounded, bought rubbish (cough drops instead of heroin, for example). In order to obtain a picture that was as complete as possible, we also asked a number of questions about such "items of loss."

Income We distinguished between legal and illegal income. In a number of cases, this distinction proved to be too sharp because there is also a grey area which is neither the one nor the other. Strictly speaking, working while receiving social benefit ("moonlighting") or working and not paying tax can also be considered illegal. Under certain circumstances, the same applies to streetwalking. To keep things simple, we regarded these grey areas as legal sources of income for the purpose of this study.

Besides working (or moonlighting) and prostitution, the questionnaire included as legal sources of income: social benefit, gambling, begging, borrowing, receiving gifts (either money or drugs), and "doing odd jobs." The latter category includes selling one's own possessions or clean needles, cleaning windows, sweeping the pavement, helping bar personnel to unload a lorry, etc.

In the field of acquisitive crime, the following offenses received special attention: shoplifting, stealing bicycles, breaking into cars, breaking into buildings, robbery, fencing, and other forms of "theft" (such as obtaining by means of false pretences, stealing from offices, etc.). In the case of shoplifting the questionnaire distinguished between theft for personal use and theft in order to subsequently sell stolen goods. In the latter case, money or drugs were actually earned, in the former expenses saved. Weekly frequency, type of goods obtained, shop value of and actual gain from those goods were registered with regard to all these offenses.

The drug trade, especially on the street, is fairly difficult to unravel because drugs are generally distributed through a number of intermediaries. The questionnaire had to be suited to asking about such networks. Respondents were asked, for example, whether they had sold drugs during the previous week and, if so, whether they were acting independently or as an intermediary. We then asked whether the respondent had played some other role in the drug trade (for example bringing clients and dealer together, acting as a lookout during a drug deal, keeping drugs for a dealer, etc.). Because many activities in the drug trade are not rewarded with money but with drugs, gains were not only calculated in guilders but also in grams.

Drug Consumption After respondents had reported items concerning spending and income during the previous week, they were asked about their drug consumption. To a certain extent, these questions acted as a check on the reliability of answers to the previous questions, because respondents had to think again about the drugs they had bought or earned on a certain day, how much they had given away, sold, or lost, and how much they had retained for personal consumption. Daily amounts consumed for heroin, cocaine, Rohypnol, other sleeping tablets, tranquilizers and alcohol, and weekly cannabis consumption were registered.

Because one of the central questions in this study concerned the influence of methadone maintenance programs on economic behavior, questions were included on consumption of this opiate and the manner in which it was obtained. Both the regular methadone distribution and the black market were taken into account. In this way we did not lose track of respondents who were not registered with a methadone program but who bought the drug on the street. Respondents who were registered with a program where they are regularly allowed to take a certain amount of methadone home were explicitly asked about what had happened to it: personal use, sale, or shared use.

Life History Interview The life history interview was a partly structured interview. A list of topics was compiled beforehand, but it left the field-workers enough scope to conduct the interview as they saw fit. Most respondents spoke freely about themselves and did not seem to identify the life history interview with the psychosocial conversations they had so often had with social workers or therapists.

A number of data from the life history interviews were processed quantitatively. The field-workers also drew up a crime profile for statistical processing of all of their respondents, while special attention was paid to prostitution activities and the spread of HIV in the research group.

The most important contribution of the life history interview to this project was "verstehend." It allowed us to penetrate more deeply into the motives of drug users.

Field Notes The third method of data collection involved an ethnographic approach. Based at a field station specially set up for this project, field-workers and researchers regularly visited the inner city and the places where methadone is distributed. Each member of the team recorded all kinds of observational information in their own diary; the field notes could be consulted by the other members at the field station.

Our fieldwork started in May 1987. The last material was collected more than two years later, in July 1989.

Reliability and Validity of Research Data

Both in and outside of the world of research, the reliability of information provided by drug users is regarded with skepticism. Nevertheless, literature (on drugs) shows that self-report data are not necessarily less reliable than other data (Amsel et al. 1976; Stephens 1972). In the Netherlands there are researchers who regard information provided by drug users as highly reliable (Hoekstra 1987; Korf 1986).

There are concrete indications that the standard of reliability of our data is acceptable. Because of the longitudinal aspect of the project, recurring patterns of behavior for each respondent could be identified. They would report having committed the same type of offense again and again, for example, while certain patterns also became apparent in their use of psychotropic substances.

Another check was provided by a number of business and friendly relations within the network of respondents. Because several respondents went out to acquire their income together, separate interviews with these "partners in crime" allowed us to check whether their information tallied. In practice, we found that it usually did.

Finally, the countless observations of and informal conversations with our respondents during the fieldwork gave us a background against which to judge the credibility of their behavior as they reported it. Direct observation was sometimes the best way to find out about their life-style. An increasingly more detailed picture of our respondents' lives often resulted from requested or unrequested information from the drugs scene.

As we were asking the respondents for retrospective information about their economic behavior during the seven days prior to the interview, it is not impossible that some information was inaccurate because respondents simply did not remember. Those with very busy lives were sometimes unable to remember what they had been doing five or six days previously. However, considering research abroad on over and underreporting and the use of drugs (Amsel et al. 1976; Ben-Yehuda 1980; McGlothlin et al. 1978), there seems to be little reason to fear any systematic loss of memory.

There are some indications that two aspects remained relatively underexposed. One is the use of alcohol, the other the use of violence. As far as alcohol is concerned, in our opinion its use was structurally underreported. This could be explained by the fact that the use of alcohol is socially accepted. As a result, respondents were less likely to remember whether they had drunk alcohol.

The fact that the use of violence was something of a background issue in this project is probably attributable to both a shortcoming in the questionnaire and to a certain reluctance on the part of the respondents. To start with, our standardized questionnaire only had room for the question of whether the respondent had used violence in the commission of acquisitive crime. Therefore, no systematic information is available on the use of physical violence during interactions with other users, dealers, or police officers. In the light of our observations we would say that this is when most violence occurs. Moreover, the number of registered robberies with violence reported on the questionnaires by no means matches the number of remarks by respondents reported in the field notes that "they had once done that." The respondents were probably more likely to give a socially desirable (negative) answer here, than if crime without violence was concerned. Offenses such as shoplifting in big department stores, bicycle theft, breaking into cars, etc., were reported candidly and even with some pride, but as soon as the subject of violence was broached, respondents became reluctant to pursue the issue.

A Closer Look at the Sample

Demographical Description of the Sample This description of the sample represents the state of affairs at the moment at which the respondents were interviewed for the first time.

Our aim was to achieve a representative sample with regard to the different ways in which methadone is distributed to drug users in Amsterdam (modality of distribution). Table A–1 shows the numbers of respondents.

TABLE A–1
Number of Respondents by Modality of Distribution

Modality of Distribution	N
Community Stations	43
Buses	41
General Practitioners	15
Consultation Bureau for Alcohol and Drugs	5
Evening Consulting Hour	1
Total	105

The methadone component of the sample takes the background characteristics of age, sex, and ethnic background into account. Table A-2 shows the composition of the sample, according to these three variables.

TABLE A–2
Composition of Sample: Age by Gender and Ethnicity

	Male		Female	
Age	Dutch	Surinamese/ Antillian	Dutch	Surinamese/ Antillian
>20	3	0	3	0
20–25	11	1	9	2
25–30	29	3	13	2
>30	38	21	13	2
Total	81	25	38	6

The average age of the respondents is over thirty. This agrees with a trend also noted in other publications (Buning 1986 1987 1988 and 1990; Bartelds et al. 1987; Intraval 1989): for a number of years now the average age of opiate users has been rising. The main cause is the fact that young people are not taking to regular opiate use. Our interviewers had great difficulty in finding young (<20 years old) users, an indication that the trend is still being maintained.

Little is known about the composition of the population of drug users who do not regularly receive methadone. This segment of the sample was put together by means of the so-called snowball method (Biernacki and Waldorf 1981). In short, the snowball method involves interviewers (or "bounty hunters" as Korf [1986] calls them) seeking out users in their "natural habitat" in order to find a starting point for a chain of respondents. Other respondents are nominated by those already interviewed. New chains are started by approaching another unknown user. This is repeated until the desired number has been achieved.

Of the 150 respondents, 89 (60 percent) completed the full cycle of interviews. For reasons that we were unable to discover, interviews with four clients somehow disappeared or got lost. There is, therefore, material available on 85 respondents for the whole cycle of interviews.

What caused people to drop out? Three respondents became suspicious and refused to participate after three interviews. Four stopped participation because they had just kicked the habit and no longer wished to be reminded of their past addiction. It is known that six respondents died during the project. One was fatally wounded by a police bullet trying to avoid arrest somewhere outside of Amsterdam; three died of AIDS; one committed suicide; we do not know the exact fate of the last.

Some respondents disappeared when they left Amsterdam, or entered a clinic or prison. Others were simply not to be found anywhere in town.

With a view to the representativity of the sample, it is relevant to ask whether any category of users contained systematic dropouts. We followed two strategies in order to provide a satisfactory answer. To start with, all field-workers checked whether the dropouts were evenly distributed over their groups of respondents, taking into account such factors as age, sex, ethnic background, patterns of crime and drug use. This information was available on the basis of the field notes kept by the field-workers. As an extra check, the eighty-nine remaining respondents were compared on a number of central variables with sixty-one dropouts by means of the chi-square test. The only variable that showed a systematic difference ($p<0.05$) between the two groups was ethnic origin. Respondents from Surinam and the Antilles dropped out of the project relatively more often than others. On numerous other variables (sex, age, modality of distribution, level of crime, level of use, duration of heroin use, etc.) the dropouts were evenly distributed over the categories.

REFERENCES

Adler, P. A., P. Adler. Wheeling and dealing: An ethnography of an upper-level drug dealing and smuggling community. New York: Columbia University Press 1985.

Albrecht, H. J., A. van Kalmthout (eds.). Drug policies in Western Europe. Freiburg: Max Planck Institut 1989.

Amsel, Z., W. Mandell, L. Matthias, C. Mason, I. Hocherman. Reliability and validity of self-reported illegal activities and drug use, collected from narcotic addicts. International Journal of the Addictions, vol. 11, no. 2 1976, pp. 325–336.

Anglin, M. D. The efficacy of civil commitment in treating narcotic addiction. In C. G. Leukefeld, F. M. Tims (eds.), Compulsory treatment of drug abuse. Research and clinical practice. Rockville: NIDA, Research Monograph 86 1988.

Anglin M. D., W. H. McGlothlin, G. Speckart. The effect of parole on methadone patient behavior. American Journal of Drug and Alcohol Abuse, vol. 8, no. 2 1981, pp. 153–170.

Anglin, M. D, M. W. Booth, T. W. Ryan, Y. Hser. Ethnic differences in narcotics addiction. II, Chicano and Anglo addiction career patterns. International Journal of the Addictions, vol. 23, no. 10 1988, pp. 1011–1027.

Ausubel, D. P. Methadone maintenance treatment. The other side of the coin. The International Journal of the Addictions, vol. 18, no. 6 1983, pp. 851–862.

Baanders, A. De Hollandse aanpak; Opvoedingscultuur, druggebruik en het Nederlandse overheidsbeleid. Assen: van Gorcum 1989.

Ball, J. C., L. Rosen, J. A. Flueck, et al. Lifetime criminality of heroin addicts in the United States. Journal of Drug Issues, vol. 12, no. 3 1982, pp. 225–239.

Bartelds, J. I. M. W., A. J. H. van Ginkel, M. Grapendaal, R. C. F. Nijhof. Evaluatie van het beleidsplan van het huis van bewaring te Rotterdam. Den Haag: Ministerie van Justitie 1987.

Beaufort, L. A. R. J. de. Strafrechtelijke marktbeheersing. In M. S. Groenhuijsen, A. M. van Kalmthout (eds.), Nederlands drugsbeleid in Westeuropees perspectief. Arnhem: Gouda Quint 1989.

Becker, H. Outsiders. New York: The Free Press 1963.

Ben-Yehuda, N. Are addicts' self-reports to be trusted? International Journal of the Addictions, vol. 15, no. 8 1980, pp. 1265–1270.
Bennett, T., R. Wright. The drug-taking careers of opioid users. The Howard Journal of Criminal Justice, vol. 25, no. 1 1986.
Berg, T. van de, M. Blom. Tippelen voor dope; levensverhalen van vrouwen in de heroïneprostitutie. Amsterdam: De Graaf stichting/SUA 1986.
Berghuis, A. C. Amsterdamse criminaliteit in cijfers en plaatjes. Den Haag: WODC, Ministerie van Justitie 1987.
Biernacki, P. Pathways from heroin addiction. Recovery without treatment. Philadelphia: Temple University Press 1986.
Biernacki, P., D. Waldorf Snowball sampling. Problems and techniques of chain referral sampling. Sociological Methods and Research, vol. 10 1981, pp. 141–163.
Brussel, G. H. A. van, S. J. M. van Lieshout. Jaarverslag drugsafdeling 1992. Amsterdam: Gemeentelijke Geneeskundige en Gezondheidsdienst (GG&GD) 1993.
Buning, E. C. De GG&GD en het Drugsprobleem in Cijfers, Deel I, II, III, IV. Amsterdam: Gemeentelijke Geneeskundige en Gezondheidsdienst (GG&GD) 1986, 1987, 1988, 1990, 1992.
Bureau regionaal coördinator voorkoming misdrijven. Achtergrondinformatie over auto-inbrekers en preventie. Eindhoven, 1985.
Burr, A. Chasing the dragon: Heroin misuse, delinquency and crime in the context of South London culture. British Journal of Criminology, vol. 27, no. 4 1987, pp. 333–357.
Carpenter, C., B. Glassner, J. Loughlin. Kids, drugs and crime. Lexington: Lexington Books 1988.
CBS (Centraal bureau voor de statistiek). Statistische zakboeken 1961–1993. Den Haag: SDU 1961–1993.
Chaiken, J. M., M. R. Chaiken. Drugs and predatory crime. In M. Tonry, J. Q. Wilson (eds.), Drugs and Crime. Chicago and London: The University of Chicago Press 1990.
Chambers, C. D., S. W. Dean, M. F. Pletcher. Criminal involvement of minority group addicts. In Inciardi (ed.). The Drugs-Crime Connection. Sage Publications: Beverly Hills, 1981.
Chein, I., D. L. Gerard, R. S. Lee, E. Rosenfeld, D. M. Wilner. The road to H. . Narcotics, delinquency and social policy. New York/London, Basic Books 1964.
Clayton, R. R., B. S. Tuchfield. The drug-crime debate: Obstacles to understanding the relationship. Journal of Drug Issues, vol. 12, no. 2 1982, pp. 153–166.
Cohen, D. A. P. Cocaïne en cannabis: een gelijk beleid voor verschillende drugs? Tijdschrift voor criminologie, vol. 29, no. 6 1987, pp. 244–268.

Cohen, D. A. P. Drugs as a social construct. Utrecht: Elinkwijk 1990.
Derks, J. Het Amsterdamse morfine verstrekkingsprogramma; een longitudinaal onderzoek onder extreem problematische drugsgebruikers. Utrecht: Nederlands centrum geestelijke volksgezondheid 1990.
Dijk, J. J. M. van. Heroïneverstrekking: kenmerken en dynamiek van het Engelse systeem. Tijdschrift voor Criminologie, vol. 26, no. 2 1984, pp. 110–122.
Dobinson, I. Making sense of the drug and crime link. Australian and New Zealand Journal of Criminology, vol. 22, no. 4 1989, pp. 259–275.
Dobinson, I., P. Ward. Drugs and crime. Sydney: NSW Bureau of crime statistics and Research 1985.
Dole, V. P. Implications of methadone maintenance for theories of narcotic addiction. Journal of the American Medical Association, vol. 260, no. 20 1988, pp. 3025–3029.
Dole, V. P., M. E. Nyswander. A medical treatment of Diacetylmorphine (heroin). Journal of the American Medical Association 1965, vol. 1 of 3, pp. 646–650.
Dole, V. P., M. E. Nyswander. Methadone maintenance treatment. A ten-year perspective. Journal of the American Medical Association, vol. 248, no. 19 1976.
Draijer, N. Seksueel misbruik van meisjes door verwanten; een landelijk onderzoek naar de omvang, de aard, de gezinsachtergronden, de emotionele betekenis en de psychische en psychosomatische gevolgen. Den Haag: Ministerie van Sociale Zaken en Werkgelegenheid 1988.
Driessen, F. M. H. M. Methadonverstrekking in Nederland. Utrecht: Bureau Driessen Sociaal wetenschappelijk onderzoek en advies 1990.
Duster, T. The legalization of morality. Law, drugs and moral judgement. New York: The Free Press 1970.
Edwards, E. D. Arrest and conviction histories before, during and after participation in a substance abuse treatment program. Drug Forum, vol. 7, nos. 3–4 1979, pp. 259–264.
Elzakker, A. van, M. Steinbusch. Heroïneverstrekking? een onderzoek onder klanten van het methadonteam. Utrecht: CAD-cahier 4 1982.
Engelsman, E. L. Responding to drug problems. Dutch policy and practice. Paper read at the International Conference on Drug Policy Reform, Washington 1988.
Engelsman, E. L. Dutch policy on the management of drug-related problems. British Journal of Addiction, vol. 84 1989, pp. 211–218.
Erkelens, L. H. Ontwikkelingen in het Nederlands Penitentiaire Drugsbeleid. Tijdschrift voor Alcohol, Drugs en andere Psychotrope Stoffen, vol. 13, nr. 4, 1987.

Erkelens, L. H., P. D. J. Haas, O. J. A. Janssen Drugs en detentie; een beschrijvend onderzoek naar harddruggebruikers in een zestal Huizen van Bewaring. Groningen: Kriminologisch instituut 1979.

Faupel, Ch. E. Drug treatment and criminality: Methodological and theoretical implications. In J. A. Inciardi (ed.), The drugs-crime connection. Beverly Hills: Sage Publication 1981.

Faupel, Ch. E. Heroin use, street crime and the "main hustle." Implications for the validity of official crime data. Deviant Behavior, vol. 7, no. 1 1986, pp. 31–45.

Faupel, Ch. E., C. B. Klockars. Drugs-crime connections: Elaborations from the life histories of hard-core heroin addicts. Social Problems, vol. 34, no. 1 1987, pp. 54–68.

Gemeente Amsterdam. Nota harddrugs, een aanzet tot een gentegreerd beleid. Amsterdam: Gemeenteblad, bijlage C 1985.

Gemeente Amsterdam. Nota harddrugs. Amsterdam: 1988.

Gemeentepolitie Amsterdam. Evaluatie afdeling lokale handel. Amsterdam: unpublished manuscript 1986.

Gemert, F. van. Mazen en netwerken. Amsterdam: Instituut voor sociale geografie, Universiteit van Amsterdam 1988.

Gerritsen, J. Een hardnekkig vraagstuk; Kanttekeningen bij de vaak vergeten samenhang tussen het drugprobleem en ontwikkelingen op de arbeidsmarkt. Tijdschrift voor Criminologie, vol. 33, no. 1 1991, pp. 3–28.

Glassner, B., J. Loughlin. Drugs in adolescent worlds. New York: St. Martin's 1987.

Goffman, E. Stigma. Englewood Cliffs: Prentice-Hall 1963.

Goldman, F. Drugabuse, crime and economy. The dismal limits of social choice. In J. A. Inciardi (ed.), The drugs-crime connection. Beverly Hills: Sage Publication 1981.

Goldstein, P. J. The drugs/violence nexus: A tripartite conceptual framework. Journal of Drug Issues, Fall 1985, pp. 493–506.

Goldstein, P. J., H. H. Brownstein. Drug Related Crime Analysis: Homicide. A Report to the National Institute of Justice; Drugs, Alcohol and Crime Program 1987.

Goldstein, P. J., H. H. Brownstein, P. J. Ryan, P. A. Bellucci. Crack and homicide in New York City 1988: A conceptually based event analysis. Contemporary Drug Problems, vol. 16, no. 4, Winter 1989, pp. 651–687.

Goldstein, P. J., B. J. Spunt, P. A. Bellucci, T. Miller. Volume of cocaine use and violence: A comparison between men and women. Journal of Drug Issues, vol. 21, no. 2 1991, pp. 345–367.

Grapendaal, M. Drugs in detentie. Justitiële Verkenningen, vol. 13, no. 3 1987, pp. 54–66.

Grapendaal, M. De tering naar de nering; middelengebruik en economie van opiaatverslaafden. Justitiële Verkenningen, vol. 15, no. 5 1989a, pp. 23–46.
Grapendaal M. De markt van wit en bruin. De Psycholoog, vol. 24, no. 7/8 1989b, pp. 357–363.
Grapendaal M. De paradox en het dilemma; effecten van politie-optreden op de Zeedijk. Ars Aequi, vol. 39, no. 10 1990a, pp. 112–118.
Grapendaal, M. The effects of methadone maintenance on the criminal behaviour of opiate users in Amsterdam. Paper presented at the first international conference on the reduction of drug related harm, Liverpool 1990b.
Grapendaal, M., R. Aidala. Duits drugstoerisme in Arnhem; een veldonderzoek onder Duitse drugsgebruikers in Arnhem. Den Haag: WODC, Ministerie van Justitie 1991.
Grund, J. P. C., N. F. P. Adriaans, C. D. Kaplan Changing cocaine smoking rituals in the Dutch heroin addict population. British Journal of Addiction, vol. 86, no. 4 1991, pp. 439–448.
Hammersley, R., V. Morrison. Effects of polydrug use on the criminal activities of heroin-users. British Journal of Addiction, vol. 82, no. 8 1987, pp. 899–906.
Hammersley, R., A. Forsyth, V. Morrison, J. R. Davies. The relationship between crime and opioid use. British Journal of Addictions, vol. 84, no. 9 1989, pp. 1029–1043.
Handelingen Tweede Kamer der Staten Generaal, 1976.
Hartnoll, R. L. Current situation relating to drug abuse assessment in European countries. Bulletin on Narcotics, vol. 28 1986, pp. 65–80.
Haverkamp, G. Carrière- en scenevorming onder autochtone heroïnegebruikers. Tijdschrift voor Criminologie, vol. 26, no. 2 1984, pp. 136–148.
Hoekstra, J. C. Handelen van heroïnegebruikers; effecten van beleidsmaatregelen. Meppel: Krips Repro 1987.
Hubert, M. C., E. A. Noorlander. Creatief omgaan met methadon in een laagdrempelige organisatie. Tijdschrift voor alcohol, drugs en andere psychotrope stoffen, vol. 13, no. 4 1987, pp. 114–121.
Hunt, D., D. S. Lipton, D. S. Goldsmith, D. L. Strug, B. Spunt. "It takes your heart." The image of methadone maintenance in the addict world and its effect on recruitment into treatment. The International Journal of the Addictions, vol. 20, no. 11–12 1985 pp. 1751–1769.
Inciardi J. A. (ed.). The drug legalization debate. Newbury Park: Sage publications 1991. Studies in Crime, Law and Justice, vol. 7.
Intraval. Harddrugs & Criminaliteit in Rotterdam. Groningen: Drukkerij Gerlach 1989.

Intraval. Minder hinder; eindrapport van het Rotterdamse Drugs Related Crime Project. Groningen/Rotterdam: stichting Intraval 1990.
ISAD (Interdepartementale Stuurgroep Alcohol- en drugbeleid). Drugbeleid in beweging: naar een normalisering van de drugproblematiek. Den Haag: Ministerie van Welzijn, Volksgezondheid en Cultuur 1985.
Jansen, A. C. M. Cannabis in Amsterdam; een geografie van hashish en marihuana. Muiderberg, Dirk Coutinho 1989.
Janssen, O., K. T. Swierstra. Heroïnegebruikers in Nederland; een typologie van levensstijlen. Groningen: Criminologisch Instituut, Rijksuniversiteit Groningen 1982.
Jarvis, G., H. Parker. Young heroin users and crime. How do the "new users" finance their habits? British Journal of Criminology, vol. 29, no. 2 1989, pp. 175–185.
Johnson, B. D., P. J. Goldstein, E. Preble, J. Schmeidler, D. S. Lipton, B. Spunt, T. Miller. Taking care of business, the economics of crime by heroin abusers. Lexington: Lexington Books 1985.
Johnson, B. D., K. Anderson, E. D. Wish. A day in the life of 105 drug addicts and abusers: Crimes committed and how the money was spent. Sociology and Social Research, vol. 72, no. 3 1988, pp. 185–191.
Junger-Tas, J., M. Kruissink. Ontwikkeling van de jeugdcriminaliteit: periode 1980-1988. Arnhem: Gouda Quint bv 1990. WODC, Ministerie van Justitie.
Kaplan, Ch. D. The heroin system: A general economy of crime and addiction. Crime and Justice, November 1977.
Kaplan, Ch. D. The uneasy consensus. Prohibitionist and experimentalist expectancies behind the international narcotics control system. Tijdschrift voor Criminologie, vol. 26, no. 2. 1984, pp. 98–109.
Kaplan, Ch. D., D. J. Haanraadts, H. J. van Vliet, J. P. Grund. Is Dutch drug policy an example for the world? In Between Prohibition and Legalization; The Dutch Experiment in Drug Policy. Ed. Leuw, I Haen Marshall (eds.). Kugler Publications: Amsterdam/New York, 1994.
Kaplan, J. The hardest drug. Heroin and public policy. Chicago: The University of Chicago Press 1983.
Korf, D. J. Heroïnetoerisme; veldonderzoek naar het gebruik van harddrugs onder buitenlanders in Amsterdam. Amsterdam: Stadsdrukkerij van Amsterdam 1986.
Korf, D. J. Heroïnetoerisme II; resultaten van een veldonderzoek onder 382 buitenlandse dagelijke opiaatgebruikers in Amsterdam. Amsterdam: Instituut voor sociale geografie, Universiteit van Amsterdam 1987.

Korf, D. J. Jatten alle junkies? Tijdschrift voor Criminologie, vol. 32, no. 2 1990, pp. 105–123.

Korf, D. J., H. Hoogenhout. Zoden aan de Dijk; heroïnegebruikers en hun ervaring met en waardering van de Amsterdamse drugshulpverlening. Amsterdam: Instituut voor Sociale Geografie, Universiteit van Amsterdam 1990.

Korf, D. J., R. Mann, H. van Aalderen. Drugs op het platteland; het drugsgebruik in een kleinere gemeente. Assen/Maastricht: Van Gorcum 1989.

Korf, D. J., H. van Aalderen, H. Hoogenhout, and J. P. Sandwÿh. Gooise Geneugten; legaal en illegaal drugsgebruik. Amsterdam: Spcp 1990.

Koster, L. Wandelaars in de nieuwmarktbuurt. Amsterdam: Universiteit van Amsterdam, Instituut voor sociale geografie 1987.

Kowalski, G. S., Ch. E. Faupel. Heroin use, crime, and the "main hustle." Deviant Behavior, vol. 11 1990, pp. 1–16.

Laan, P. H. van der. Afscheid van het welzijnsmodel; ontwikkelingen in jeugdbescherming en jeugdstrafrecht. Justitiële Verkenningen, vol. 16, no. 2 1990, pp. 8–42.

Lemert, E. M. Human deviance, social problems and social controls. Englewood Cliffs: Prentice-Hall 1967.

Leune, J. Illegale Drogen. In R. Hinghorst, B. Ness, B. Wünschmann (eds.), Jahrbuch Sucht 1991. Geesthacht: Neuland Verlag 1992, pp. 19–35.

Leuw, Ed. Heroïnegebruik, criminaliteit en de mogelijke effecten van methadonverstrekking. Tijdschrift voor Criminologie, vol. 28, no. 3 1986, pp. 128–136.

Leuw, Ed. Enkele dilemma's van rationeel sociaal drugsbeleid. Justitiële Verkenningen, vol. 13, no. 3 1987, pp. 7–27.

Leuw, Ed. Over gokken en de hernieuwde humanisering van het verslavingsbegrip. Tijdschrift voor alcohol, drugs en andere psychotrope stoffen, vol. 14, nos. 5–6 1988, pp. 178–185.

Leuw, Ed. Verslaving en criminaliteit: een verkenning. Justitiële Verkenningen, vol. 15, no. 5 1989, pp. 8–22.

Leuw, Ed. Dwangopname voor hypercriminele druggebruikers. Justitiële Verkenningen, vol. 17, no. 2 1991, pp. 106–124.

Leuw, Ed. Drugs and Drug Policy in the Netherlands. In M. Tonry (ed.), Crime and Justice, a review of research. Vol. 14, pp. 229–276. Chicago and London: The University of Chicago Press 1991a.

Loor, A. de. Het middel Ecstasy bestaat niet; een onderzoek. Amsterdam: Info/adviesburo Drugs 1989.

MacCoun, R. J. Drugs and the Law. A psychological analysis of drug prohibition. Psychological Bulletin, vol. 113, no. 3 1993, pp. 497–512.

McBride, D. C., C. B. Mc Coy. Crime and Drugs. The issues and the literature. Journal of Drug Issues, vol. 12, no. 12 1982, pp. 137–152.

McGlothlin, W. H., M. D. Anglin, B. D. Wilson. Narcotic addiction and crime. Criminology, vol. 16, no. 3 1978, pp. 293–315.

Mead, G. H. Mind, self and society. Chicago: University Press of Chicago 1939.

Merton, R. K. Social theory and social structure. Glencou, Illinois: The Free Press 1957.

Mol, R., F. Trautmann. Normalisering als ideaal van het Nederlandse drugsbeleid; de Amsterdamse praktijk. Tijdschrift voor alcohol, drugs en andere psychotrope stoffen, vol. 16, no. 4 1990, pp. 129–141.

Mott, J. Opiate use and crime in the United Kingdom. Contemporary drug problems, vol. 9, no. 4 1980, pp. 437–453.

Musto, D. F. The American disease. Origins of narcotic control. New Haven: Yale University Press 1973.

Nadelmann, E. A. The case for legalization. In J. A. Inciardi (ed.), The drug legalization debate. Newbury Park: Sage Publications 1991, pp. 17–44.

National Institute of Justice, Research in Action. Drug use forecasting. Research Update. Washington: December 1989.

Nelen, H. Het gebruik van psychofarmaca in de Amsterdamse drugsscene. Justitiële Verkenningen, vol. 15, no. 5 1989, pp. 47–66.

Nelen, H. Drug misuse in local communities: Amsterdam. In T. Bennett (ed.), Drug misuse in local communities: Perspectives across Europe. London: Police Foundation 1991, pp. 81–88.

NeVIV. Everybody wants to go to Disneyland; Verslag van een studiereis naar de Verenigde Staten van Amerika. Utrecht: NeVIV 1993.

Nurco, D. N., I. H. Cisin, J. C. Ball. Crime as source of income for narcotic addicts. Journal of Substance Abuse Treatment, vol. 2, no. 2 1985, pp. 113–115.

Nurco, D. N., J. W. Shaffer, I. H. Cisin. An ecological analysis of the interrelationship among drug abuse and other indices of social pathology. International Journal of the Addictions, vol. 17, no. 4 1984, pp. 441–452.

Nurco, D. N., L. Rosen, J. A. Flueck, T. E. Hanlon, T. W. Kinlock. Differential criminal patterns of narcotic addicts over an addiction career. Criminology, vol. 38, no. 3 1988, pp. 407–423.

Parker H., K. Bakx, R. Newcombe. Living with heroin. The impact of a drugs "epidemic" on an English community. Milton Keynes, Philadelphia: Open University Press 1988.

Pearson, G. The new heroin users. Oxford: Blackwell 1987.

Pearson, G. Drug-control policies in Britain. In M. Tonry (ed.), Crime and Justice, a review of research, vol. 14. Chicago and London: The University of Chicago Press 1991.

Pearson, G. Pharmacology and fashion. The uses and misuses of cultural relativism in drug policy analysis. European Journal on Criminal Policy and Research, vol. 1, no. 2 1993, pp. 9-29.
Peele, S. The meaning of addiction. Compulsive experience and its interpretation. Lexington: Lexington Books 1985.
Peele, S. Diseasing of America; addiction treatment out of control. Lexington: Lexington Heath 1989.
Preble, E. Methadone, wine and welfare. In R. S. Weppner (ed.), Street ethnography, selected studies of crime and drug use in natural settings. Beverly Hills/London: Sage Publications 1977.
Preble E., Casey J. J. Taking care of business- The heroin user's life on the street. International Journal of the Addictions, vol. 4, no. 4 1969, pp. 1-24.
Reijneveld, M. Methadon maakt je nog zieker dan heroïne. Amsterdams Drug Tijdschrift, vol. 7, no. 3 1990, pp. 4-5.
Reuter, P. Hawks ascendant. The punitive trend of American drug policy. Daedalus, vol. 121, no. 3 1993, pp. 15-52.
Reuter, P., R. MacCoun, P. Murphy. Money from crime. A study of the economics of drug dealing in Washington D. C. Santa Monica: the RAND Corporation, Drug Policy Research Center 1990.
Rook, A., J. J. A. Essers. Vervolging en strafvordering bij opiumwetdelicten. Den Haag: Staatsuitgeverij 1988. WODC, Ministerie van Justitie, no. 80.
Rosenbaum, M. Women on heroin. New Brunswick, New Jersey: Rutgers University press 1981.
Rüter, C. F. Drugs and the criminal law in the Netherlands. In J. van Dijk, Ch. Haffmans, F. Rüter (eds.), Criminal law in action. An overview of current issues in Western societies. Arnhem: Gouda Quint 1986.
Rüter, C. F. Die Strafrechtliche Drogenbekämpfung in den Niederlanden: Ein Königreich als Aussteiger? Zeitschrift für Strafrechtswissenschaft, vol. 100, no. 2 1988, pp. 121-139.
Scheerer, S. The new Dutch and German Laws: Social conditions for criminalization and decriminalization. Law and Society, vol. 12 1978, pp. 585-605.
Schoone, E. Het waarom van methadon. Amsterdam: Universiteit van Amsterdam, Sociologisch Instituut, 1989 (doctoraalscriptie).
Sechrest, D. K. Methadone programs and crime reduction: a comparison of New York and California addicts. International Journal of the Addictions, vol. 14, no. 3 1979, pp. 377-400.
Senay, E. C. Methadone Maintenance Treatment. International Journal of the Addictions, vol. 20, nos. 6/7 1985, pp. 803-821.
Sengers, W. J. Scheiding van methadonverstrekking en behandeling. Tijdschrift voor alcohol, drugs en andere psychotrope stoffen, vol. 13, no. 3 1987, pp. 52-55.

Shaffer, J. W., D. N. Nurco, J. C. Ball, T. W. Kinlock, K. R. Duszynsky, J. Langrod. The relationship of preaddiction characteristics to the types and amounts of crime committed by narcotic addicts. International Journal of the Addictions, vol. 22, no. 2 1987, pp. 153-166.
Speckart, G., M. D. Anglin. Narcotics and crime, a causal modeling approach. Journal of Quantitative Criminology, vol. 2, no. 1 1986a, pp. 3-28.
Speckart, G., M. D. Anglin. Narcotics use, property crime and dealing. Structural dynamics across the addiction career. Journal of Quantitative Criminology, vol. 2, no. 4 1986b, pp. 355-375.
Spunt, B. J., P. J. Goldstein, P. A. Bellucci, T. Miller. Race/Ethnicity and gender differences in the drugs-violence relationship. Journal of Psychoactive Drugs, vol 22, no. 3 1990, pp. 293-303.
State Secretary for Welfare, Health and Cultural Affairs Policy on drug use. Letter in preparation for the meeting of the Special Committee on Drugs Policy June 13 1983, Session 17867. 's Gravenhage: 1983.
Stephens, R. The truthfulness of addict respondents in research projects. The International Journal of the Addictions, vol. 7, no. 3 1972, pp. 549-558.
Sutherland, E. H. The professional thief. Chicago: University of Chicago Press 1937.
Swierstra, K. E. Drugscarrières; van crimineel tot conventioneel. Groningen: Stichting Drukkerij C. Regenboog 1990.
Swierstra, K. E., O. Janssen, J. H. Jansen. De reproductie van het heroïnegebruik onder nieuwe lichtingen; heroïnegebruikers in Nederland, deel II. Groningen: Rijksuniversiteit Groningen, Criminologisch instituut 1986.
Tweede kamer der Staten-Generaal. Handelingen Tweede Kamer (Proceedings of the House of Representatives). 's-Gravenhage: Staatsuitgeverij 1976.
U. S. Embassy in the Netherlands. A Report on Drug Policy in the Netherlands. 's Gravenhage: U. S. Embassy, unpublished manuscript 1989.
Verbraeck, H. T. De staart van de Zeedijk. Amsterdam: Universiteit van Amsterdam, Instituut voor sociale geografie 1988.
Verbraeck, H. T., G. van de Wijngaart. "Nu ik alleen methadon haal voel ik mij helemaal geen junk meer"; Ervaringen van cliënten met methadonverstrekking. Tijdschrift voor alcohol, drugs en andere psychotrope Stoffen, vol. 15, no. 4 1989, pp. 146-155.
Visser, A. Meester methadon. NRC Handelsblad, 18-2-1989.
Waldorf, D. Careers in dope. Englewood-Cliffs: Prentice-Hall 1973.
Wever, L. Drugs in alle staten; een verslag van het Amerikaanse drugbeleid. Den Haag: Ministerie van Welzijn, Volksgezondheid en Cultuur, September 1990.

White Raskin H., V. Johnson, C. Gozansky Garrison. The Drug-Crime nexus on adolescents and their peers. Deviant Behavior, vol. 6, no. 2 1985, pp. 183–204.

Wijngaart, Govert F. van de. Methadone in the Netherlands: An evaluation. International Journal of the Addictions, vol. 23 1988, pp. 913–925.

Wijngaart, G. F. van de. Competing perspectives on drug use. The Dutch experience. Amsterdam/Lisse: Swets & Zeitlinger b. v. 1991.

Wisotsky, S. Breaking the impasse in the war on drugs. Westport, Connecticut: Greenwood Press 1986.

WVC (Ministry of Welfare, Public Health and Culture). Notitie Drang en Dwang. Den Haag: 1987.

WVC (Ministry of Welfare, Public Health and Culture). Het drugbeleid. Den Haag: Fact Sheet 1989. d

WVC (Ministry of Welfare, Public Health and Culture). Registration figures of the Inspection for Mental Health. Den Haag: 1992.

Zinberg, N. E. Drug, set, and setting. The basis for controlled intoxicant use. New Haven and London: Yale University Press 1984.

Zwart de, W. M. Alcohol, Tabak en Drugs in cijfers. Utrecht: Nederlands Instituut voor Alcohol en Drugs 1989.

INDEX

Activities habit, 156, 158
Adler, P., 35
Adler, P. A., 35
Aidala, R., 142
AIDS, 204, 223
Albrecht, H. J., 8
Alcohol(ics), 22, 38, 46, 48, 73, 77, 84, 151, 193
America(n): see U.S.
Amsel, Z. W., 220, 221
Anglin, M. D., 33, 165
Antecedent variables, 32
Ausubel, D. P., 163, 166, 167, 168

Baanders, A., 6, 7
Ball, J. C., 26
Beaufort, L. A. R., de, 9, 201
Becker, H., 36
Bennett, T., 26, 59
Berghuis, A. C., 17, 18
Biernacki, P., 74, 223
British: see Great Britain
Black box, 195
Brownstein, H. H., 18
Brussel, G. H. A., van, 10
Buning, E., 4, 10, 81, 201, 223
Burr, A., 19, 32

Cannabis, 22, 23, 46, 48–49, 77, 152, 199–200
  shops, 9, 215
  pseudo-legalization, of 203–204
Career, 16, 198
  drugs, 35–39, 196
  deviant, 35–39, 130, 183, 186, 197
Carpenter, C., 37
Casey, J. J., 61, 62
Causal
  reinforcement, 29
  chains, 32

Causes
  of crime, 15, 19, 27, 28, 30, 33, 34, 117, 118, 164, 189
  of drug use, 33, 41–42, 190
CBS, 45
Chaiken, J. M M. R., 32
Chambers, C. D., 21
Chasing the dragon, 57, 68, 143, 175
Chein, I., 18, 120
Child Protection Council, 45
Clayton, R. R., 32
Cohen, D. A. P., 142, 200, 204
Community station, 71–73, 124, 169–171, 173, 175, 181, 184, 192
Competence in crime, 29, 70, 79
Compulsive(ness), 27, 28, 135, 148
Cost-gain perspective, 42, 61
Crack, 27, 28, 142
Craving, 163, 193
Criminal user, 125, 126, 129–131, 182–185, 193
Cultural rebels, 15, 54, 77

Dealing user, 125, 127, 129–131, 182–185, 193
Decrease of intravenous drug use, 144
Decreasing tolerance, 85
Decriminalization, 199
Derks, J., 170, 207
Determinants of drug use, 41–42
Deviancy, 36, 37
Deviant
  development, 38, 50, 60
  subculture, 38
  drug use, 16, 34, 163, 167
  life style, 28, 34, 50, 54, 82, 75, 125, 177, 192, 202–203
Dijk, J. J. M., van, 207
Division of labor (on the drugsmarket), 100–108

Dobinson, I., 19, 21, 26, 122
Dole, V. P., 159, 162, 184
Dominant sources of income, 116, 123, 182–183, 193
Double selectivity, 166
Draijer, N., 46
Driessen, F. M. H. M., 10, 12, 201
Duster, T., 16

Economic depression, 16
Edwards, E. D., 165
Elasticity of demand, 154–155
Elzakker, A., van, 207
Employed/employment, 44, 165–166.
Engelsman, E. L., 7, 205
England: see Great Britain
Epidemiology, 10–11
Erkelens, L. H., 23
Essers, J. J. A., 201
Explained variance, 152, 178–179

Factor analysis, 152
Faupel, Ch. E., 63, 156, 165
Fence/fencing, 100, 102
Full time job, 186
Function(ality),
   of drug use, 34, 41, 42, 59, 61–62, 168, 196
   of rituals, 68
   of methadone, 156, 163, 178, 183, 186, 188, 205

Gangs, 51
Garbage men, 107, 135–136
Gemert, F., van, 87, 92
Gerritsen, J., 16
Glassner, B., 37
Goffmann, E., 38
Goldman, F., 29, 155
Goldstein P. J., 18, 27, 28, 91
Grapendaal, M., 23, 142
Great Britain, UK, England, British, 15, 18–19, 20, 22–24, 43, 44, 194, 207
Grund, J. P. C., 142

Habit size, 155
Hammersley, R., 22
Harm reduction, 214
Hartnoll, R. L., 11
Hashish, 8. 53
Haverkamp, G., 156
Hell's Angels, 51
Hepatitis, 204
Heroin structure, 168
HIV, 89, 107, 144, 158, 201, 207, 219
Hoekstra, J. C., 117, 132, 200, 220
Hubert, M. C., 161
Hunt, D., 160, 163

Increase of police pressure, 200
Increase of crime, 17–20
Increasing availability of drugs (when legalized), 203–204
Inevitability, 27, 29–30, 37, 191, 196
Informal economy, 100–101, 192
Institutional reactions, 159–160
Interacting factors, 165
Internal consistency, 195
Intervening variables, 32

Jansen, A. C. M., 8, 200
Janssen, O., 54, 77
Jarvis, G., 15, 25, 27
Johnson, B. D., 4, 25, 117, 118, 155
Junger-Tas, J., 54, 77
Junkie territory, 81, 94

Kalmthout, A., van, 8
Kaplan, Ch. D., 160, 168
Klockars, C. B., 63
Korf, D. J., 25, 44, 117, 118, 132, 144, 194, 220, 223
Koster, L., 96
Kruissink, M., 45

Laan, P. H., van der, 45
Labeling theory, 36–38
Legalization, 7, 199–200, 202–204
Lemert, E. M., 36, 37
Leune, J., 10

Leuw, Ed., 205, 211
Lieshout, S. J. M., van, 10
Life style, 26, 28, 30, 34, 48, 50, 54, 56, 59, 63, 99, 117, 133, 160, 167–168, 187–188, 192
Life history, 3, 35, 39, 41,–58, 111
Liverpool, 19, 118
London, 19, 24
Loor, A., de, 142
Loughlin, J., 37

MacCoun, R. J., 205
Marihuana, 8
Maximum consumption, 139–140, 148
McBride, D. C., 29
McCoy, C. B., 29
McGlothlin, W. H., 221
Mead, G. H., 37
Merton, R. K., 61
Metabolic disease, 162
Methadone, 23, 31, 66–67, 87, 124, 125, 128, 135, 147, 150–154, 156, 158, 206
   programs, 4, 12, 71–72, 139, 189, 192, 201
   treatment, 12, 164
   free, 12, 169, 187
   bus, 71, 124, 169, 173, 175, 181, 182, 186
   theoretical justification of, 162–163
   orthodoxy of treatment, 162, 163, 177, 180
   modalities of distribution, 169–171, 173
   high/low thershold, 169, 175, 177, 180, 183, 186, 192, 195, 206
   black/street market, 171, 173–174, 177, 178, 182
   non-participants in program, 172, 175, 182, 192
   policy, 188
Methodology, 3, 4, 217–224
Mol, R., 201
Money habit, 156, 158
Monocausal effect, 165

Moral boundaries/resistance, 75–77, 192
Morrison, V., 29
Mott, J., 15
Multiplier of crime, 29
Musto, D. F., 16

Nadelmann, E. A., 204
Natural experiment, 164
Needle exchange/selling, 107, 130, 143
New York, 20, 25, 118, 201
New heroin users, 15, 19, 43
Noorlander, E. A., 161
Normalization, 5, 142
Normalized user, 124, 125, 129–131, 182–185, 193
Normative transgressions/limits, 37, 157
Nurco, D. N., 19, 26, 122
Nyswander, M. E., 159, 162, 184

Open scene, 81
Opium Act (Dutch), 5–10, 85, 118, 189, 210
Opportunities/opportunistic, 17, 25, 58, 103, 115, 120, 168, 186, 191, 193–194
   structures, 168

Parker, H., 15, 19, 23, 25, 27, 117, 118
Pearson, G., 10, 15, 16, 19, 207
Peele, S., 3, 30, 67
Periods of intensive (drug) use and abstinence, 26, 94, 121–122, 198
Policy, 2, 6–10, 164, 194–195
   alternatives, 190
   reformation, 199
   pragmatic, 5–6, 204–205
   goals, 159, 206, 208
   alterations/modifications, 209–210, 212
   differentiated, 212
   applicability to U.S. 213–215
   outcome indicators, 214
   law enforcement, 8–9, 208–209

Poly drug use, 125, 164, 173, 184, 208
Preble, E., 23, 61, 62, 163–164, 198
Predictor of crime, 178
Prohibition, 7, 199–200, 202–203, 205
Promotion system (of methadone maintenance), 170, 171, 174, 186
Prostitute/prostitution, 47, 52, 59, 61, 76, 78, 84, 100, 102, 107, 123, 128, 147, 149, 170

Reciprocity approach in treatment, 209–210
Recreational drug(s) (use), 152, 158
Red light district, 84, 100, 193, 197
Regression analysis, 178
Reijneveld, M., 160
Retired junkie, 72, 74, 177, 197
Reuter, P., 117
Rituals/ritualism, 68, 135, 142, 161
Rook, A., 201
Rosenbaum, M., 58–60, 160
Rüter, C. F., 7, 8, 9, 10, 201

Scheerer, S., 6
Schoone, E., 162
Sechrest, D. K., 165
self-medication, 140, 145, 146
Senay, E. C., 163
Sengers, W. J., 161
Sexual abuse/victimization, 46, 51, 52
Shaffer, J. W., 74
Shooting gallery, 97, 107
Social control, 159–160, 194
Social integration of drug use, 7–8
Social security, 115–117, 123, 129, 132
Social cultural differences, 159
Social casework, 12
Specialization in crime, 100–103, 131
Speckart, G., 33
Spunt, B. J., 28
Steinbusch, M., 207
Stephens, R., 220
Surinam(ese), 45, 55–58, 71, 81, 86, 88–89, 125, 143, 172
Sutherland, E. H., 36
Swierstra, K. E., 28, 32, 36, 54, 74, 77, 122
Synthesis of theory and empirical data, 189, 195–198

Theoretical models, 16
    of drugs and crime, 27–28, 32–33, 189–190
    of methadone distribution, 161–169
Trautmann, F., 201
Treatment, 12
Tripartite conceptual framework, 27
Tuchfield, B. S., 32

UK: *see* Great Britain
U.S., America(n), 16, 18, 20, 21, 26, 43, 44, 73, 91, 132, 142, 143,
    Embassy, 8
    Nat. Inst. of Justice, 23
    methadone programs in, 159–169

Variability of drug use, 135, 150, 191
Verbraeck, H. T., 92, 114, 160
Victimless crime, 116–117, 201–202
Violent/Violence, 18, 30, 46, 50, 75–76, 91, 102, 103, 112, 192, 200, 211, 213–214
Visser, A., 160, 185

Waldorf, D., 223
War on drugs, 5, 204, 213
Ward, P., 19
Wever, L., 201
White Raskin, H., 74
Wijngaart, G., van de, 5, 160, 205
Wirral, 19, 25
Wright, R., 26, 59
WVC, 12, 13

Zinberg, N. E., 204